The Best of Proctor's West

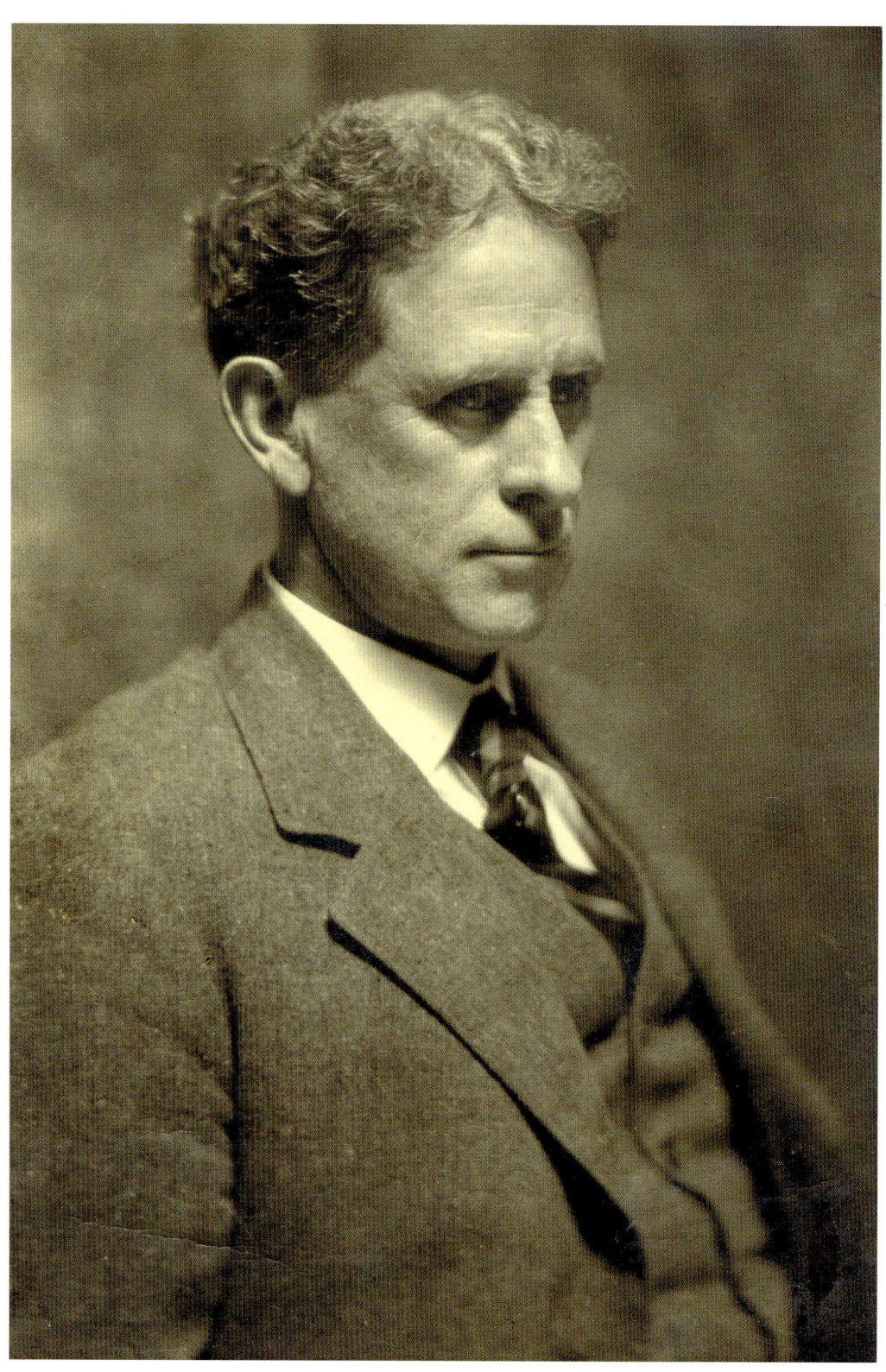

The Best of Proctor's West

AN IN-DEPTH STUDY

OF ELEVEN OF PROCTOR'S BRONZES

BY PETER H. HASSRICK

WITH CONTRIBUTIONS BY

KAREN B. McWHORTER AND ALLISON ROSENTHAL

FOREWORD BY BRUCE B. ELDREDGE

Buffalo Bill Center of the West

**BUFFALO BILL
CENTER
OF THE WEST**

Buffalo Bill Center of the West
720 Sheridan Avenue, Cody, Wyoming
centerofthewest.org

FOR BUFFALO BILL CENTER OF THE WEST
Project Manager: Sylvia Huber

Designer: Renée Tafoya, WordsWorth, Cody, WY
Editor: Steven Baker, Oklahoma City, OK
Indexer: Amron Gravett, Wild Clover Book Services, San Louis Obispo, CA

Library of Congress Cataloging-in-Publication Data

 Names: Hassrick, Peter H., author. | Proctor, Alexander Phimister, 1860-1950.
 Title: The Best of Proctor's West : an in-depth study of eleven of Proctor's
   bronzes / edited by Peter H. Hassrick ; with contributions by Karen
   McWhorter and Allison Rosenthal ; foreword by Bruce B. Eldredge.
 Description: Cody, Wyoming : Buffalo Bill Center of the West, 2017. |
   Includes bibliographical references and index.
 Identifiers: LCCN 2017006432 | ISBN 9780931618710 (alk. paper)
 Subjects: LCSH: Proctor, Alexander Phimister, 1860-1950--Criticism and
   interpretation. | West (U.S.)--In art.
 Classification: LCC NB237.P74 H37 2017 | DDC 700/.45878--dc23 LC record
 available at https://lccn.loc.gov/2017006432

ISBN 978-0-931618-71-0
Printed in South Korea

PROCTOR ONLINE DATABASE

www.proctor.centerofthewest.org

The online database complements and expands upon the publication by providing thorough documentation on each of the eleven Proctor bronzes. Visitors to the website can access foundry and casting information, listings of known castings' locations, provenance records, and some metallurgic analyses.

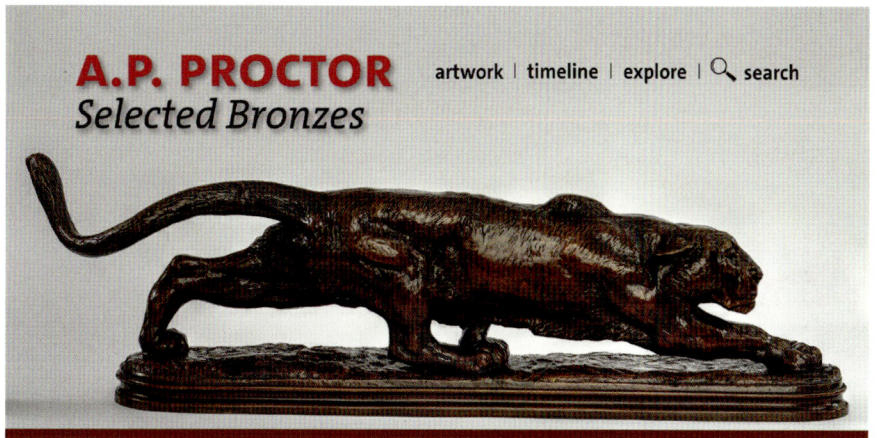

Proctor spent his childhood in the West, hunting and hiking in the backcountry of Colorado. With his artistic talent and a little money from his Colorado homestead, Proctor went to New York to train as an artist. While there, he turned to sculpture and began to achieve national recognition. Several major monuments at the World's Columbian Exposition of 1893 confirmed his status as an impressive figure in American art —only furthered by awards at the Paris Universal Exposition in 1900.

It was more than academic training and skill that set Proctor apart from the other artists of his day. He based his work on his experiences in the West. Hunting, hiking, and wild adventure inspired Proctor's sculptures, both monumental and small.

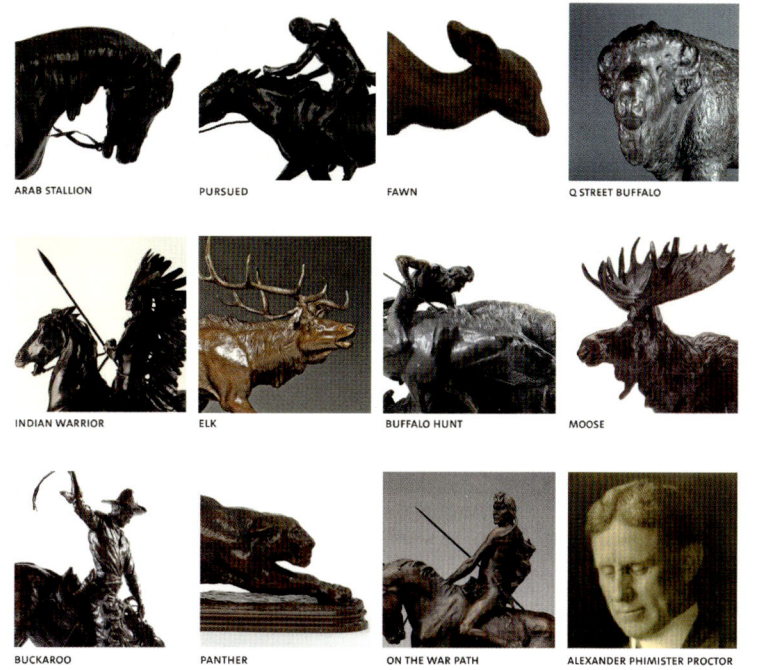

ARAB STALLION | PURSUED | FAWN | Q STREET BUFFALO

INDIAN WARRIOR | ELK | BUFFALO HUNT | MOOSE

BUCKAROO | PANTHER | ON THE WAR PATH | ALEXANDER PHIMISTER PROCTOR

DEDICATION

This book is dedicated to the Proctor family with special recognition to the artist's staunchly committed grandson, Phimister Proctor "Sandy" Church and devoted great-granddaughter, Laura Proctor Ames.

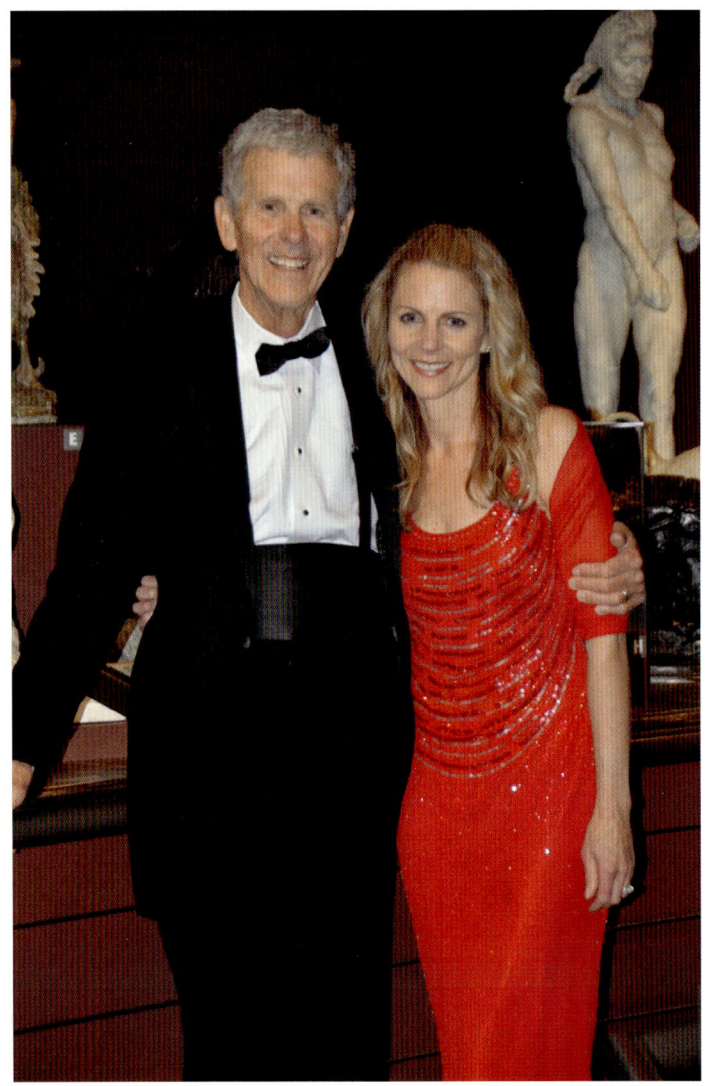

CONTENTS

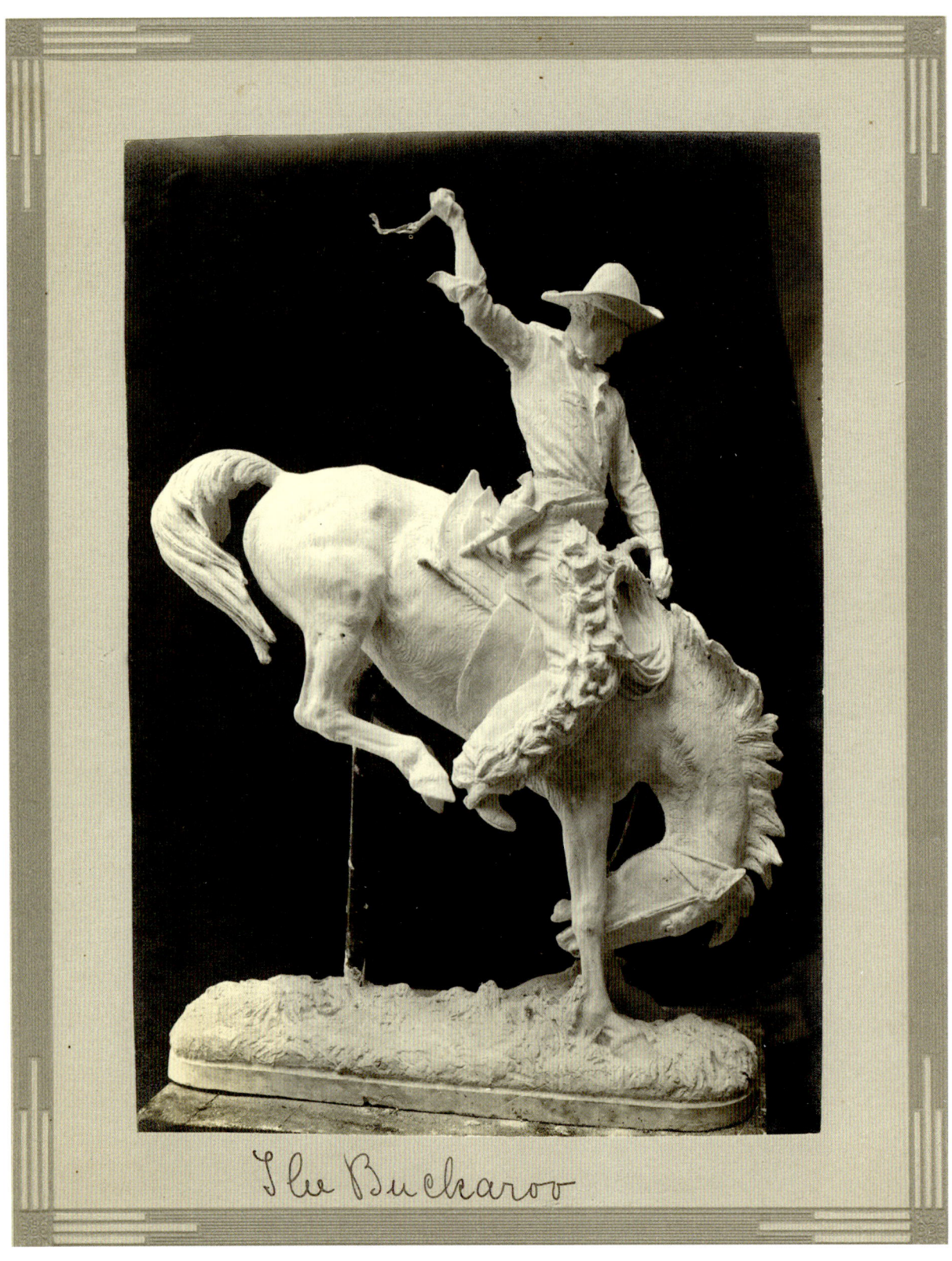

The Buckaroo

UNKNOWN PHOTOGRAPHER, *The Buckaroo.* Photograph, sepia tone. Alexander Phimister Proctor Collection, MS 242, Harold McCracken Research Library, Buffalo Bill Center of the West, Cody, Wyoming. P.242.942A

FOREWORD

Bruce B. Eldredge
Executive Director & CEO
Buffalo Bill Center of the West

In the summer of 2003, the Buffalo Bill Center of the West hosted a landmark exhibition on one of America's premier sculptors, Alexander Phimister Proctor. There had been few western one-man sculpture exhibitions prior to this, so our eyes were opened not only to the mastery and vision of Proctor's art but also to bronze casting in general as a medium for revealing the essence of our national legacy, both historic and modern. Remarkably, it was not many years later that the Center received a profoundly generous gift of the artist's complete studio collection and archives from Sandy and Sally Church. Concurrently, our curator at the time, Dr. Mindy Besaw, created a concept for presenting the Proctor studio as part of a major reinstallation of the Whitney Western Art Museum. From that point forward the public was offered a supreme view of the artist's environment as well as many of his true masterworks.

The Center has continued to acquire important castings of Proctor's work as well as archival support material. Most of these acquisitions have come from the Proctor Foundation that until recently was headed by Sandy Church but has recently been turned over to one of his daughters, Laura Ames. The Proctor Foundation has generously underwritten the costs of this volume as part of its commitment to support scholarship in American sculpture and especially the career of its namesake, Alexander Phimister Proctor. This current endeavor combines connoisseurship with science in an effort to establish an in-depth understanding of eleven of Proctor's signature works. The book, part of an ongoing set of annual publications known as *Whitney West*, seeks to sustain and enhance research and study of Proctor's extraordinary oeuvre.

ACKNOWLEDGEMENTS

Peter H. Hassrick
Director Emeritus and Senior Scholar
Buffalo Bill Center of the West

This volume, an in-depth study of eleven of Alexander Phimister Proctor's most famous bronzes, has taken shape over several years of art historical research and scientific inquiry. In an effort to contribute to a better understanding of the artist's work methods, creative process, and his patronage, we have called upon many individuals, galleries, and institutions for help. Primarily, it is thanks to this museum, the Buffalo Bill Center of the West, its leadership, its trustees and advisors, and its staff that such a project could take shape. The Conservation Department led by Beverly Perkins and supported by numerous interns provided invaluable guidance and countless hours of study. The administration, especially Bruce Eldredge offered encouragement and direction. The staff of the Whitney Western Art Museum—Karen McWhorter, Nicole Harrison, and Emily Wilson—buttressed the effort and welcomed it into their busy schedule of projects. And my assistant, Sylvia Huber, worked tirelessly to collect images, assist with research, and oversee publication design, schedule, and production.

The Proctor Foundation supplied inspiration, fiscal guidance and underwriting, and moral support during the full tenure of the project. Its first director, Sandy Church, vetted the manuscript, guided and encouraged the scientific studies, supplied countless insights into the history of the eleven bronzes discussed here, and provided endless reassurance and stimulation. The current director, Laura Ames, has continued the model and standards that Sandy Church set.

The scientific base of the project was developed under the aegis of Dr. Bruce Kaiser, former Chief Scientist of Bruker Elemental. Bruce developed the method used to analyze Proctor's sculptures and tested over 140 of his bronzes throughout the United States and Canada. My co-author, Allison Rosenthal worked with Bruce and under the knowledgeable eye of the Center's Chief Conservator, Beverly Perkins, to assess and analyze many of the bronzes under discussion in this volume. Allison's insights have been invaluable.

Also, playing a vital role in the project's success were the members of the Center's staff: Harold McCracken Research Library, Mary Robinson, Nicholle Gerharter, Mack Frost, and Karen Preis for research and image production; Information Technology Department, Seth Johnson for development of the online resource; Data Entry Specialist, Rosemary Ginger for production and data entry of the online resource; and Graphics Department, Jessica McKibben for designing the online homepage.

I appreciate the help of friends and colleagues: Alice Levi Duncan; Michael Frost, J.N. Bartfield Galleries; Gerald Peters Gallery; Adam Duncan Harris, National Museum of Wildlife Art; Belle Clegg Hays, Comptche, California; Thomas Nygard, Thomas Nygard Gallery; Cameron Shay, James Graham & Sons; and Thayer Tolles, The Metropolitan Museum of Art.

I would like to thank the many colleagues, museums, art galleries, institutions, associated personnel and individuals who gave invaluable assistance in making available the beautiful images included in this publication. Amon Carter Museum of American Art, Emily Olson; Art Institute of Chicago, Aimee Marshall; Art Resource, Inc., Jennifer Belt; Bridgeman Images, Inc., Amanda Gaspari; Brooklyn Museum, Monica Park; C.M. Russell Museum, Brenda Kornick; Chicago Park District, Julia Bachrach; Cleveland Museum, James Kohler; Cyrus Dallin Art Museum, Heather Leavell; Denver Art Museum, Renee Miller; Gilcrease Museum, Diana Cox; Grey Towers Heritage Association, Rebecca Philpot; Haggin Museum, Tod Ruhstaller; Mead Art Museum; Metropolitan Museum of Art; National Academy of Design, Diana Thompson; National Cowboy & Western Heritage Center, Melissa Owens; National Gallery of Art, Peter Dueker; National Museum of Wildlife Art, Emily Winters; Nordica Homestead Museum, Erik Nichols; Oregon Historical Society, Kim Buergel; Portland Art Museum, Anne Crouchley; Proctor Foundation; R.W. Norton Gallery, Loren Culver; Smithsonian American Art Museum, Richard Sorensen; Stark Museum of Art, Katherine Barry; Tacoma Art Museum, Ellen Ito; and private collectors who gave generously of their permissions.

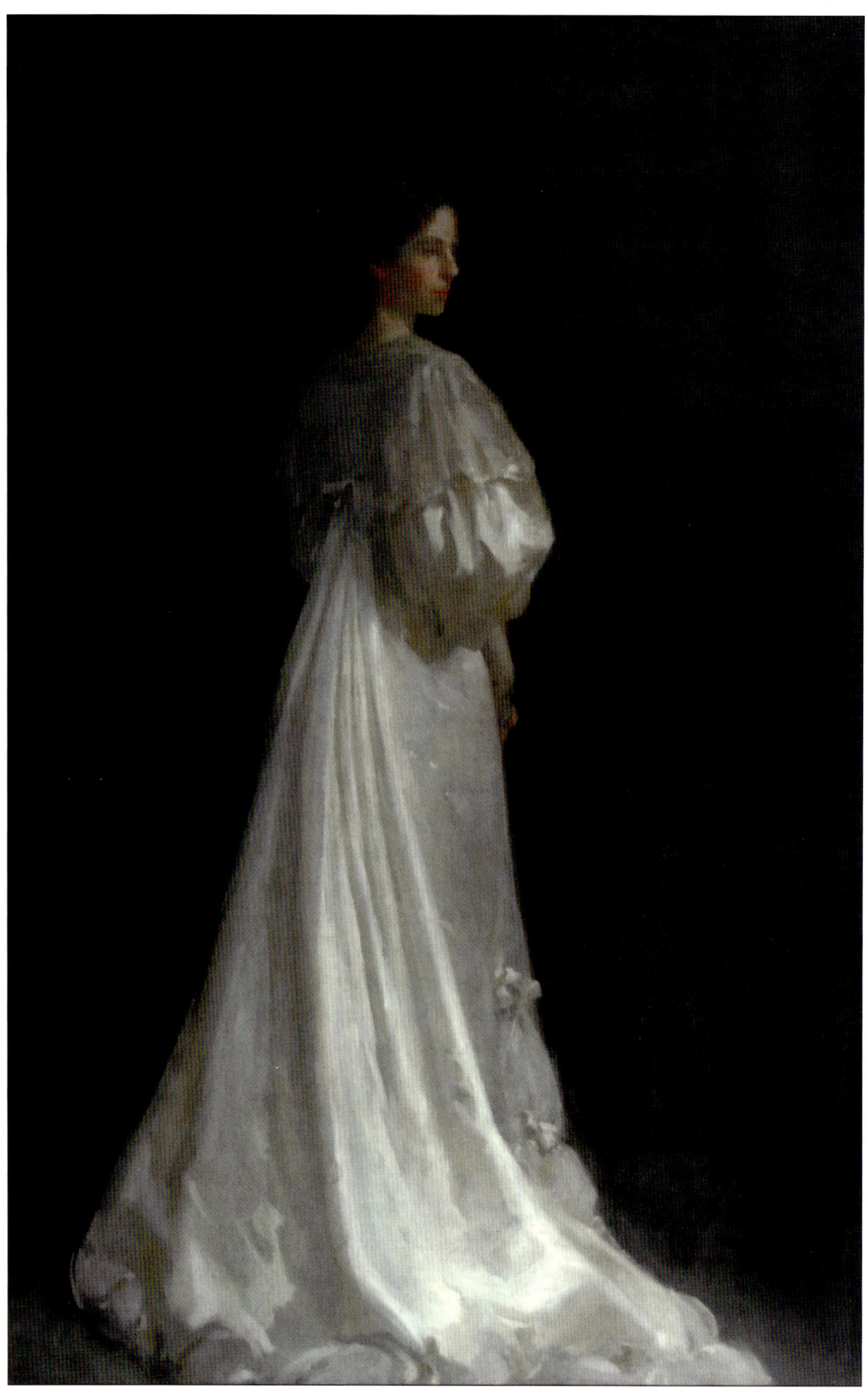

ROBERT VONNOH, (1858 – 1933), *(Mrs. A. Phimister Proctor), Portrait in Wedding Dress,* 1893,
Margaret Daisey Gerow. Oil on canvas, 78 x 50 in. Courtesy, The Proctor Foundation

MARGARET "MODY" PROCTOR (1875–1942)

Margaret Daisey Gerow met Alexander Phimister Proctor at the World's Columbian Exposition in Chicago in 1891. Both young artists participated in the festive, spectacular event; Gerow assisted sculptor Lorado Taft, and Proctor was commissioned to create large outdoor sculptures to decorate the fairgrounds. Two years after a chance encounter in Taft's tent, the couple was married. Together, they raised eight children and, over the course of their almost fifty-year marriage, traveled extensively and moved frequently to support Proctor's career. "Mody" Proctor was her husband's most dedicated champion and art critic. She celebrated her husband's optimism and dedication to his craft in this charming poem.

A POEM BY MARGARET "MODY" PROCTOR

As the sculptor, working upon his clay,

Adds and takes away each day,

So we our characters form and mold,

And the good and evil there unfold.

Both sculptor and child begin with glee,

Each sure its ideal will perfect be.

But only to him who, with clay or life

Thru the discouragements so rife,

Can hold to the good, the fine, the strong,

Spend all his efforts to right the wrong,

Comes joy in work that to whole worlds gives

The glorious soul or statue that lives.

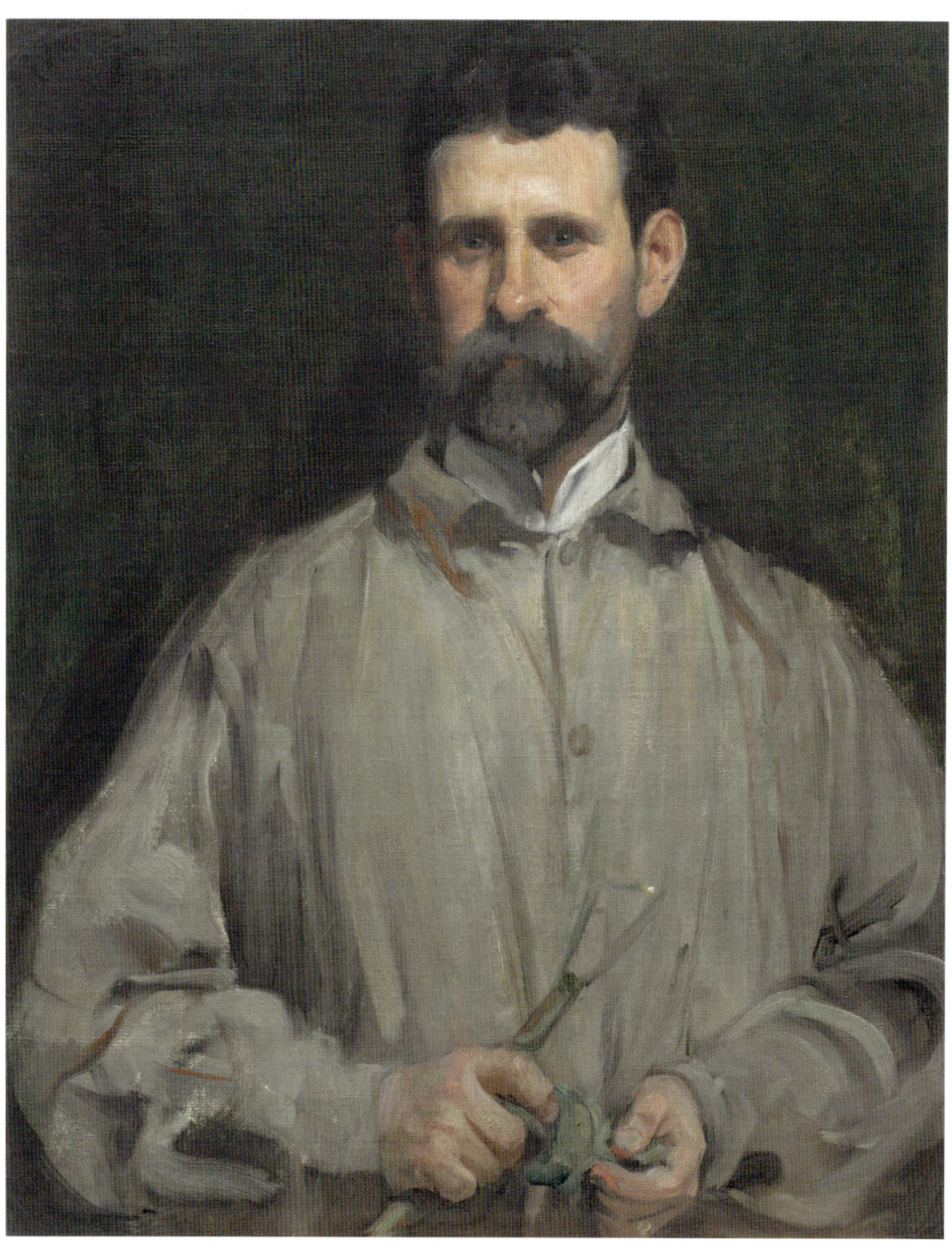

ROBERT VONNOH, (1858 – 1933), *Alexander Phimister Proctor,* 1903. Oil on canvas, 30 x 24 in. National Academy Museum, New York, New York / Bridgeman Images

THE PROCTOR STUDIO
Its Antecedents and History at the Whitney

Karen B. McWhorter
Scarlett Curator of Western American Art
Whitney Western Art Museum
Buffalo Bill Center of the West

In 1959, the Whitney Gallery of Western Art (now the Whitney Western Art Museum) opened its doors to the public. A crowd gathered in the small town of Cody, Wyoming, to see a remarkable presentation of western American art hung on the Whitney's wood-paneled walls and reflected in its polished travertine floors. Most of the paintings and sculpture in that inaugural show were borrowed to supplement the nascent collection, but the exhibition also included a groundbreaking recent gift.

The W. R. Coe Foundation had purchased and donated the Frederic Remington Studio Collection—an extraordinary array of objects comprising artwork by Remington, items the artist collected on western excursions, and artifacts and furnishings from his New Rochelle, New York, studio. From palettes and paintbrushes once wielded by the artist to Plains Indian regalia and cowboy gear that inspired his artwork, these personal effects helped provide a deeper context for more than one hundred oil sketches and paintings also included in the Coe Foundation's gift. In and of themselves, the studio materials could seem inconsequential, even mundane—exceptional mainly for their provenance. But when assembled alongside the paintings and sculpture for which Remington is best known, they became exceedingly important. As do individual musical notes in an orchestra, these individual artifacts gave substance to a grander composition of the artist's life history.

It is not hard to imagine a different fate for the Remington Studio Collection—the group broken up, sold piecemeal, and scattered across the country or the world. But, thanks to the generosity of Mrs. William Robertson Coe, Mr. William Rogers Coe, the Honorable Robert Coe, and Mr. Henry H. R. Coe, the collection remained intact. In 1981, much of its contents were installed in a reconstructed studio modeled after Remington's East Coast atelier, a project made possible by a generous grant from Laurance S. Rockefeller. A perennial favorite among guests to the Whitney, the Remington Studio is a light-filled space with rose-colored walls upon which hang an astounding assortment of props, paraphernalia, and artwork. As a period room, it evokes the era and environment in which Remington blended fact and fiction to create his own distinctive vision of the American West, a vision that would inspire generations to come.

And so it was that a studio collection formed the Whitney's foundation and set the stage for Cody to become a recognized repository of such exceptional and historically important assets. As the Buffalo Bill Historical Center (now the Buffalo Bill Center of the West) grew and its campus expanded to encompass five museums, a conservation laboratory, and a research library, the institution developed a distinctly interdisciplinary character, making it even better suited to house, preserve, and interpret the varied objects that constitute artists' studio collections.

Over the years, the Whitney accessioned the studio collections of three other celebrated western artists. Each of these acquisitions reflected a forging of mutual interests among donors and museum staff who recognized the Whitney's unrivaled ability to make artists' stories available to the world. A shared commitment between the Whitney's founding director, Dr. Harold McCracken, and the Coe Family enabled the Center to become the steward of the Remington Studio Collection. Peter Hassrick, Peg Coe, and Laurence Rockefeller established the Center as the site of the artist's re-created workspace. In 1978, Ruth Koerner Oliver and William H.D. Koerner, heirs of W.H.D. Koerner, donated the artist's studio effects in that same spirit. In 1986, Mr. and Mrs. Forrest Fenn donated the studio-cabin of Joseph Henry Sharp, and, thanks to Joseph and Miriam Sample, Thomas J. Watson, and IBM Corporation, Sharp's "Absarokee Hut" was renovated and relocated to the museum grounds. And, in the 2000s, as discussed below, the family of Alexander Phimister Proctor entered into a partnership with the Whitney and made monumental gifts of the sculptor's work and archives, heralding a long-term collaboration between the museum and Proctor's descendants. The Center's four studio collections constitute the cornerstones of the Whitney's holdings and are what truly distinguishes the Whitney from its sister institutions. Each offers unrivaled insight into the artists' private worlds and encourages deeper appreciation for human ingenuity and the artistic process.

One can admire a handsome bronze sculpture from a purely aesthetic point of view, assessing its craftsmanship, subject, and composition. On a deeper level, one may seek the context in which the work was made, the artist's intent, or its reception by looking to scholarly assessments or contemporaneous narratives written by critics, peers, or the artist during his or her lifetime. But undoubtedly richer and more complex is an understanding garnered from an in-depth investigation of an extensive archive of correspondence, diaries, photographs, preliminary drawings, studies in plaster or bronze, and casting records of that bronze. This kind of object-based study is possible at the Buffalo Bill Center of the West, where curators and independent scholars have only just begun to scratch the surface of a treasure trove of material in its studio collections. The eleven in-depth studies of Alexander Phimister Proctor's iconic bronzes that comprise the corpus of this publication poignantly reveal the fruitful results of one expert's dedicated exploration of the Center's cache of Proctor materials. Thoughtfully composed by leading scholar Peter Hassrick, the following essays shed new light on a selection of Proctor's best western sculptures. Hassrick has established his distinguished reputation in the field of American art history in large part by scrutinizing the work of important nineteenth- and early-twentieth-century artists, including Frederic Remington, Ernest Blumenschein, E. Martin Hennings, William Tylee Ranney, John Mix Stanley, and Allen Tupper True. In 2003, Hassrick served as guest curator of the first major exhibition of Proctor's sculpture, *Wildlife and Western Heroes: Alexander Phimister Proctor, Sculptor*, organized by the Amon Carter Museum and authored the accompanying catalogue, the first in-depth study of Proctor's work. In this publication, Hassrick turns once again to Proctor and with a connoisseur's perspective invites readers to look more closely at the sculptor's enduring contributions to the field of western American art.

Proctor was a prolific artist best known for his bronze depictions of western and wildlife subjects and his public monuments. Though born in Canada, Proctor spent his youth in Denver, Colorado, where boyhood escapades and family camping trips in the Rockies and their foothills kindled in him a lifelong wanderlust. Proctor was, from an early age, "at home in the open," as he wrote, and his interest in outdoor adventure fed his artistic practice throughout his career. In the West's wild reaches, the artist sought solace, pursued his passions for hunting and fishing, and sketched the landscape and the creatures that roamed its great expanses. And although he became restless after too long a stint in town, the dusty streets of Denver with their cattle drives and the antics of roughneck cowboys, miners, and hunters also provided ample inspiration for the budding artist. Proctor established a pattern in his teens and early twenties of summering in the high country and spending winters in a downtown studio where he fulfilled commissions for illustrations and worked up sketches into finished paintings. He would continue this itinerant lifestyle long after he moved away from the Colorado frontier; the mountains of the West beckoned him, and whenever he could, he answered their call.

Proctor worked under the tutelage of several established artists in Denver, but was predominantly self-taught during his early years. His artistic growth was also encouraged by his cohorts, fellow artists with whom he shared studio space and exhibited work in venues across the growing local cultural scene. An 1883 trip to Yosemite catalyzed his resolve to become a professional artist, but several years would pass before Proctor could afford to move to New York City, a longtime goal of both the artist and his father, who supported his son's aspirations wholeheartedly. In the winter of 1885, Proctor traded the open spaces of the West—his early classroom—for the museums, galleries, and studios of New York. Although he continued to sketch and paint, he increasingly turned to sculpting as his preferred form of artistic expression. He undertook formal training at the National Academy of Design and the Art Students League and, on his own time, sketched and modeled animals at the Central Park and Bronx Zoos. Working alongside (and sometimes *inside*) the animal paddocks, he honed his skill as a sculptor not only of western wildlife but of more exotic species as well. His intimate understanding of animal anatomy and locomotion, based on close study of live and dissected specimens (which he harvested himself in the field or examined in the lab of the American Museum of Natural History), lent his compositions an air of authenticity that few other animalier artists of his era achieved.

Throughout his life, Proctor was an eager student with an almost insatiable hunger for knowledge. He sought beauty and ideal forms in nature, looked to classical Greek statuary for inspiration, and solicited advice from instructors and artist peers. Proctor's pursuit of perfection was inexhaustible, and his career was marked by an intense passion for his subjects and commitment to his craft.

For his first major commission, Proctor was invited to create life-size sculptures to decorate the grounds of the 1893 World's Columbian Exposition in Chicago. His subjects were western animals and equestrian models of a cowboy and an Indian, the latter inspired by William F. "Buffalo Bill" Cody's Wild West performers. His work earned him accolades, and, encouraged by this success, he decided to travel to Paris, the veritable center of art and culture, to broaden his horizons. There, he studied at the Académie Julian and the Académie Colarossi, frequented the city's historic museums, and continued to study animals at local menageries. He would later return to Paris, and spent time in Rome as the Resident Sculptor of the American Academy.

Proctor traveled extensively not only to further his studies but also to fulfill commissions, satisfy his adventurous whims, and seek new, compelling subjects. As he wrote in his autobiography, "Smoke from my tent has curled into the sky in many places." Often with his wife, Margaret "Mody"—a talented artist herself and Proctor's most dedicated supporter and critic—and their family in tow, the sculptor ventured from the bustling cities of continental Europe and America's East Coast to quieter locales west of the Mississippi and Missouri Rivers. The American West proved an endless source of inspiration and rejuvenation for Proctor, and some of his best-known works featuring American Indian and cowboy subjects and wildlife were based on his experiences visiting Cheyenne, Nez Perce, and Blackfeet Indians on the northern plains; observing buckaroos at roundups and rodeos from California to Oregon; studying and sketching bison at a game preserve; and roaming wild places from Colorado to Alaska.

Proctor became one of the most acclaimed artists of his time, garnering public and private patronage that placed his sculptures, from small bronzes to heroic-size monuments, in prominent private collections, city centers, and renowned museums. He collaborated with the leading artists of his day, including Augustus Saint-Gaudens. He was a member of more than twenty-five professional organizations and won significant national and international awards and honors for his sculptures and paintings. He befriended American presidents, European dignitaries, influential figures in America's emerging conservation movement, distinguished artists and collectors, and many among the upper echelons of academia and business. Some of these illustrious friends he immortalized in bronze and stone portraits.

Although Proctor trained in traditional art academies and espoused classical European models, his career was equally shaped by his lifetime of experiences in the western American wilds. The sculptor felt as much at home in the backcountry as he did in urban art capitals, and his ability to nimbly navigate these disparate worlds contributed greatly to his success. Illustrative of what Hassrick has called Proctor's "duality" was the artist's application of a refined French Beaux-Arts style, which he mastered through years of committed study, to fundamentally American subjects and themes. Drawing on his own personal history and the larger social and natural histories of the American West, Proctor's paintings and sculptures celebrated—with all the elegance and grace of the Beaux-Arts aesthetic—some of the characteristics often associated with the West and North America, traits he himself also embodied: independence, optimism, industriousness, and bravery.

In the years following Proctor's death, the sculptor's family strove to preserve his memory and then passed the torch to subsequent generations to continue the quest. Much credit for Proctor's increasing renown after his passing should go to his daughter Hester, who edited and published her father's autobiography, *Sculptor in Buckskin*, in 1971. It seems that all of the other Proctors were enchanted by their family's patriarch as well, and one needn't look further than the final passage of his autobiography to see why. Proctor wrote: "I am eternally obsessed with two deep desires—one, to spend as much time as possible in the wilderness, and the other, to accomplish something worthwhile in art. With a fine wife as inspiration in my work and as a companion in the wilderness, with a fine family of children, and with good friends, my cup has been full to overflowing."

Such passion and optimism were contagious and spread even to the youngest among the Proctor clan. Sitting on his grandfather's lap, patiently posing for a sculpture, or laughingly fleeing a lasso's loop wielded by Proctor himself—these were the moments that sparked a special bond between the artist and his grandson and namesake, Phimister Proctor "Sandy" Church. As a young man Sandy struck out on a journey to amass and study Proctor's artwork and share his legacy with the world, and has been "following in Granddad's footsteps" ever since. Together with his wife, Sally, and his daughter, Laura Proctor Ames, Sandy Church has indescribably enriched our understanding of the sculptor's life and art by sharing the family's personal recollections and his intimate knowledge gained through years of devoted research. The Churches have also shared their treasures, choosing the Center as the ultimate locus for the collection they thoughtfully assembled.

For more than a decade, the Center has been the beneficiary of donations on behalf of the Proctor family, the A. Phimister Proctor Museum (founded by Sandy and Sally Church in Poulsbo, Washington, in 1997), and the Proctor Foundation. Between 2003 and 2006, the Center accessioned the artist's personal papers, artifacts from his life and work, and an extraordinary collection of art objects, thereby establishing the institution as the steward of the largest collection of Proctor material in the country. In 2016, the Center was fortunate to receive a culminating gift of paintings, plasters, and bronzes created by Proctor, along with related historical material. Among the treasures were exceptional casts of Proctor's *Q Street Buffalo* and *Buckaroo,* both of which are examined in this publication alongside other of Proctor's best western works.

In 2009, a large alcove within the Whitney was redesigned and dedicated to the display of a representative cross-section of the Proctor collection, including significant examples of the artist's opus. The space commemorates Proctor's long and impressive career, in particular his love of outdoor adventure and dedication to his craft. The Proctor Studio, with its rich burgundy walls and brick architectural details, has the feeling of a turn-of-the-century bronze foundry. A large-scale photographic reproduction of Proctor's *Rough Rider* (Theodore Roosevelt) statue and a painted plaster model of the same heighten the effect. Displayed in sections as if ready for assembly, the monumental model and its interpretation through written and visual means help pull back the curtain on the complicated process of casting a bronze statue. The space is otherwise filled with Proctor's models and sculptures in plaster and bronze, works on paper, and finished oil paintings in a display that illustrates the artist's expertise in multiple media and his facility in depicting a wide range of subjects from bronc riders and Indian leaders to all manner of western wildlife. While the Proctor Studio Collection cannot, because of its size, be shown in its entirety within the Whitney, an active schedule of rotations in the gallery space regularly brings new works and fresh perspectives to the display, and the Center's staff can provide scholars access to those objects not on view.

The ancillary, supporting materials related to Proctor—those shown in the gallery and a larger group held in the Center's research library and collections storage—allow for a more complete understanding of Proctor's finished artwork: its meaning and import, the context in which his works were originally made, their reception, the artist's intent, and his interactions with fellow artists and patrons concerning the works. As this publication illustrates, the study of these broad and deep collections can result in new, connoisseurial perspectives on Proctor, a great American artist.

The Alexander Phimister Proctor Studio Collection at the Center comprises a wide range of objects, but what makes the Proctor collection unique, aside from its nearly comprehensive nature and its kaleidoscopic diversity, is the family's long-term involvement in and support of its development and preservation. Like the Coe, Koerner, and Fenn families before them, the Proctors, through their benevolence and passion, have realized in a grand way their commitment to promoting a broader appreciation for the artist and his oeuvre. The reverberations of this commitment are felt far beyond the Center, particularly by other institutions whose holdings include works by Proctor and in other cities where Proctor's monuments stand. The Proctor family and the A. Phimister Proctor Foundation have underwritten preservation projects that help to ensure the collection's longevity and appreciation by future generations.

They have supported research, notably by empowering museum interns and fellows to work alongside top scholars in the fields of conservation, art history, and technical studies. One of these fellows is Allison Rosenthal, whose essay on the elemental analyses of Proctor's bronzes undertaken by Sandy Church and Dr. Bruce Kaiser is included herein.

Though long a topic of art historical interest, the study of bronzes having western American subjects has lately experienced a renaissance. Illustrative of this trend was the highly successful and well-received exhibition and publication *The American West in Bronze, 1850–1925*, co-organized in 2014 by the Metropolitan Museum of Art, New York, and the Denver Art Museum. Eight of Proctor's bronzes were included in that important exhibition, a number exceeded in representation only by Proctor's contemporary Charles M. Russell. Beyond, but complimentary to, the field of art history, new scientific technologies such as X-ray fluorescence (XRF) are being employed to investigate western bronzes at a molecular level. We hope that *The Best of Proctor's West*, in its interdisciplinary approach combining aesthetic, connoisseurial, and analytical inquiry into Proctor's iconic western bronzes, advances further the burgeoning interest in the subject of western American bronze sculpture at large. All are invited to join the conversation and to explore Proctor's legacy through the studio collection at the Buffalo Bill Center of the West, the museum's website, and this publication. The opportunities in research and exhibition made possible by the treasure trove of art, artifacts, and archival material are endless.

During 2017, the centennial year of the Buffalo Bill Memorial Association (the Center's founding body), it seems especially pertinent to highlight one among the Center's many great strengths, its studio collections, and one of western American art's luminaries, Alexander Phimister Proctor. This publication stands as part of a larger suite of programming coordinated to commemorate the organization's hundred years of growth, fueled by a passion to share the spirit of the American West the world over.

Few artists embodied the spirit of the West to a greater extent than did Proctor. A self-proclaimed "sculptor in buckskin," Proctor dedicated his life to exploring the West with his hunting rifle and with pad and pencil. In towns and cities across the nation, Proctor's monuments (twenty-seven of them) and sculptures pay homage to western heritage. Proctor's *Buffalo* decorate the Dumbarton (Q Street) Bridge in Washington, D.C.; his *Broncho Buster* and *On the War Trail* stand sentry in Civic Center Park in Denver; his *Pioneer Mother* honors women's heroic roles in western settlement in Kansas City, Missouri; and his monument to U.S. president and conservationist Theodore Roosevelt stands in both Portland, Oregon, and Minot, North Dakota. But it is in Cody, Wyoming, a small town situated at the heart of the Rocky Mountain West, where the most comprehensive collection of Proctor's work is held and where scholarly inquiry into the artist's life and legacy will continue to flourish.

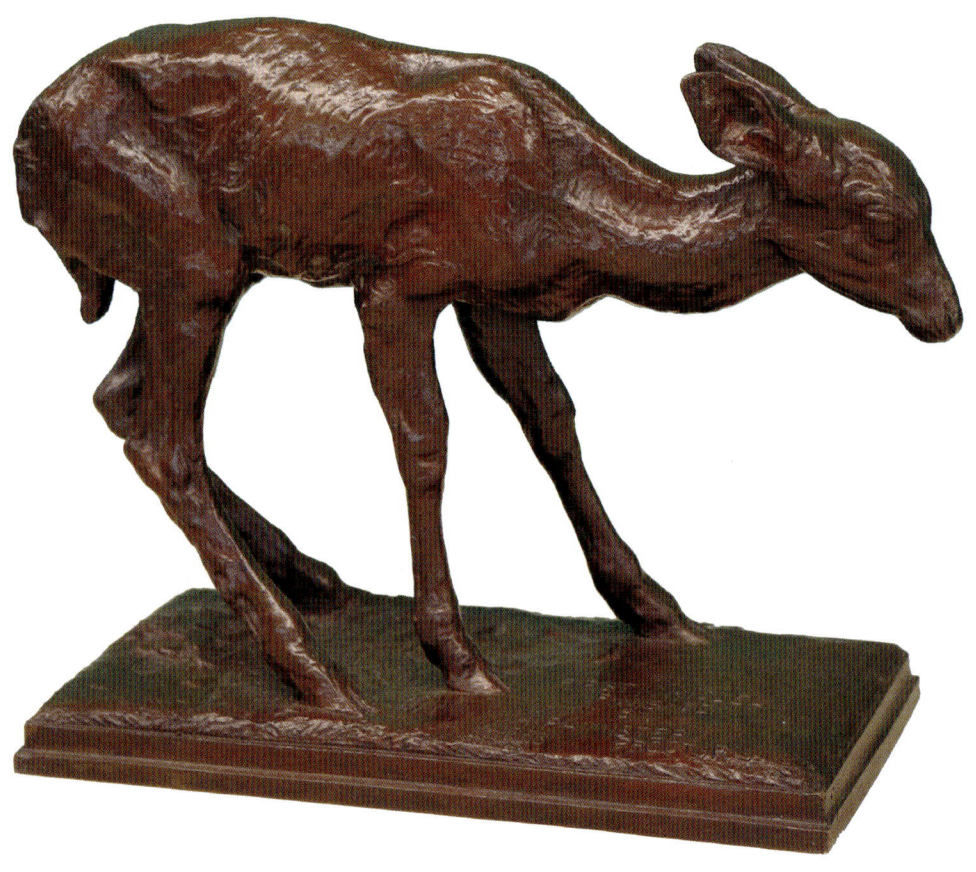

ALEXANDER PHIMISTER PROCTOR, *Fawn* (first model), 1914. Bronze, 6 ¾ in. (height). R. W. Norton Art Gallery, Shreveport, Louisiana

FAWN (FIRST MODEL, 1888)
AND
FAWN (SECOND MODEL, 1892)

The Fawn's First Step; Young Fawn; First Step; Mule Deer

From the first time Proctor's initial version of the *Fawn* received critical acclaim in the newspapers, the sculpture was paired with another work. That was in January 1893 in Chicago. Proctor had just cast in bronze the earliest variation of the *Panther*. A reporter from the *Chicago Inter Ocean* saw the two works and remarked: "The panther recently completed in bronze is an excellent example of the forceful power of his creations, and the shivering fawn overtaken by a storm shows the keen and sensitive perceptions of the sculptor."[1]

This comment provides not only a cogent review of the two works but also an assessment of the artist himself. The reviewer grouped the two sculptures together, and together they have a broader meaning. As a pair they reflected the complex character of the artist and made subtle reference to his biography as it had developed to this point. Revealed in his panther was Proctor's prowess as a wilderness hunter and, in the newborn deer, his own emergence in a competitive world as an artist of note. Proctor explored the hunter theme again in his early work when he produced his lumbering *Polar Bear*, which, like the *Panther*, was first cast in 1893. At the same time, he could not forget his inherent empathy for the prey as well as the predator. By the end of 1893, he had apparently conceived at least two other variations of the baby deer.

The first instance of the *Fawn* being pictured on the printed page came in mid-October 1893 when Proctor's first model was illustrated as a plaster [PLATE 1.1] in an extended article on the artist in Denver's *Rocky Mountain News*.[2] The writer praised Proctor's "knowledge of animals acquired by close study" in the Colorado backcountry.

---

1 "Phimister Proctor Is a True Natural Sculptor," *Sunday Inter Ocean* (January 1, 1893).
2 "To Fame in a Year," *Rocky Mountain News* (October 15, 1893). This is probably the same plaster that Proctor had exhibited in New York that spring. See *Fourteenth Exhibition of the Society of American Artists* (New York: Society of American Artists, 1892), no. 172.

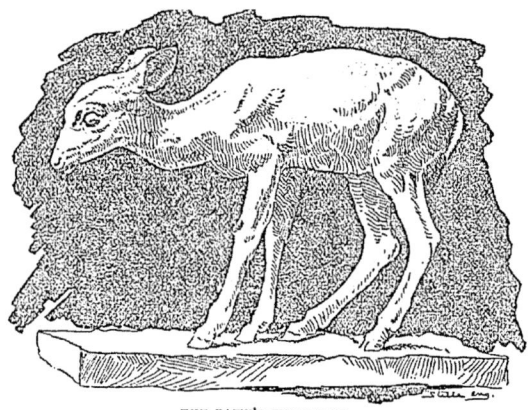

THE FAWN'S FIRST STEP.

[PLATE 1.1]

ALEXANDER PHIMISTER PROCTOR

Fawn, 1893

Wood engraving
Illustration in (Denver), *Rocky Mountain News*
(October 15, 1893), 10
Buffalo Bill Center of the West, Cody, Wyoming

[PLATE 1.2]

ALEXANDER PHIMISTER PROCTOR

Fawn (first model), ca. 1899

Bronze, 7 ¼ in. (height)
Buffalo Bill Center of the West, Cody, Wyoming. Gift
of A. Phimister Proctor Museum with special thanks
to Sandy and Sally Church. 4.08.8

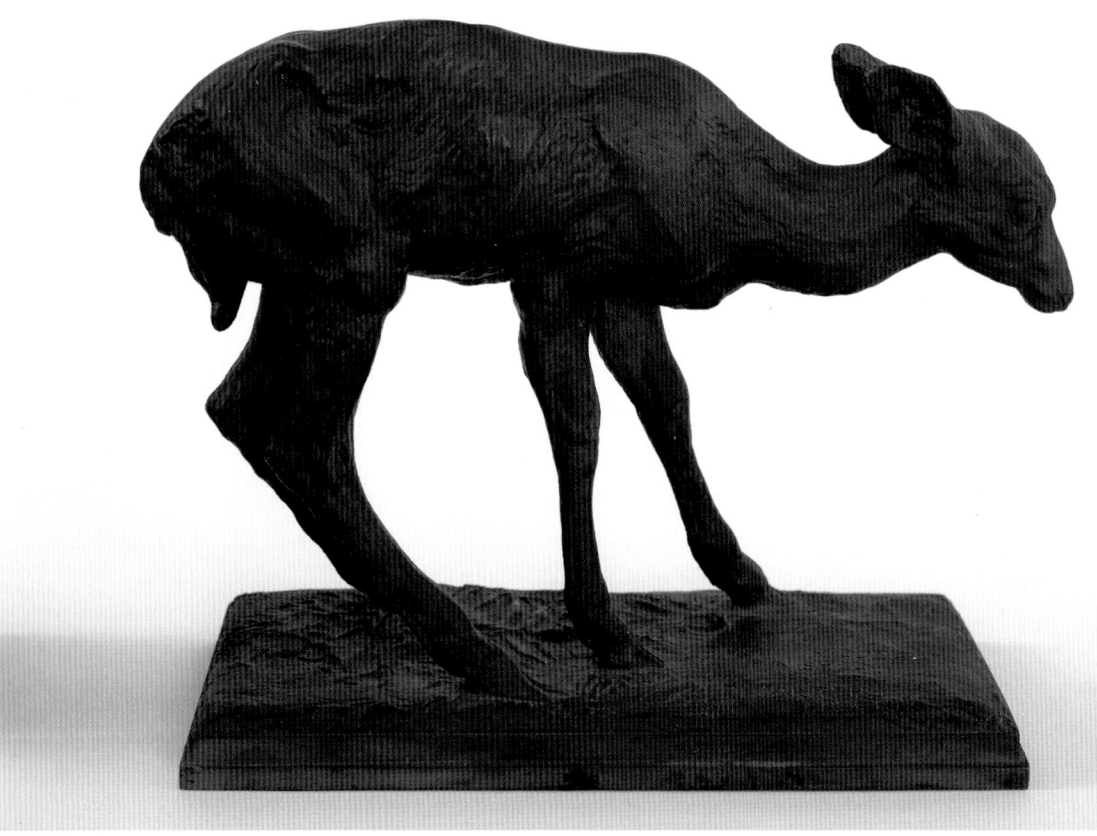

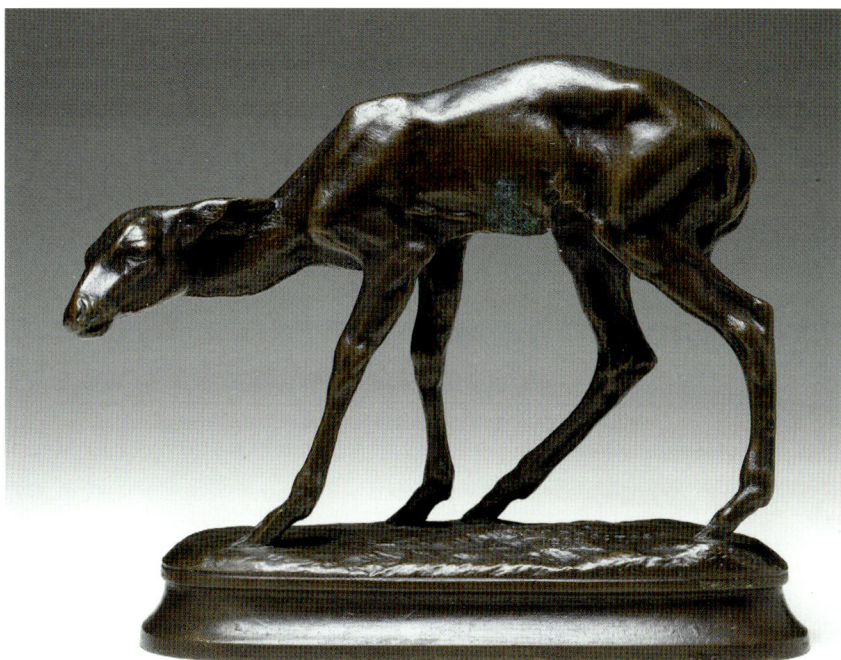

He also mentioned the fact that Proctor had been married only a few weeks before, so that this first model of the *Fawn* [PLATE 1.2] may have provided a metaphor for familial expectations.

The *Rocky Mountain News* writer went on to comment about "one of the artist's most recent efforts," called "The Orphans," a model projected to be cast in bronze in Paris, where the newlyweds were soon to travel. It is unknown what *The Orphans* looked like, as it was never cast, though it is presumed to have portrayed twin fawns. But the group was described as "so tender, graceful, touching and beautiful that those of his friends who have been permitted to see them are unmeasured in praise."[3] Here, then, is another pairing for the infant deer.

Although it is not known whether the second model of the *Fawn* [PLATE 1.3] was one of the orphans, it certainly shared all the characteristics of the orphan model—grace, tenderness, and beauty. Possibly, then, the second model, which bears the date of 1893 stamped boldly into its base, was one of the pair. In any event, by autumn of 1893 in Paris, Proctor had at least two versions of the *Fawn* in his studio.

Because of his busy schedule as a student in Paris and his two big commissions with Augustus Saint-Gaudens, Proctor entered few public exhibitions between 1894 and 1899.[4] In 1900, though, at the Paris Exposition, Proctor reversed the pattern. He submitted eight small sculptures for the American display, including one he titled *Young Fawn*.

[PLATE 1.3]

ALEXANDER PHIMISTER
PROCTOR

Mule Deer (Fawn)
(second model), ca. 1898

Bronze, 6 ¾ in. (height)
Amherst Library, New York, New York.
Gift of George D. Pratt / Bridgeman
Images

3   "To Fame in a Year." The model is presumed lost.
4   The exception was the *Panther*. See *Sixteenth Annual Exhibition of the Society of American Artists* (New York: Society of American Artists, 1894), no. 313. He had exhibited three animal sculptures at the Chicago World's Fair in 1893, but not a *Fawn*. See *World's Columbian Exposition, 1893, Official Catalogue: Fine Arts* (Chicago: W. B. Gonkey Company, 1893), nos. 100a–100c.

The group of eight won him a gold medal.[5] This fawn was probably the same *Young Fawn* that he sent to the Pan-American Exposition in Buffalo, New York, the following year.[6] In neither case, nor in several subsequent exhibitions in New York and Toronto, is there any indication which version of the *Fawn*, the first or second model, was included. However, a hint may have surfaced in 1915. That year, he submitted eleven small bronzes to the Panama-Pacific International Exposition in San Francisco. He loaned only

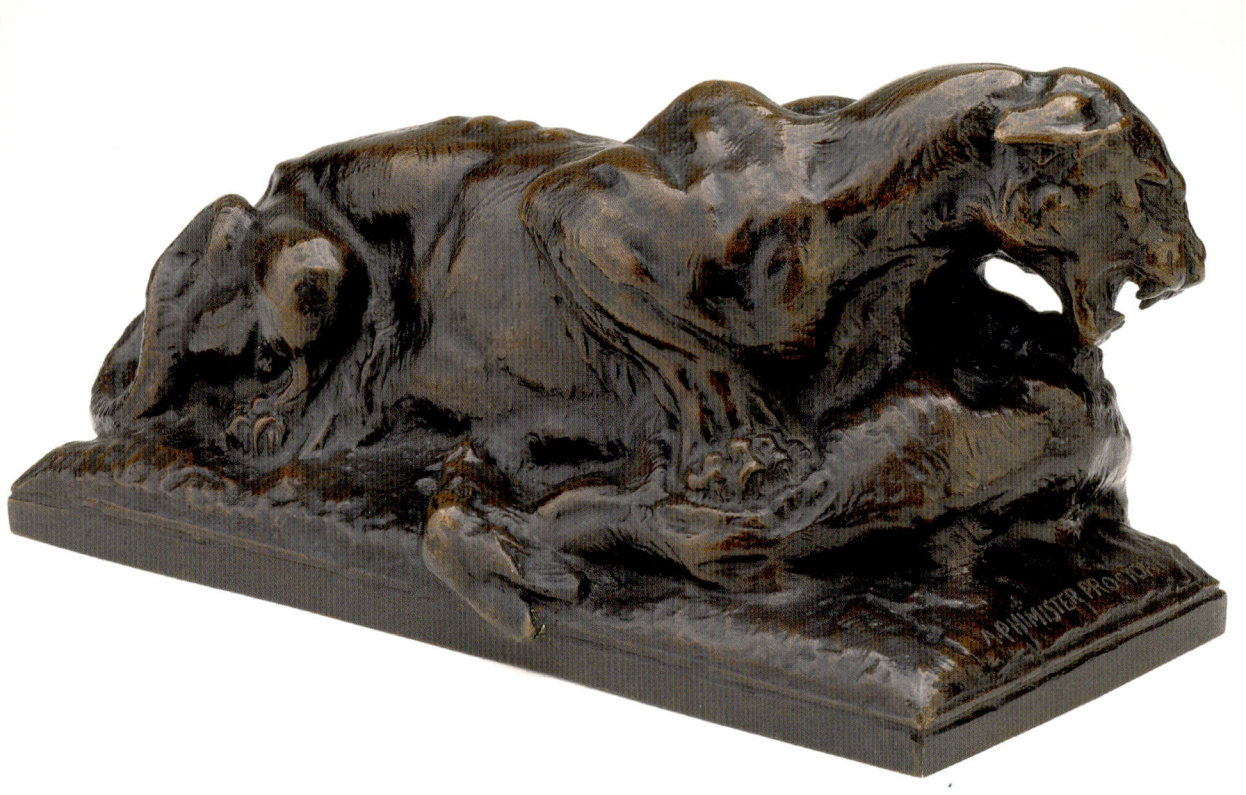

[PLATE 1.4]

ALEXANDER PHIMISTER
PROCTOR

Cougar Feasting on Fawn
(*Panther with Kill*), 1909

Bronze, 5 ¼ in. (height)
National Museum of Wildlife Art,
Jackson, Wyoming

one of his fawn pieces, and it was clearly labeled *Fawn: First Model*.[7] This distinction was made again at the Albright Art Gallery in Buffalo and at the Art Institute of Chicago in 1916.[8] Early that year, in a special one-man show of Proctor's work at the Art Institute, the artist included both versions.

5   *Official Illustrated Catalogue: Fine Arts Exhibit, United States of America, Paris Exposition of 1900* (Boston: Noyes, Platt & Company, 1900), nos. 43–50.

6   *Pan-American Exposition: Catalogue of the Exhibition of Fine Arts* (Buffalo: n.p., 1901), no. 1638.

7   *Official Catalogue of the Department of Fine Arts, Panama-Pacific International Exposition* (San Francisco: Wahlgreen Company, 1915), no. 3531.

8   See *Catalogue of Contemporary American Sculpture* (Buffalo: Buffalo Fine Arts Academy, 1916), no. 616; and *Catalogue of the Twenty-Ninth Annual Exhibition of American Oil Paintings and Sculpture* (Chicago: Art Institute of Chicago, 1916), no. 871.

One was titled simply *Fawn* and the other *Fawn* (*First model*).[9] This would suggest, then, that when he displayed the earlier work, he made sure to note that it was the first model.

In 1908, Proctor decided to combine the subjects of his two contrasting sculptural pieces *Panther* and *Fawn* into one composition he titled *Panther with Kill*. [PLATE 1.4] It revealed the bitter, raw truth of nature's predator-prey relationship. A fawn has fallen victim to a mountain

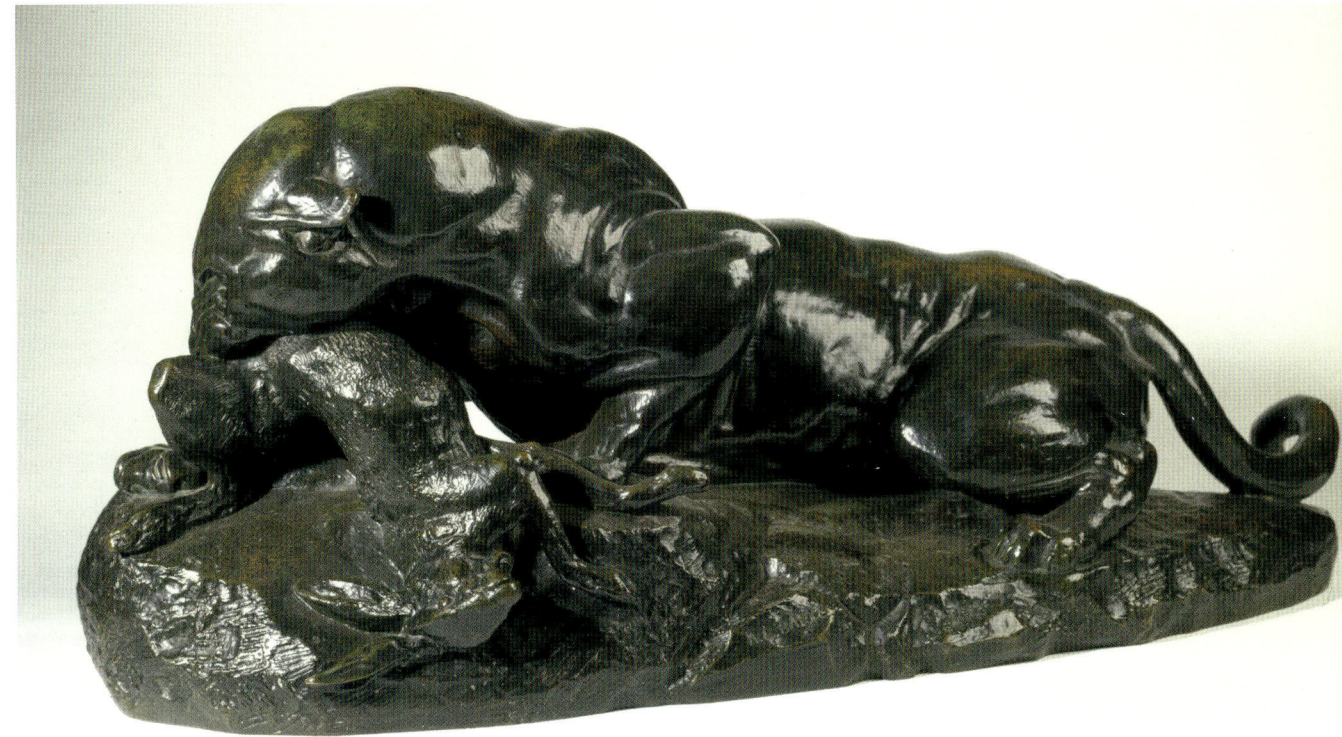

lion's voracious appetite. It was a theme that Proctor chose to explore primarily for artistic reasons as it mirrored a work by the Frenchman Antoine-Louis Barye, one of his sculptural heroes from the mid-nineteenth century, *Jaguar Devouring a Hare*.[10] [PLATE 1.5] Proctor's version, unlike that of his predecessor, was not popular. *Panther with Kill* was the ultimate and fatal pairing of deer and lion. Only two casts are known to exist today.

[PLATE 1.5]

ANTOINE-LOUIS BARYE
(b. France, 1795 – 1875)

Jaguar Devouring a Hare, ca. 1850

Bronze, 23 in. (height)
National Museum of Wildlife Art,
Jackson, Wyoming

9   *Small Bronzes by A. Phimister Proctor* (Chicago: Art Institute of Chicago, 1916),
     nos. 11 and 22.

10   I am grateful to Adam Duncan Harris of the National Museum of Wildlife Art in Jackson,
     Wyoming, for bringing this connection to my attention.

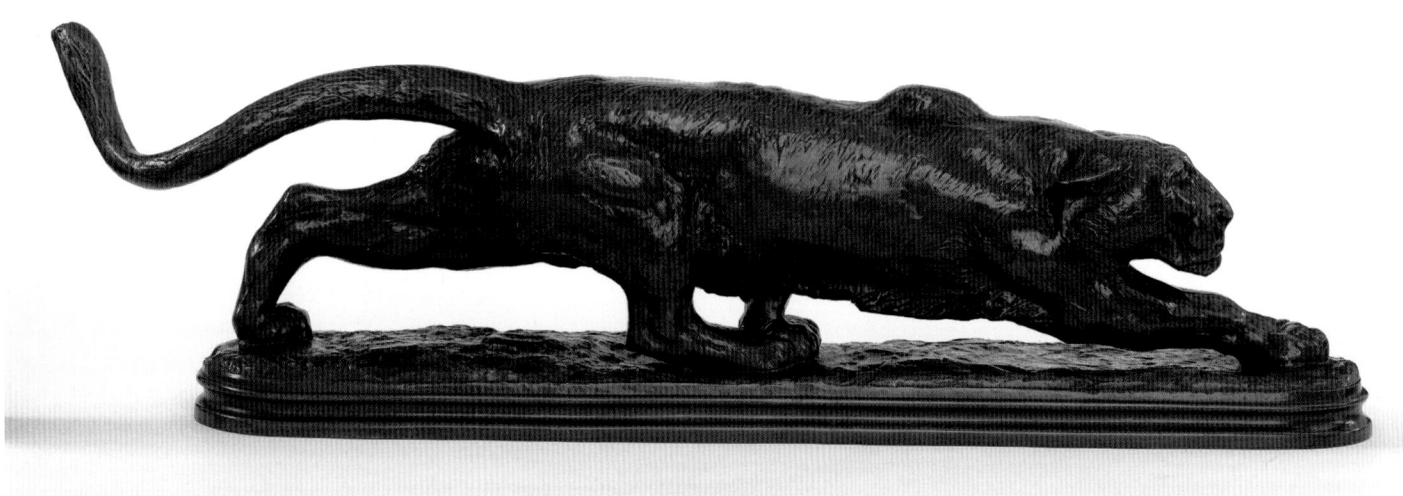

ALEXANDER PHIMISTER PROCTOR, *Stalking Panther,* ca. 1893. Bronze, 9 ¾ in. (height). Buffalo Bill Center of the West, Cody, Wyoming. Gift of A. Phimister Proctor Museum with special thanks to Sandy and Sally Church. 4.08.1

PANTHER

Prowling Panther; Charging Panther; Stalking Panther; Crouching Panther; Panther-Fate; Fate; Roosevelt Panther

Proctor began to dream of exploring in art the mountain lion of the Rockies during one of his hunting trips in the Flat Tops of the Colorado Rockies in the summer of 1887. He shot and killed at least a couple of bears, numerous deer and elk, and an adult panther. The lion was perhaps his favorite trophy. He sketched it, skinned it, and then had the pelt packed up to take back to his studio at the Art Students League in New York.[1] He continued to pursue his passion for these wild cats at New York's menagerie, just a few blocks away from his studio. Using various studies, he made his first model in wax at the Art Students League.[2]

When, in 1891, Proctor received an invitation to model monumental plaster sculptures of western animals as decorations for the grounds of the World's Columbian Exposition, one of the subjects he chose was his western mountain lion. [PLATE 2.1] It may have looked something like the first wax model that he had fashioned in New York, but that is not known. What is for certain is the impression it made on the visitors. In what one reviewer referred to as "Nature's mountain school, among the wild play-fellows of canyon and forest," Proctor had learned from "the lion's roar or the cunning panther's plaintive cry" the essence of wilderness. Yet, beyond that, through his personal studies, he had also become a savant of the cat's "anatomy, which is a more valuable accomplishment for a sculptor."[3]

As a subsequent tabletop bronze, this work seems to have undergone more alterations over the long course of its life than any

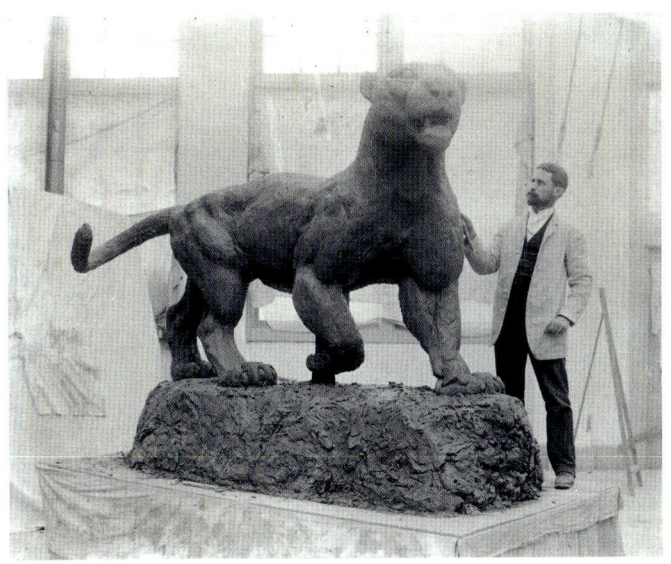

[PLATE 2.1]

UNKNOWN PHOTOGRAPHER

Proctor and World's Fair *Panther,* 1893

Photograph, b&w
Alexander Phimister Proctor Collection, MS 242, Harold McCracken Research Library, Buffalo Bill Center of the West, Cody, Wyoming. P.242.429

1 Katharine C. Ebner (ed.), *Sculptor in Buckskin: The Autobiography of Alexander Phimister Proctor* (Norman: University of Oklahoma Press, 2009), 83–84.

2 Ibid., 88.

3 "About the Studios: Phimister Proctor Is a True Natural Sculptor," *Chicago Inter Ocean* (January 1, 1893).

other Proctor sculpture. Although the work was copyrighted under the title *Panther* in 1897, most early versions of the piece are marked with the dates "1891–1892." The first known record of the work being cast in bronze appeared in the *Chicago Inter Ocean* on January 1, 1893, which reported its having been "recently completed in bronze."[4] That 1892 casting (current location unknown), also referred to simply as *Panther*, was exhibited in the American art section of the World's Columbian Exposition in Chicago in 1893 and the next spring in New York City at the Society of American Artists.[5]

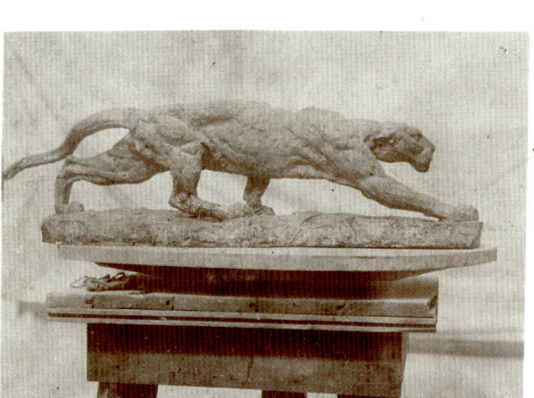

At the showing in New York, Proctor's early venture in animalier bronze drew a good deal of notice. When it was seen in the Society of American Artists exhibition, one reviewer admired *Panther* for its "rough energy" and "truth," another for its evident fierceness, and a third for its anatomical correctness.[6] Proctor could not have asked for more complete coverage or a more thorough assessment of his skills. In a comparison of what is thought to be the plaster for this early version (preserved in an extant photograph) [PLATE 2.2] to later iterations, the tail seems to droop, the body is more elevated, the foreleg is attenuated, and the head is substantially smaller.

[PLATE 2.2]

ALEXANDER PHIMISTER PROCTOR, PHOTOGRAPHER

Panther (one of Proctor's first models), 1893

Photograph, b&w
Alexander Phimister Proctor Collection, MS 242, Harold McCracken Research Library, Buffalo Bill Center of the West, Cody, Wyoming. P.242.432

When the Proctors moved to Paris in the fall of 1893, they took with them what the artist referred to as a "three-foot plaster model of the stalking panther."[7] They must have left the first bronze casting at home to be shown in New York during their absence. But Proctor felt that he could make improvements on the piece, ultimately by studying the anatomy of a Parisian alley cat, and a new model was thus created in France. So pleased was Proctor with the subsequent revisions that he exhibited a "sketch" of it, presumably a plaster, in the Pennsylvania Academy of the Fine Arts in 1895.[8] He went to the expense of having that second version cast in bronze. Proctor referred to it, albeit incorrectly, as "our first real bronze."[9]

---

4   Ibid.

5   *World's Columbian Exposition, 1893, Official Catalogue: Fine Arts,* no. 100a; and *Sixteenth-Annual Exhibition of the Society of American Artists* (New York: Society of American Artists, 1894), no. 313.

6   See "The Chronicle of Arts," *New-York Daily Tribune* (April 10, 1894); "Society Show Soon to Close," *New York Times* (April 18, 1894); and "Juggling with Brushes . . . ," *Morning Journal* (March 18, 1894). I am grateful to Thayer Tolles for bringing these reviews to my attention.

7   Ebner, *Sculptor in Buckskin,* 102.

8   See Peter Hastings Falk (ed.), *The Annual Exhibition Record of the Pennsylvania Academy of the Fine Arts,* Vol. 2, 1876–1913 (Madison, CT: Sound View Press, 1989), 390.

9   Ebner, *Sculptor in Buckskin,* 102. A second bronze, identical except for the date, now in a private collection, was shown in 1899 at the Pennsylvania Academy of the Fine Arts. See Falk, *Annual Exhibition Record of the Pennsylvania Academy of the Fine Arts,* 2:390.

This may be the bronze owned by the famous operatic soprano Madame Lillian Nordica (1857–1914), who was in Europe performing that year. That casting has a unique marking on the base, not found on other castings, in which it is signed and dated 1894. [PLATE 2.3A and 2.3B] The head is shorter and less streamlined, the lower jaw does not protrude, the tail is straighter and bends more abruptly upward at the end, and the left forepaw is pointed outward to the left, quite differently from the later castings as well, suggesting that subsequent alterations were made after Proctor's

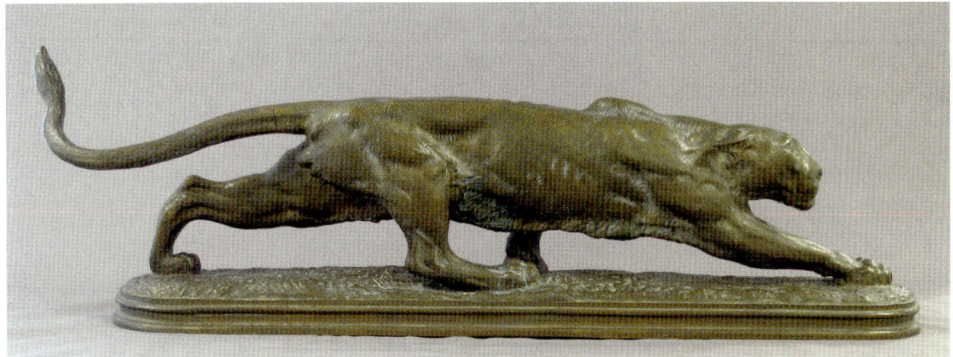

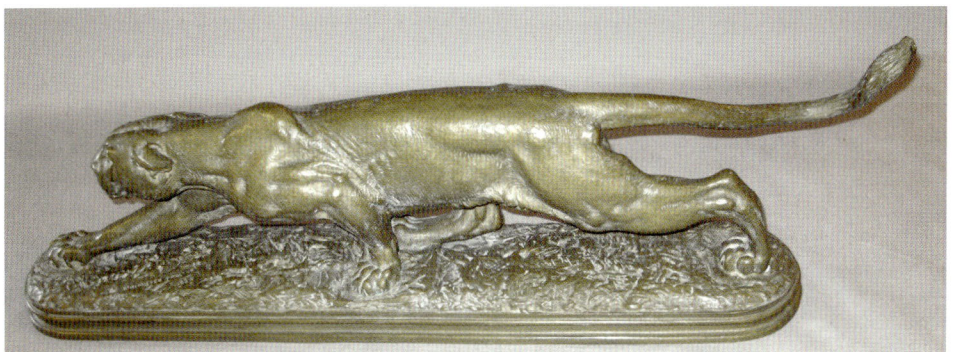

second attempt to further perfect the pose. A second casting of this version in bronze was exhibited in Philadelphia in 1899.[10]

When the third and most commonly known of the *Panther* versions was first modeled is not known. It varies from the earlier known version in that the tail is lowered and more curved, the left forepaw is placed in line with the cat's body, which is closer to the ground, and the jaw is brought forward in line with the nose. Proctor exhibited a casting under the title *Panther-Fate* in the U.S. Pavilion at the Paris Exposition in 1900,[11] and again—possibly as a plaster—under the title *Charging Panther* in the

[PLATES 2.3A AND 2.3B]

ALEXANDER PHIMISTER PROCTOR

Panther (views 1 and 2, second version), ca. 1894

Bronze
Nordica Homestead Museum, Farmington, Maine

---

10   Falk, *Annual Exhibition Record of the Pennsylvania Academy of the Fine Arts*, 2:390. This casting, with a Pennsylvania Academy of the Fine Arts sticker, was sold by the Thomas Nygard Gallery to a private collection in 2011.

11   *Official Illustrated Catalogue: Fine Arts Exhibit, United States of America, Paris Exposition of 1900* (Boston: Noyes, Platt & Co, 1900), no. 47.

Pan-American Exposition in Buffalo in 1901.[12] One sand casting of this work, currently in the collection of the Portland Art Museum in Oregon, was marked "1901" on the base, which suggests that this was possibly the inception date of the third version. It was cast by Gorham Co. Founders after 1913. At about the same time, Proctor started casting lost-wax versions of the bronze using the Roman Bronze Works. The earliest known example of this, cast number 4 produced in about 1902, is in the collections of the Metropolitan Museum of Art in New York. [PLATE 2.4] Between 1900 and

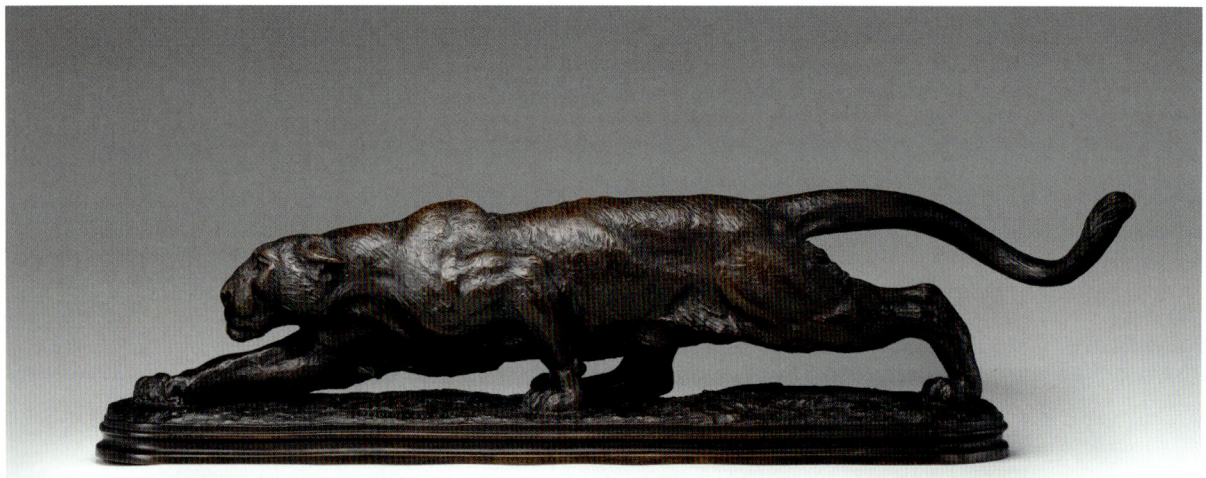

[PLATE 2.4]

ALEXANDER PHIMISTER
PROCTOR

Stalking Panther, ca. 1902

Bronze, 9 ½ in. (height)
The Metropolitan Museum of Art, New York, New York. Purchase, William Cullen Bryant Fellows Gifts and Maria DeWitt Jesup Fund, 1996. 1996.561. Art Resource, NY

1915 he cast twenty-two pieces with the Roman Bronze Works.[13]

In 1908, at Proctor's major retrospective exhibition in New York's prestigious Montross Gallery, the famous silversmith and brother-in-law of Proctor's friend Alden Sampson, Henry Blanchard Dominick, loaned a casting called *Prowling Panther* to the show. In the same exhibition, suggesting that a new variant of the piece was under way, Proctor exhibited what might be assumed to be the genesis of another, fourth version under the title "Prowling Panther: Later Study of the Above."[14] In his magazine, *The Craftsman,* Gustav Stickley referred to Proctor's show at the Montross Gallery as "one of the most important exhibits of the season," claiming also that his "'Prowling Panther' . . . is considered second to no other bronze in its vivid suggestion of swift stealthy action."[15] Presumably the review concerns the bronze casting, version four.

These later castings are somewhat sleeker than the third version. The hump over the panther's front shoulder is less accentuated, and the rear hip is lowered. As if to push the cat forward, the tail lifts slightly more upward than in earlier castings. [PLATE 2.5]

12   *Pan-American Exposition: Catalogue of the Exhibition of Fine Arts* (Buffalo: David Gray, 1901), no. 1636.

13   See note 20.

14   *Catalogue of Sculpture, Bronzes, Water Colors, and Sketches Exhibited by A. Phimister Proctor* (New York: Montross Gallery, 1908), nos. 4 and 4a.

15   "Music: Drama: Art: Reviews," *The Craftsman,* 15 (January 1909), 501.

The earliest documented example of what is probably this fourth variation was a sand-cast bronze produced by the New York foundry Jno. Williams, Inc., and acquired by Theodore Roosevelt in February 1909. The artist had received a letter from his close friend Henry L. Stimson, whom President Roosevelt had appointed as U.S. district attorney for the Southern District of New York. Stimson had been asked by members of the president's "Kitchen Cabinet" to acquire a casting of the *Panther* to be given to Roosevelt as a token of their respect for and appreciation of the

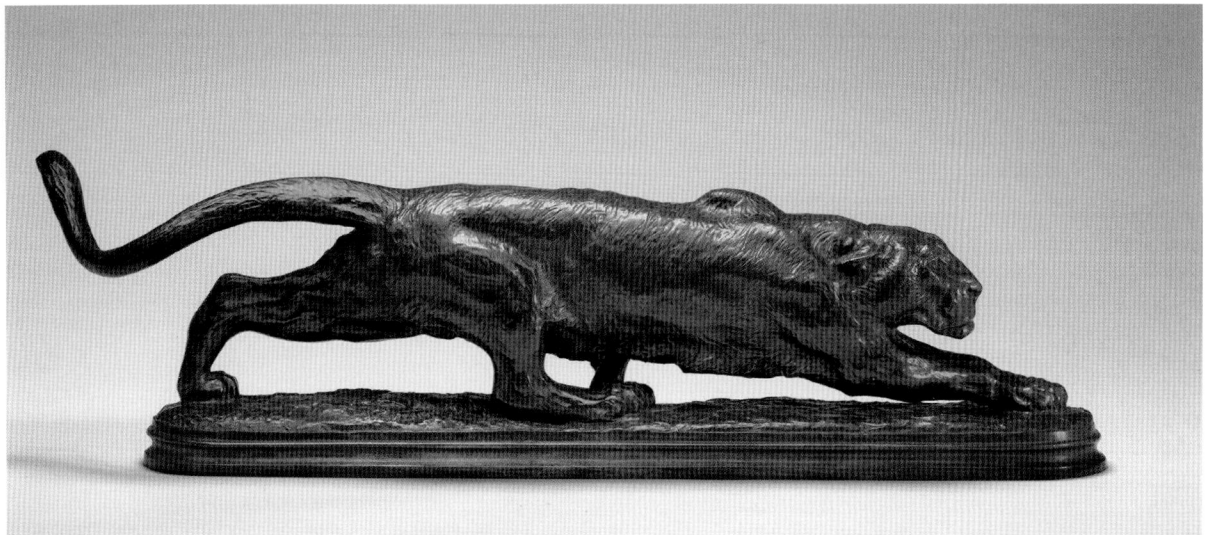

[PLATE 2.5]

ALEXANDER PHIMISTER PROCTOR

Stalking Panther, ca. 1905 – 1913

Bronze, 10 ¼ in. (height)
National Gallery of Art, Corcoran Collection, Washington, DC. Bequest of James Parmelee. 2015.19.3686

president's years of service as the nation's leader. Proctor was thus called upon to gratify the outgoing president of the United States, his own friend and supporter. Presented on February 26, 1909, the casting still resides at Sagamore Hill, Roosevelt's Oyster Bay, New York, home.[16] Roosevelt thereafter made the *Panther* a national symbol of power and fortitude.

Shortly on the heels of that commission, events moved forward that resulted in another casting of the fourth version, finding a home at the National Gallery of Canada in 1909. Proctor had become a member of the Canadian Art Club that year and was invited in March to show with his new associates at their second annual exhibition in Toronto. He displayed twelve bronzes, including a casting of *Prowling Panther*.[17] The club purchased this Jno. Williams, Inc., casting and donated it to the National Gallery of Canada in honor of its new member.

The Montross Gallery continued to feature Proctor's bronzes into the early teens.[18] But in 1913, the Gorham Company took center stage in Manhattan when, in its splashy new downtown gallery, Gorham presented a monumental one-man exhibition of Proctor's work. Among the twenty bronzes and twenty-five plasters was a bronze of what the catalogue called

16   See Ebner, *Sculptor in Buckskin,* 196.
17   *Canadian Art Club: Second Annual Exhibition* (Toronto: Canadian Art Club, 1909), no. 51.
18   See *Exhibition of Sculpture* (New York: Montross Gallery, 1912).

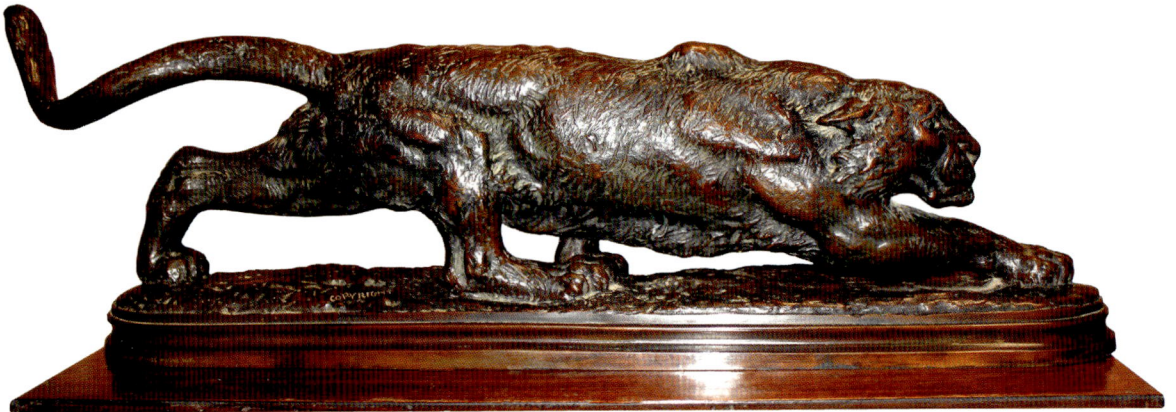

[PLATE 2.6]

ALEXANDER PHIMISTER
PROCTOR

Panther, ca. 1925

Bronze, 11 ¼ in. (height)
Belle Clegg Hays, Comptche, California

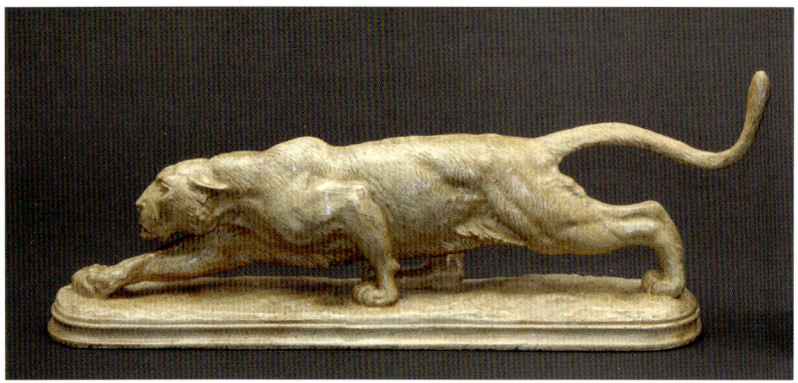

[PLATE 2.7]

ALEXANDER PHIMISTER
PROCTOR

Panther (small version), ca. 1922

Plaster, 6 ⅞ in. (height)
Buffalo Bill Center of the West, Cody,
Wyoming. Gift of A. Phimister Proctor
Museum with special thanks to Sandy
and Sally Church. 11.06.384

Charging Panther.[19] Orders could be taken, once that show piece was sold, and current research indicates that more than a half-dozen Gorham sales, mostly of sand-cast bronzes, occurred from that date forward into the 1940s. The same research notes that there are three known sand-cast bronzes produced by Jno. Williams Founders of New York between about 1900 and 1905, and another twelve known castings made after the foundry was incorporated as Jno. Williams, Inc., in 1905. Some of the latter are inscribed with cast numbers ranging from 3 (Agnes Etherington Art Centre) to 32 (private collection, Michigan), suggesting that Jno. Williams, Inc., was a major producer of these works. In addition, at least twenty-two, in lost wax, were produced by the Roman Bronze Works between 1900 and 1915.[20]

About a dozen years later, in 1922, Proctor again undertook modifications to the *Panther.* One result of this effort has been referred to as the remodeled large version, while the other was a substantially smaller interpretation. The former variation was made to satisfy the artist, who had evidently tired of the original pose, and the latter was initiated to accommodate patrons by introducing a work of similar spirit but at a reduced price.

19   *Exhibition of Bronzes and Plaster Models by A. Phimister Proctor* (New York: Gorham Co., 1913), no. 8.

20   The Roman Bronze Works ledger books at Amon Carter Museum record eight castings, numbers 8 through 15, made between 1904 and 1905 alone. Subsequent castings, up to number 22, were noted in the records up to 1915. If it can be assumed that the Roman Bronze Works began casting *Panthers* in around 1900, the firm averaged about three castings every two years for fifteen years.

The remodeled large version was sculpted in Palo Alto while Proctor was putting the finishing touches on a maquette for the monument *The Pioneer Mother* in Kansas City. The sculptor, ever conscious of costs, wished to realize serious economies by having the monument pointed up and cast in Italy. To that end he moved back to New York in the fall of 1925 to clean out his studio there and prepare for the trip to Europe. In early October, while Proctor was still in New York, Theodore Roosevelt's son Kermit and his friend Alfred Ernest Clegg visited the studio.[21] Clegg wanted to buy a casting of the *Panther* like the one Kermit's father had received as a gift in 1909. Proctor encouraged him to purchase a casting of the newly remodeled version from Roman Bronze Works. [PLATE 2.6] Clegg not only did that but also ordered castings of the *Indian Warrior* and the maquette size of the Kansas City *Pioneer Mother*. All three sculptures were passed down in the Clegg family.

The remodeled large version of the *Panther* is altered in a number of ways from its earlier prototype. In the new model the panther's face is shortened, resembling the first bronze castings of the piece. The forward shoulder is given more mass, the back left leg is strengthened and shortened, and the tail is somewhat further extended.

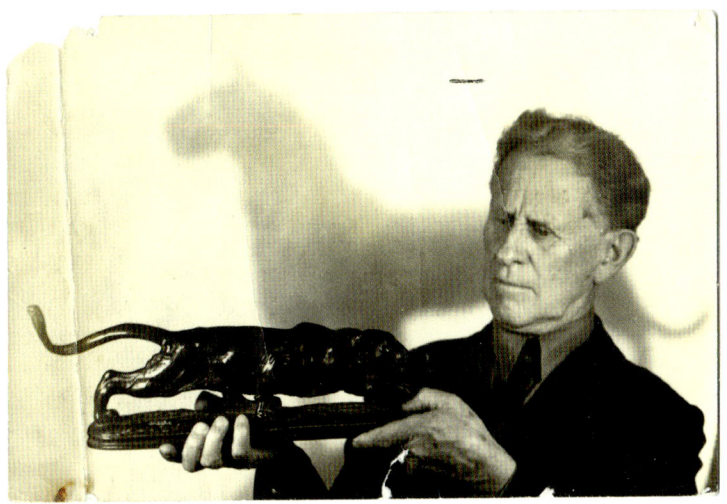

The small version of the *Panther* [PLATE 2.7] is reduced in size by half, measuring in length about 19 inches instead of 39 inches. These bronzes, quite rare today, were derived from a model conceived in 1922, the same date as the remodeled large version.[22] Cast in the 1920s from a plaster used by at least two foundries, the new model of the wild cat gratified the artist for nearly three decades and brought closure to Proctor's experience begun sixty-five years earlier. [PLATE 2.8] That hunting adventure in the Flat Tops of western Colorado in 1887, where—alone in the wilderness—he shot a mountain lion and spent several days sketching it in his hunting camp, was still a fond memory. Proctor's passion for and identification with one of nature's most iconic hunters had served him as a sculptor throughout his career. The multiple variations that he imposed on the theme only clarified how vital that experience and that model were to the development of his life's oeuvre.

[PLATE 2.8]

UNKNOWN PHOTOGRAPHER

Proctor reviewing small *Panther*, 1943

Photograph, b&w
Alexander Phimister Proctor Collection, MS 242, Harold McCracken Research Library, Buffalo Bill Center of the West, Cody, Wyoming. P.242.435

---

21   This story is recounted in Ebner, *Sculptor in Buckskin*, 196. I am grateful to Belle Clegg Hays, A. C. Clegg's daughter, for confirming the story from her family's perspective.

22   Proctor seems to have retained the 1897 copyright for both the remodeled and the small version. An article about his 1923 Stendahl Gallery exhibition in Los Angeles, in which he showed both new versions, mentions specifically that the small work had been first produced the previous year. See "Proctor, a Sculptor of Unusual Power," *Los Angeles Times* (April 1, 1923).

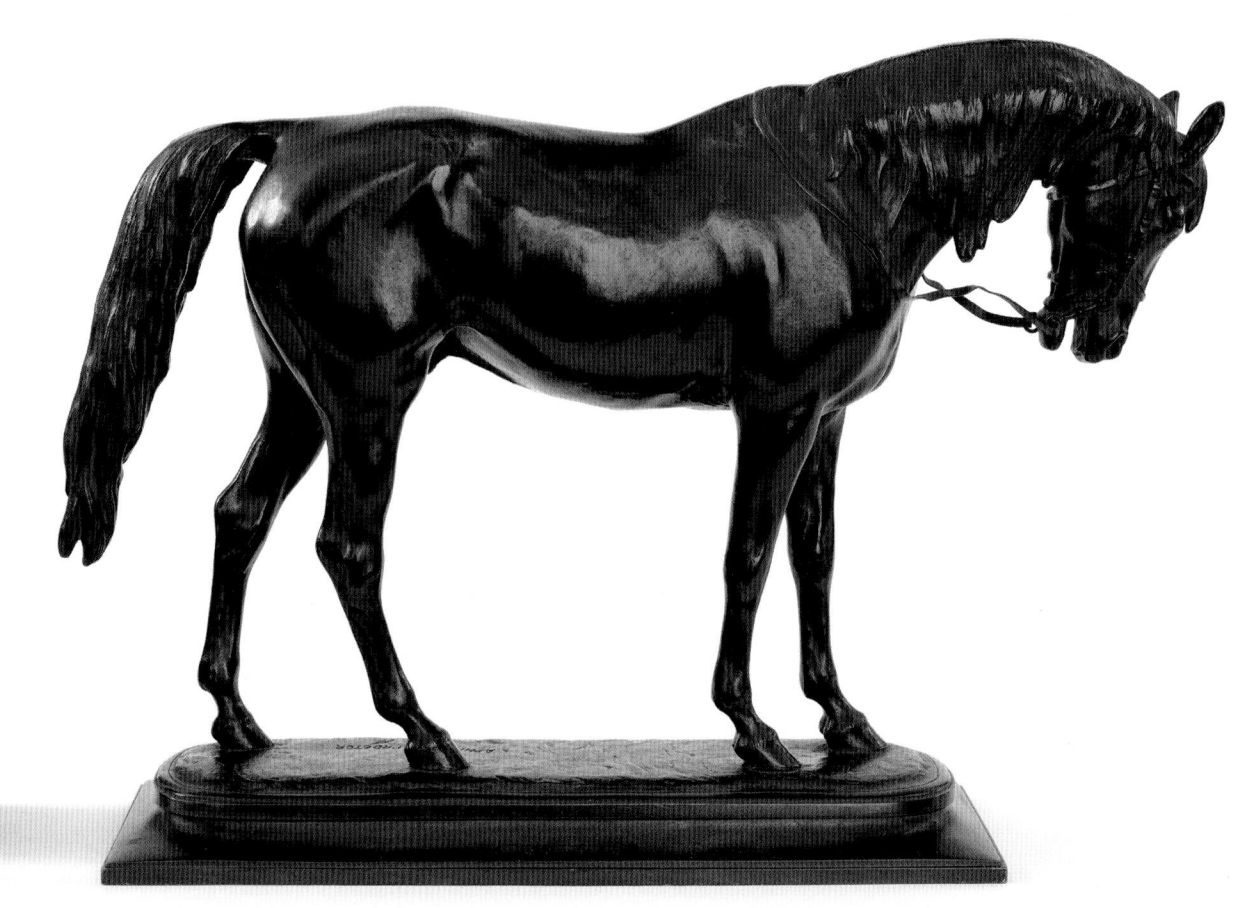

ALEXANDER PHIMISTER PROCTOR, *Arab Stallion,* ca. 1914. Bronze, 12 ½ in. (height). Buffalo Bill Center of the West, Cody, Wyoming. Gift of A. Phimister Proctor Museum with special thanks to Sandy and Sally Church. 18.08.3

ARAB STALLION (1895)

Bronze Horse; Stallion; Arabian Stallion

Proctor loved horses and was known as an accomplished horseman. Though never a cowboy himself, he explored this equestrian theme throughout his professional life. His first and last sculptures drew on the theme: his *Buckaroo* of 1915 created a sensation among art and western aficionados alike, and his heroic-sized *Broncho Buster* was his first human-themed bronze monument ever. He initially came under the wing of his great mentor Augustus Saint-Gaudens because of his facility at rendering horseflesh, and his early career was bolstered by orders from patrons who wanted spectacular, three-dimensional portraits of their favorite mounts.

Proctor's *American Horse* of around 1895, for example, portrayed a famous jumper named Ontario (also referred to as Transport) who was jointly owned by the cofounders of the famous Belmont Park racetrack, Samuel S. Howland and August Belmont II. The artist had also used that steed as the model for Saint-Gaudens's *Sherman Monument* in New York in the early 1890s. In 1904 he flattered a New Hampshire friend of his, Austin Corbin, by sculpting a likeness of Corbin's famous Morgan horse, Croydon Prince, in his bronze *Morgan Stallion.*

But it was a New York lawyer friend known today only by his last name, Dixon, who provided Proctor with his two most dramatic models. One was a horse from Dixon's Central Park stables that served as the dignified, spirited mount for Proctor's *Indian Warrior* of 1898. When, in 1901, Proctor was made an associate member of the National Academy of Design, he was required to submit a diploma piece to the academy's permanent collection. He chose to send a bronze casting of the *Indian Warrior*'s horse without the rider, suggesting that he considered it of sufficient merit as an equine sculpture to represent his institutional, artistic legacy (see the *Indian Warrior* entry in this volume).

Dixon allowed the sculptor to use that horse without charge. However, Dixon had a favorite mount of his own, an Arabian stud, and in 1895, he commissioned Proctor to create a likeness of it. He paid the artist $500.[1] The horse's name is not known, but he was certainly spectacular with his regal bearing and graceful elegance. He had been bred in Czar Nicholas II's stables in Russia and bore the symbol of

---

1 Ebner, *Sculptor in Buckskin*, 125.

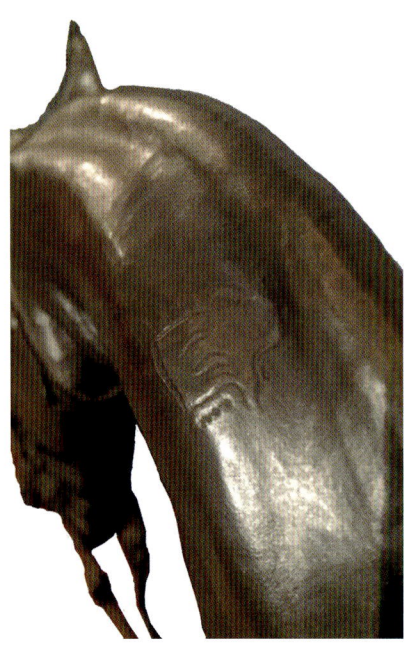

[PLATE 3.1]

ALEXANDER PHIMISTER
PROCTOR

Arab Stallion (detail – czar crown
brand), ca. 1896

Bronze
Private Collection

imperial power, the czar's crown, branded on the left side of his neck. [PLATE 3.1] Proctor proved that his skill was commensurate with the lofty lineage of his model. The resulting bronze became the subject of one of Proctor's most engaging horse portraits, *Arab Stallion*. [PLATE 3.2]

It is not known which casting Dixon received or where it is today. The piece was copyrighted in 1895 as *Arab Stallion*. There are nine castings that are known to exist today, including what may be the first. This was produced in Paris, probably in 1896, [PLATE 3.3] by the E. Gruet Juene Foundry when the artist began his Rinehart Scholarship work. This was probably the foundry operated by Edmond Gruet, the youngest son of Charles-Antoine Gruet, who worked with Proctor's hero Antoine-Louis Barye on several of his animalier sculptures.[2] Most of the other casts were made as sand casts by Gorham Co. Founders in Providence. They are marked with Gorham's record indicator, "QRD," and, in early castings, with an additional boxed inscription, "G/she wolf symbol/C." [PLATE 3.4]

A photographic reference in the Proctor Archives indicates that Jno. Williams Foundry of New York cast one or more of these works as well. None of the latter, however, has been found. Proctor was a great admirer of Barye. When the young American sculptor first visited Paris as a student in 1893, he purchased a number of Barye bronzes. He was likely familiar with Barye's bronze *Pure Blood Arab Horse*, [PLATE 3.5] which had first been cast in 1873 and which, despite its slightly less animated pose, may well have inspired Proctor's *Arab Stallion*.

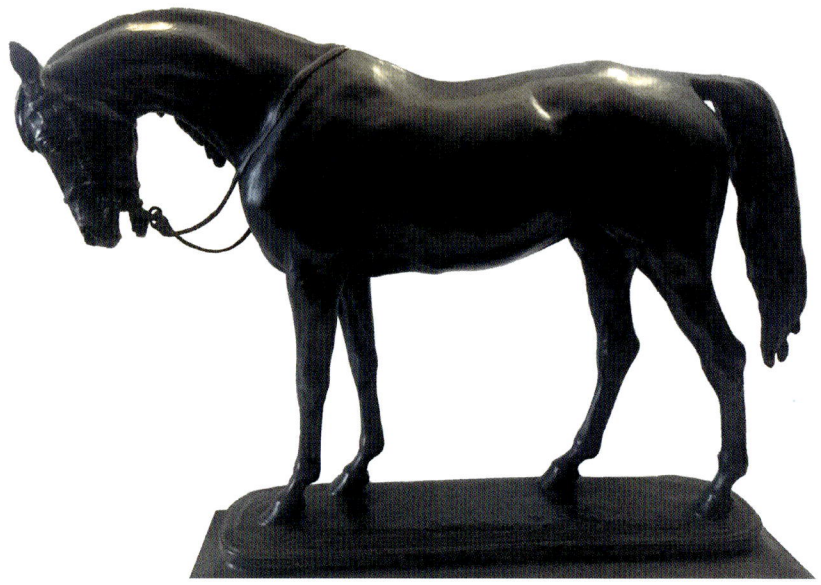

[PLATE 3.2]

ALEXANDER PHIMISTER
PROCTOR

Arab Stallion, ca. 1896

Bronze
Private Collection

2   For a discussion of the Gruet Foundry, see J. G. Reinis, *Founders and Editors of the Barye Bronzes* (New York: Polymath Press, 2007), 99–100.

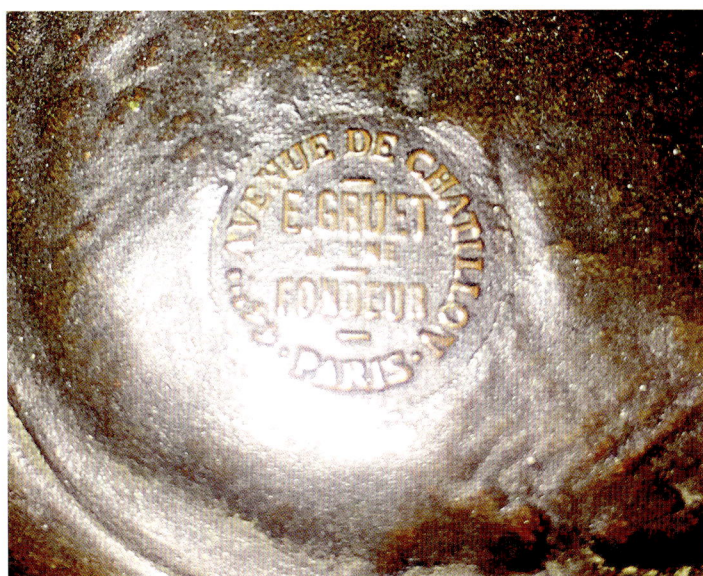

[PLATE 3.3]

ALEXANDER PHIMISTER PROCTOR

Arab Stallion (E. Gruet Juene, detail – foundry mark), ca. 1896

Bronze
Private Collection

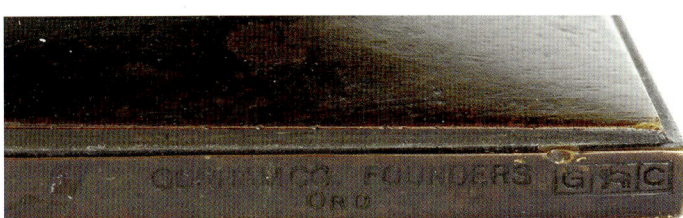

[PLATE 3.4]

ALEXANDER PHIMISTER PROCTOR

Arab Stallion (Gorham, detail – foundry mark), ca. 1915

Bronze
Buffalo Bill Center of the West, Cody, Wyoming. Gift of A. Phimister Proctor Museum with special thanks to Sandy and Sally Church. 18.08.3

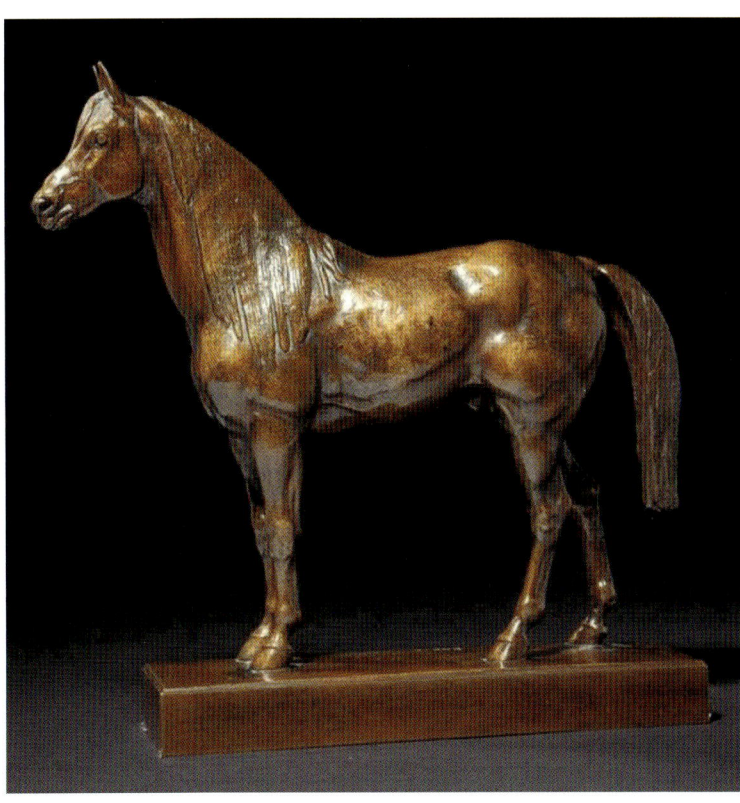

[PLATE 3.5]

ANTOINE-LOUIS BARYE

(b. France, 1795 – 1875)

Pure Blood Arab Horse, ca. 1880

Bronze, 11 7/16 in. (height)
Private Collection

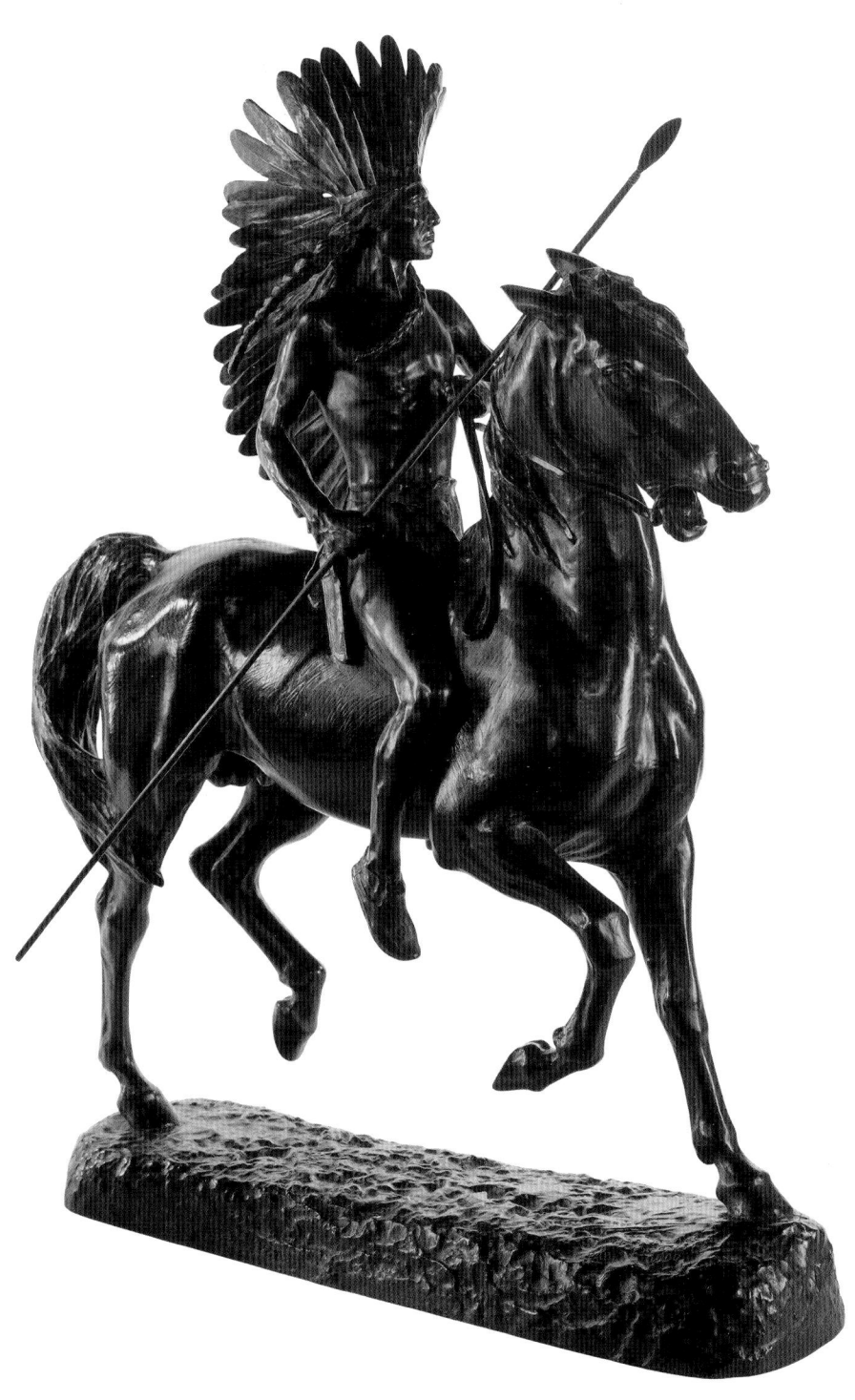

ALEXANDER PHIMISTER PROCTOR, *Indian Warrior,* ca. 1900. Bronze, 39 ½ in. (height). Amon Carter Museum of American Art, Fort Worth, Texas. Purchase with funds provided by the Council of the Amon Carter Museum of American Art. 2002.5

INDIAN WARRIOR

Indian Chief; Indian Hunter; Indian on Horseback; Equestrian Warrior; Indian Warrior on Horseback

The *Indian Warrior* had its genesis within three quite disparate milieus—one in the far northern, rustic reaches of the Rocky Mountain frontier, another among the scrubbed paddocks of Manhattan's finest riding clubs and horse stables, and a third among the cosmopolitan community of expatriate American artists in Paris. Not only is it a bold statement about Indian identity and artistic aspiration, but it also embraces lofty international achievement, supreme academic endorsement, and youthful adventure in the American West. The story of the sculpture's development, which began in the fall of 1895, also highlights the eclectic forces subsumed in the service of Proctor's fertile artistic vision. Having just completed the second of two monumental horse commissions for Augustus Saint-Gaudens at that time, he was ready for a break. In appreciation of Proctor's excellent work, Saint-Gaudens had given him a shiny new Mannlicher rifle, and Proctor planned to put his new prized possession to use on a western hunting trip with his friend the New York lawyer Henry Stimson. They headed for the northwest corner of Montana and the area that fifteen years later would become Glacier National Park.

As a side trip, Proctor spent some time on the nearby Blackfeet Reservation. It was there that he made studies of two Blackfeet men and, as he told it, "began a small model of an Indian Warrior, which I later finished in New York and Paris."[1] One of the portraits, a side view in high relief of a Blackfeet chief named Weasel Head, became the likeness used on the finished equestrian sculpture.[2] For a model for the rider's horse, Proctor reportedly searched closer to home in New York City. While he was working on his second commission for Saint-Gaudens in the mid-1890s, a friend introduced him to a New York lawyer named Dixon. Dixon retained him to sculpt his favorite horse, an Arabian

---

1 Ebner, *Sculptor in Buckskin*, 128.

2 Peter H. Hassrick, *Wildlife and Western Heroes: Alexander Phimister Proctor, Sculptor* (Fort Worth: Amon Carter Museum, 2003), 123–24. A plaster casting of *Weasel Head* is in the Proctor collections of the Buffalo Bill Center of the West.

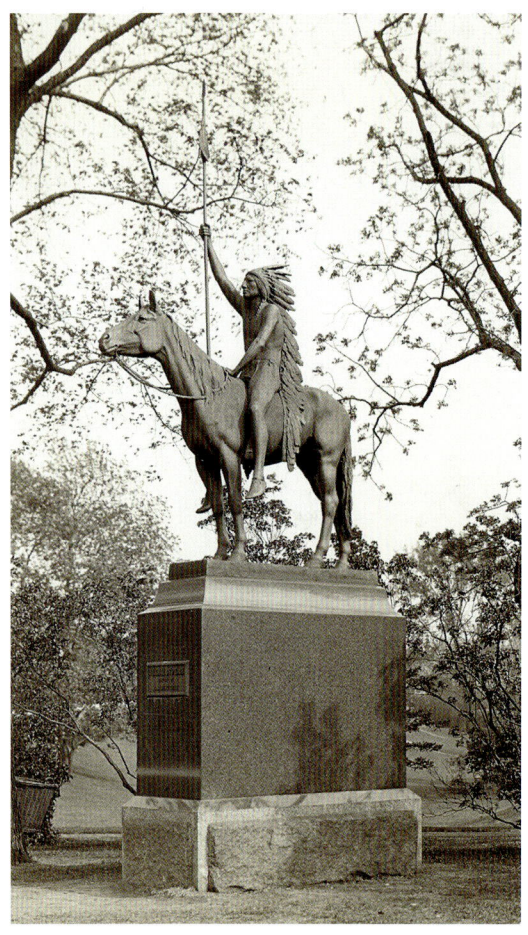

[PLATE 4.1]

CYRUS EDWIN DALLIN

(1861 – 1944)

Signal of Peace, 1893

Bronze, monumental
Chicago Park District Records:
Photographs, Photo 1-199-70C, Special
Collections, Chicago Public Library,
Chicago, Illinois

stallion, which Proctor did with alacrity. Dixon also gave him permission to make a model of another of his horses, one that Proctor acknowledged was "not a thoroughbred," though nonetheless a fine specimen.[3] The latter horse was done before his Montana trip. When Proctor returned from the West, he combined the Montana Blackfeet rider and Dixon's second horse into one of his most spectacular works, the *Indian Warrior*.[4]

In 1894, when Proctor began working on Saint-Gaudens's General John Logan monument for Grant Park in Chicago, he would have seen another monument that had been dedicated there a few years earlier. It was Cyrus Dallin's *Signal of Peace*. A small plaster version of this sculpture, inspired by Dallin's time amid the set of Buffalo Bill's Wild West in Paris in 1889, had already garnered him international fame.[5] When Dallin's monumental version was unveiled in Chicago in 1893, [PLATE 4.1] one critic remembered its smaller counterpart that had been exhibited in the 1890 Paris Salon, remarking that it was the "first distinctive American statue ever exhibited at the Salon."[6] Proctor would have been impressed, and anxious to join the competition. His own version of the theme, without the reference to amity, was shown eight years later in the same venue, the Paris Salon.[7]

By the time Proctor had completed that version of his *Indian Warrior* and begun to exhibit it internationally, he would also have come under another powerful influence, one that would possibly have dissuaded him from making any reference to peace in his sculpture of a mounted Indian. That was his friend the painter George de Forest Brush. In 1886, Brush, having recently lived in the West and painted among the Shoshone and Arapaho Indians in Wyoming Territory and the Crow of Montana Territory, had produced one of his early classical, academic

3 Ebner, *Sculptor in Buckskin*, 125–26.

4 Despite Proctor's story, the horse in the *Indian Warrior* looks remarkably like Ontario, the famous jumping horse that Saint-Gaudens and Proctor had chosen in 1895 for the *Sherman Monument*. The head, the pose, and the thrust of the horse are hauntingly similar. I am grateful to Sandy Church for this insight.

5 Rell G. Francis, *Cyrus E. Dallin: Let Justice Be Done* (Springville, UT: Springville Museum of Art, 1976), 35–40.

6 "Dallin's Famous 'Signal of Peace' to Stand in Lincoln Park," *Chicago Herald* (December 24, 1893).

7 See Lois Marie Fink, *American Art at the Nineteenth-Century Paris Salon* (Washington, DC: National Museum of American Art, Smithsonian Institution, 1990), 382. Proctor would have also seen a bronze casting of the small version of Dallin's piece in the Art Palace at the World's Columbian Exposition. See *The Official Directory of the World's Columbian Exposition* (Chicago: W. B. Conkey Co., 1893), 885. This small bronze was considered by critic William A. Coffin as "one of the best things shown by the Americans." See William A. Coffin, "The Columbian Exposition.—I; Fine Arts: French and American Sculpture," *The Nation* (August 3, 1893).

masterpieces. Titled *Before the Battle,* [PLATE 4.2] it embodied all the nobility and monumentality of a true homage to the Plains Indians. It was also all about bellicosity rather than concord. Proctor was probably familiar with the painting from his student days in New York when it was displayed at the 1886 annual exhibition of the Society of American Artists.[8] He could also have seen it illustrated in early anthologies of American art, such as George Sheldon's *Book of American Figure Painters* (1886) and *Recent Ideals of American Art,* the latter of which went through several

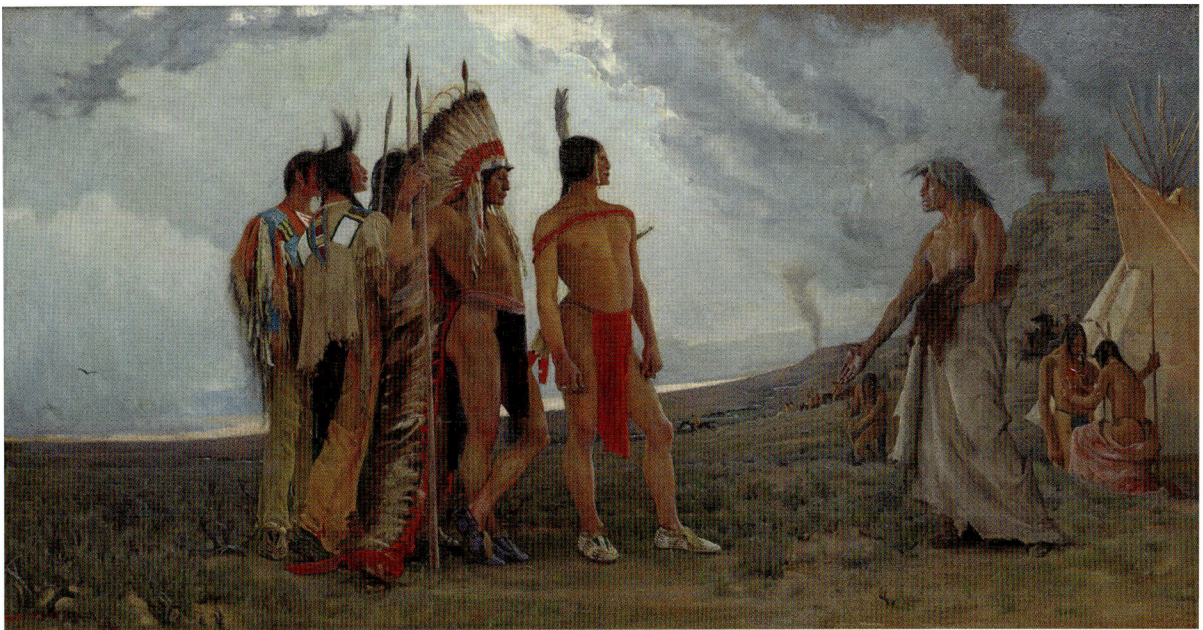

editions in the late 1880s and early 1890s.[9] Brush sold the painting to the famous New Jersey collector of American art William T. Evans. A reviewer for *Lippincott's Monthly Magazine,* assessing Brush's work in Sheldon's first book, referred to "the vigor and precision with which these figures are presented" as going "well beyond the range of ordinary praise."[10] Proctor would certainly have aspired, when his own art turned to portraying Native people, to share Brush's "vigor and precision."

Proctor and Brush were the closest of friends, enjoying many intimate moments together in Paris in the late 1890s. Their families vacationed together a couple of summers on the French coast at Boulogne-sur-Mer, and the two men relished the frequent opportunities to share their mutual

[PLATE 4.2]

GEORGE de FOREST BRUSH
(1855 – 1941)
Before the Battle, 1886

Oil on canvas, 14 ⅜ x 28 ¾ in.
The Rees-Jones Collection, Dallas, Texas

8   See Nancy K. Anderson, *George de Forest Brush: The Indian Paintings* (Washington, DC: National Gallery of Art, 2008), 148.

9   George William Sheldon, *Book of American Figure Painters* (Philadelphia: J. B. Lippincott Company, 1886), plate 30; idem, *Recent Ideals of American Art: One Hundred and Seventy Five Oil Paintings and Watercolors in Private Collections* (New York: D. Appleton and Co., 1890).

10   "The Book of American Figure Painters," *Lippincott's Monthly Magazine* (December 1886), 38).

experiences in the West among the Native people of the Great Plains.[11] The bonneted figure in Brush's *Before the Battle* could have served as much as a model for the mounted warrior in Proctor's bronze as did the Blackfeet man Weasel Head, who modeled for the figure's head.

Proctor recorded that when he returned to Paris in 1896 to pursue his Rinehart Scholarship, he packed his model for the *Indian Warrior* in his belongings. Once he got settled into a new studio on the Boulevard Montparnasse, he not only finished a small, 19-inch version of the piece but also embarked on one twice that size measuring some 39 inches in height. He proudly boasted that over the years he had "sold a good many statuettes of both sizes."[12] Although Proctor produced about half as many *Indian Warriors* as *Panthers*, around twenty-five lifetime casts are known to exist in the two sizes, from five different foundries.

The first completed *Indian Warrior* was the smaller version, measuring about 20 inches high. It featured a bonneted Plains warrior carrying a spear in his right hand and, over his left forearm, a shield decorated with relief designs (possibly beaded) and two large eagle feathers. The first bronze casting was available in 1898 for exhibition in the Paris Salon.[13] It garnered notice in the American press soon thereafter. One critic grasped immediately the emotional complexity of the piece when he commented how masterfully Proctor had resolved the tension between the "restrained action of the horse" and the "easy unconcern with which the rider sits him." "The face and the carriage of the man are noble and dignified," concluded the writer, as if he knew exactly what lessons Proctor had recently learned from Brush and from his mentor, Saint-Gaudens, whose mantra those words reflected.[14] Moreover, the sculpture was an important accomplishment for another reason, as pointed out by the sculptor and art savant Lorado Taft. Proctor's reputation had up to

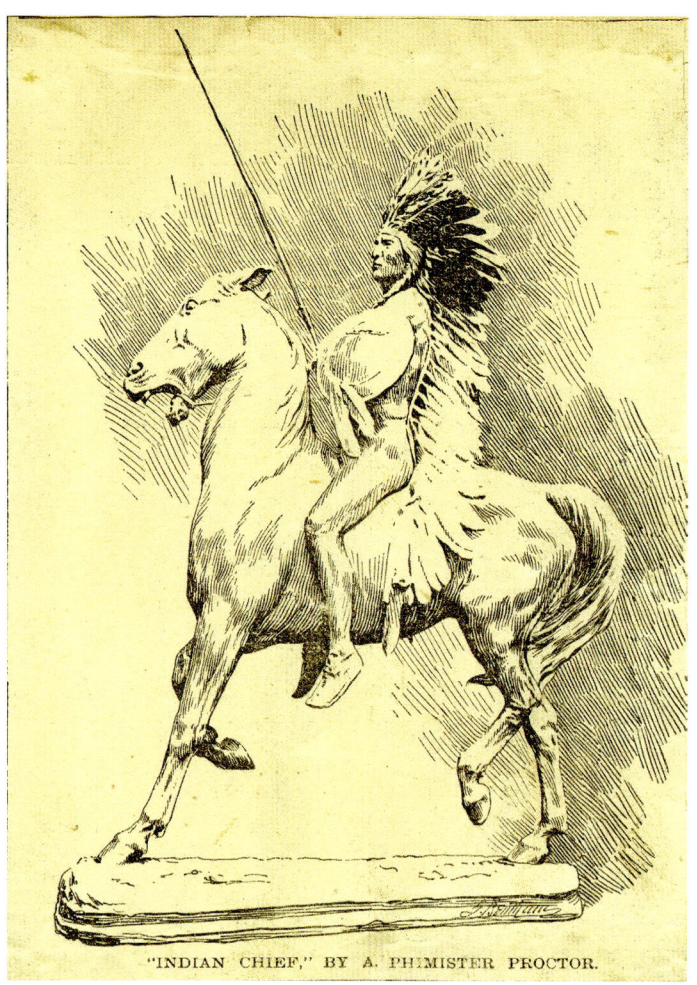

"INDIAN CHIEF," BY A. PHIMISTER PROCTOR.

[PLATE 4.3]

ALEXANDER PHIMISTER PROCTOR

Indian Chief

Wood engraving
Illustration in *Chicago Evening Post*, 1899
Alexander Phimister Proctor Collection, MS 242, Harold McCracken Research Library, Buffalo Bill Center of the West, Cody, Wyoming. MS242.OS2.07.01.01

11   See Mary Mears, "What the Masters Knew," *Christian Science Monitor* (April 1, 1938); and Nancy Douglas Bowditch, *George de Forest Brush: Recollections of a Joyous Painter* (Peterborough, NH: Noone House, 1970), 48–49.

12   Ebner, *Sculptor in Buckskin*, 126.

13   Société des Artistes Français, *Explication des Ouvrages de Peinture, Sculpture, Architecture, Gravure et Lithographie des Artistes Vivants* (Paris: C. de Mourgues frères, 1898), no. 3758.

14   Unidentified 1898 clipping in the Proctor Papers, McCracken Research Library, Buffalo Bill Center of the West, Cody, Wyoming.

that point been made essentially as an animalier artist. "The 'Indian Warrior' shows us that Mr. Proctor is fully equal to the difficult problem of the human figure," Taft wrote in 1898. "This admirable group," he concluded, "is the most important thing which he has thus far given us."[15] A casting of the bronze that is thought to have made its way to Chicago in the summer of 1898 was mentioned in the *Chicago Evening Post.* [PLATE 4.3] Although an accompanying illustration pictured the warrior with a shield, the article noted a change. "In the first model of this spirited figure the chief bore a shield on his left arm which now shows bare and sinewy."[16] It seems, then, that the shield was probably made optional rather early in the process as patrons were evidently allowed to order the small *Indian Warriors* with or without the shield. Castings with the shield are quite rare; only three are currently located. Of those, one was cast by the Thiébaut Frères of Paris around 1898, [PLATE 4.4] another by Roman Bronze Works of New York—probably sometime shortly after 1900—and a third by Gorham Co. Founders of Providence after 1913.[17]

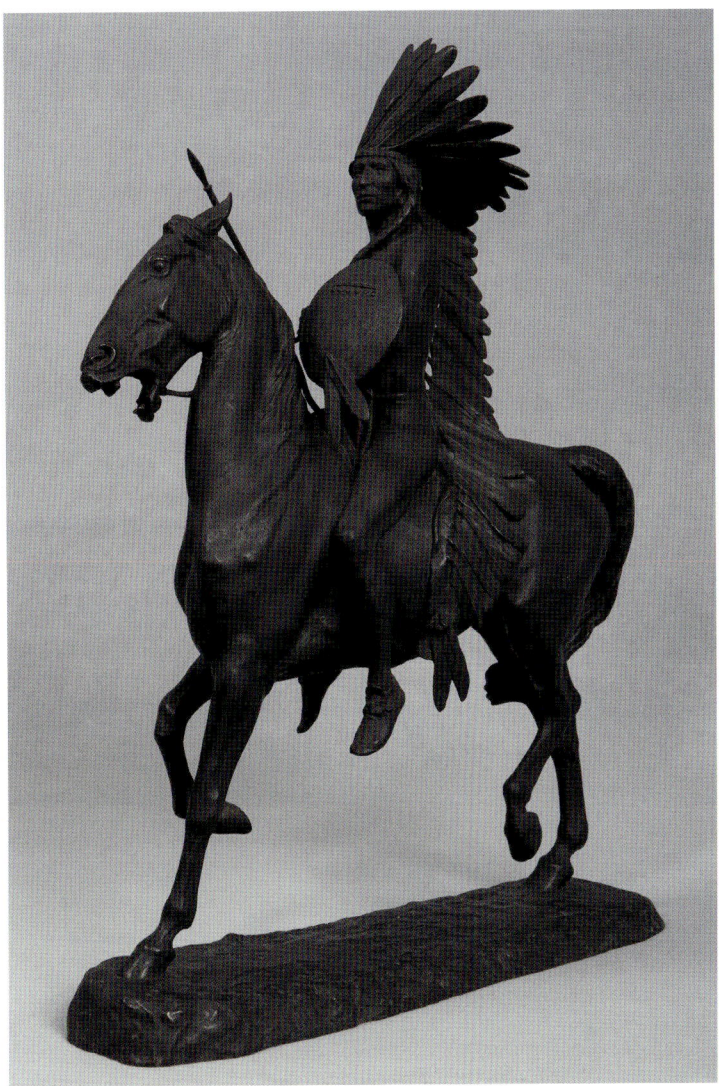

A number of the small versions of the *Indian Warrior* cast in Paris by Thiébaut Frères are known. It can be assumed that these were produced between 1898, when an iteration of Thiébaut Frères (Thiébaut Frères, Fumiere et Gavinot Successors) was established, and late 1900, when Proctor left France for the United States for good.[18] They tend to be exquisite bronzes. The casting at the Stark Museum of Art is exemplary.

[PLATE 4.4]

ALEXANDER PHIMISTER PROCTOR

Indian Warrior, ca. 1898

Bronze, 19 ½ in. (height)
Brooklyn Museum, Brooklyn, New York.
Gift of George D. Pratt. 12.898

15 Lorado Taft, "A. Phimister Proctor," *Brush and Pencil* (September 1898), 224.

16 *Chicago Evening Post* (June 24, 1898).

17 In one of the surviving casts, at the Brooklyn Museum, there is no foundry mark, though comparisons with other Thiébaut Frères castings suggest that this bronze was cast by that firm in Paris. On one other casting, sold at Christie's in New York in 1990, the foundry mark is from Roman Bronze Works. Since Roman Bronze Works did not start up until 1900, this casting would have to have been made after that date. For information on the early history of Roman Bronze Works, see Michael Shapiro, *Bronze Casting and American Sculpture* (Newark: University of Delaware Press, 1985), 137. And regarding Gorham Co. Founders, Proctor is not known to have used this foundry until 1913, when he had a major retrospective showing that autumn. *Exhibition of Bronzes and Plaster Models by A. Phimister Proctor.*

18 Reinis, *Founders and Editors of the Barye Bronzes*, 132–33.

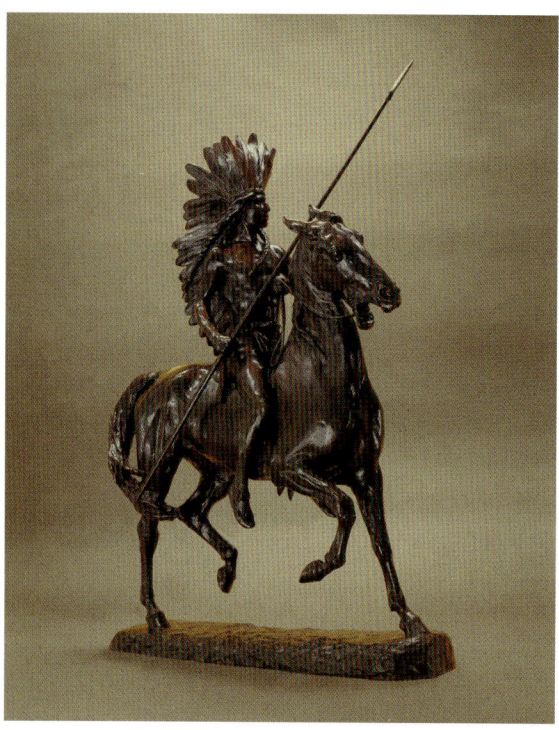

[PLATE 4.5]

ALEXANDER PHIMISTER
PROCTOR

Indian Warrior, ca. 1898

Bronze, 19 ½ in. (height)
Stark Museum of Art, Orange, Texas.
Purchase of the Nelda C. and H.J.
Lutcher Stark Foundation, 1983. 21.11.2

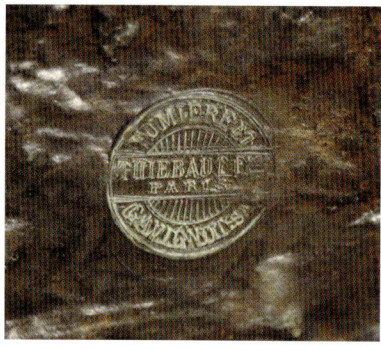

[PLATE 4.6]

ALEXANDER PHIMISTER
PROCTOR

Indian Warrior (Thiébaut, detail –
foundry mark), ca. 1898

Bronze, 19 ½ in. (height)
Stark Museum of Art, Orange, Texas.
Purchase of the Nelda C. and H.J.
Lutcher Stark Foundation, 1983. 21.11.2

Its velvety surface texture reveals the soft tone of a fine sand–cast bronze [PLATE 4.5], its founder's medallion mark is crisp [PLATE 4.6], and the underpinning is representative of the other Thiébaut Frères Proctor castings. [PLATE 4.7]

During his first stay in Paris, in 1897–98, Proctor rented studio space from the French sculptor Alfred Bouché at 11 Impasse Ronsin. It was there, immediately following his arrival in 1897, that he said he "began work on . . . a three-foot equestrian Indian figure for the Rinehart Scholarship Committee."[19] When this sculpture was completed is not known. He mentioned that it was cast in bronze (probably by Thiébaut Frères) and submitted as part of a group of works for exhibit in the American Pavilion at the Paris Exposition Universelle of 1900.[20] In his autobiography Proctor notes that he was represented there by "some small animals, a standing puma, and the *Indian Warrior* I had done for the Rinehart Scholarship. My exhibit received a gold medal."[21] At some point following the Paris exposition, that large bronze *Indian Warrior* was shipped to the Baltimore Museum as his "contribution to the Rinehart Prix de Paris Collection." Sadly, the cast was lost in shipment, and despite Proctor's later statement that he eventually cast a replacement work in the United States, no record of either casting has appeared.[22]

Other castings of the *Indian Warrior* have mysteriously disappeared as well. In 1909, Proctor, whose family lived in the Seattle area, donated three bronzes, including an *Indian Warrior*, to the Washington Art Association, the precursor to the Seattle Art Museum. The *Seattle Post-Intelligencer* announced Proctor's gift that year, but the sculptures have never been seen since.[23]

The *Indian Warrior* made a splash from coast to coast in the United States and beyond during the first decade of the twentieth century. Some version of the *Indian Warrior* was exhibited in Philadelphia at the Pennsylvania Academy of the Fine Arts in 1900.[24] The large version was shown once in 1901, at the Pan-American Exposition in Buffalo, New York, and twice in 1902 at the Century

19 Ebner, *Sculptor in Buckskin*, 130.

20 *Official Illustrated Catalogue, Fine Arts Exhibit, United States of America, Paris Exposition of 1900* (Boston: Noyes, Platt & Company, 1900), 96.

21 Ebner, *Sculptor in Buckskin*, 136. Proctor was represented by eight sculptures, including the *Indian Warrior*, according to the *Official Illustrated Catalogue*.

22 Ebner, *Sculptor in Buckskin*, 132.

23 "Seattle Museum's Catalogue Grows . . . Sculptor Makes Gift," *Seattle Post Intelligencer* (October 28, 1909).

24 Falk, *Annual Exhibition Record of the Pennsylvania Academy of the Fine Arts*, 2:390.

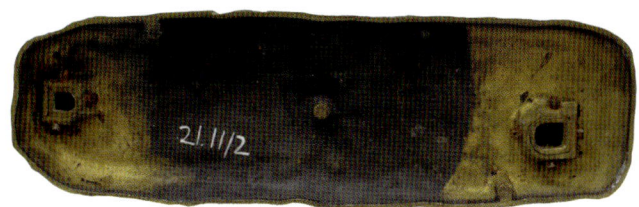

[PLATE 4.7]

ALEXANDER PHIMISTER
PROCTOR

Indian Warrior (Thiébaut, detail –
underside), ca. 1898

Bronze, 19 ½ in. (height)
Stark Museum of Art, Orange, Texas.
Purchase of the Nelda C. and H.J. Lutcher
Stark Foundation, 1983. 21.11.2

Association in New York City.[25] Then, a casting was again displayed in 1904 at the Louisiana Purchase Exposition in St. Louis, where it won another gold medal.[26] Following those showings, Proctor mounted a major retrospective exhibition of his work in 1908 at the prestigious Montross Gallery on Fifth Avenue in New York City. The exhibition included both versions of the *Indian Warrior*.[27]

A casting of the large version produced by the bronze foundry Jno. Williams, Inc., of New York was purchased by the National Gallery of Canada in 1909. Proctor had exhibited a dozen bronzes, including his *Indian Warrior*, in the second annual exhibition of the Canadian Art Club in Toronto during the spring of 1909.[28] He was a new member of the group and a welcome compatriot, having been born in Canada. Encouragement from that quarter may well have helped his pursuit of placing a major work in the National Gallery, Canada's premier art museum. The Portland Art Museum in Oregon acquired a similar large version of *Indian Warrior* in 1911. [PLATE 4.8] In that case, nine Oregon patrons and friends of Proctor collected $750 to see that the Portland Art Museum obtained this elegant work as its first sculpture acquisition.[29] A casting of the small version (unmarked, but cast by the Thiébaut Frères foundry) was donated to the Brooklyn Museum by Proctor's friend and patron George D. Pratt in 1912. Thus, within just over a dozen years after the first castings of the *Indian Warrior* arrived in the United States, the work had been widely exhibited in a variety of important venues, and four castings were safely (or unsafely, as in the case of Seattle)

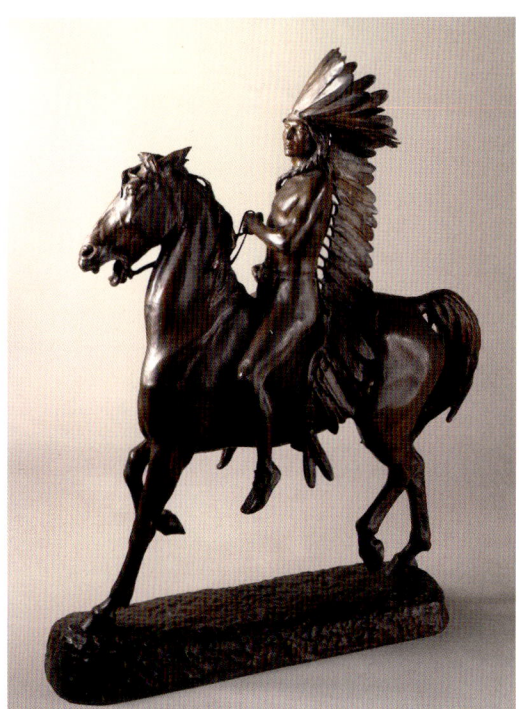

[PLATE 4.8]

ALEXANDER PHIMISTER
PROCTOR

Indian on Horseback (*Indian
Warrior*), 1898

Bronze, 39 in. (height)
Portland Art Museum, Portland, Oregon.
Gift of Mrs. A.L. Mills, Mrs. T.H. Bartlett,
Henrietta E. Failing, Mary Forbush
Failing, Mrs. H.C. Cabell, Charles Francis
Adams, John C. Ainsworth, William D.
Cartwright, and T.B. Wilcox. 11.2

25   Typescript listing of the Century Association Proctor showings in 1902, Proctor Papers, McCracken Research Library, Buffalo Bill Center of the West; William A. Coffin, *Pan-American Exposition: Catalogue of the Exhibition of Fine Arts* (Buffalo, NY: David Gray, 1901), 70.

26   "A Successful Canadian Sculptor," *Toronto Saturday Night* (January 8, 1910).

27   *Catalogue of Sculpture, Bronzes, Water Colors, and Sketches Exhibited by A. Phimister Proctor*, nos. 3 and 4.

28   *Canadian Art Club: Second Annual Exhibition*, no. 47.

29   This was a gift of a group of men and women from Portland: Mrs. A. L. Mills, Mrs. T. H. Bartlett, Henrietta E. Failing, Mary Forbush Failing, Mrs. H. C. Cabell, Charles Francis Adams, John C. Ainsworth, William D. Cartwright, and T. B. Wilcox. See "Portland's Art Taste Commended by One of Great Animal Sculptors," *Sunday Oregonian* (December 17, 1911).

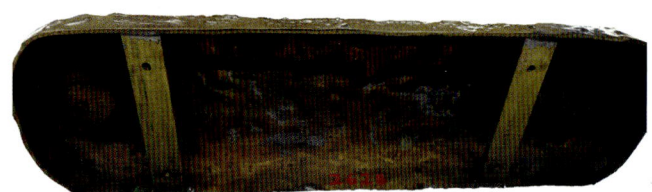

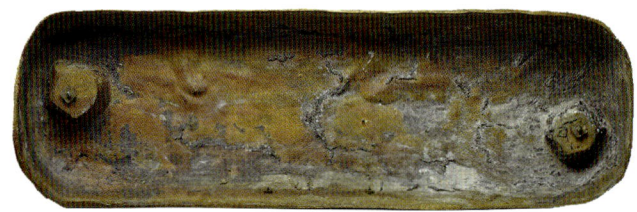

ensconced in important museums on the East and West Coasts of the
United States and in Canada.[30] Without doubt, the *Indian Warrior* was the
Proctor bronze most sought after by museums, at least in the first decade
of the twentieth century.

One or more of the large versions of *Indian Warrior* may have been cast
in Europe, but none has surfaced to date. Proctor started to produce this
bronze as sand castings in the United States with Jno. Williams Foundry
in the early 1900s. Two castings marked simply "J.W." are in the collections
of the Wilton Public Library, Connecticut (1900) and the R. W. Norton
Art Gallery in Shreveport, Louisiana (ca. 1900). [PLATE 4.9] Jno. Williams
incorporated in 1905,[31] and five castings from the newly structured
foundry are known to exist. Some of these are clearly marked, as in the
case of the National Gallery of Canada's, which reads "jno williams. inc. /
bronze foundry. n.y." Other castings are unmarked but reveal their foundry
through inspection of the underside of the bases. The Amon Carter
Museum's casting [PLATE 4.10], for example, bears no foundry marks but
shares a favorable comparison of its underpinning with that of the National
Gallery of Canada's.

In 1913 Proctor switched to Gorham Co. Founders and continued
to produce bronzes with that firm as sand casts. The early Gorham
castings are marked "QRM," with the company's standard number
for that work, but also with a small boxed notice reading "G/she wolf
symbol/C," which is thought to have been employed by Gorham
between 1913 and 1918. This insignia is found on castings belonging
to the Buffalo Bill Center of the West [PLATE 4.11], the Seattle Art
Museum, the National Gallery of Art, and the collection of Daniel

---

30 According to an article dated after 1902 titled "Indian Chief on Horseback," sales of the
    small version at that time were controlled exclusively in New York by Tiffany and Company
    (unidentified clipping, Proctor Papers, McCracken Research Library, Buffalo Bill Center of
    the West). The article illustrates a casting of the small version from "Jno. Williams Bronze
    Founders of New York." No such casting has surfaced in the present research, however.
31 See Shapiro, *Bronze Casting and American Sculpture, 1850–1900*, 175.

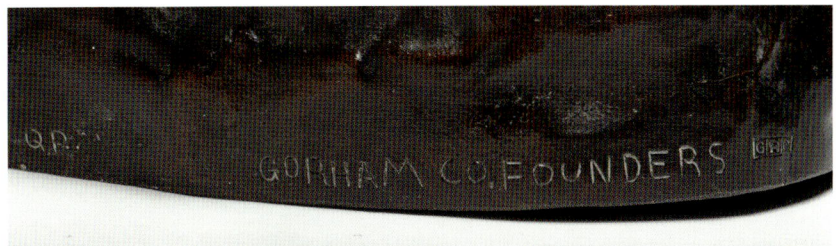

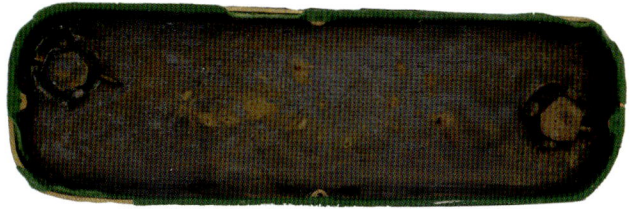

and Mathew Wolf. Gorham castings have a different system of underpinning than Jno. Williams castings, as seen in the underside view of the Buffalo Bill Center of the West's casting. [PLATE 4.12]

In 1904, Proctor released an abridged version of the work: the horse without the Indian. That year he was elected as a full member of the National Academy of Design in New York. As his required "diploma presentation" for admission to that lofty organization, he sent a casting of the horse with a single rein but no rider.[32] It was reluctantly accepted, and might be considered today as a variation of the larger work. [PLATE 4.13]

Part of what possibly attracted museums and art expositions to feature or collect Proctor's *Indian Warrior* were its classical elegance and ideal, chivalrous presence. For American audiences it was truly iconic, representing characteristics of self-confidence, masculine vigor and valor, bellicosity, mobility, and readiness, all of which symbolized the common perceptions of national identity in the Theodore Roosevelt years. Roosevelt, a lover of the West and a proponent of moral rectitude and nationalist ambitions, was a friend and supporter of Proctor. Both men viewed the West and Indians in similar ways, both agreeing that the Native people of the West were true national symbols.

Such a lofty vision of Native people was not universal, however. Cyrus Dallin certainly did not agree at the time that the Indian represented a belligerent America. Walter Winans, whose sculpture *Sioux Indian Chief* [PLATE 4.14] was shown in the Paris exposition in 1900 and was awarded a silver medal at the same time that Proctor's *Indian Warrior* won the gold, favored a more casual, less iconic presentation. Though armed and adorned similarly to the *Indian Warrior*, Winans' portrayal accentuated action and fluid motion, rather than nobility and majestic stature. In another vein, Cyrus Dallin's monument to defeat, *Appeal to the Great Spirit*

[PLATE 4.11]

ALEXANDER PHIMISTER PROCTOR

Indian Warrior (Gorham, detail – foundry mark), ca. 1918

Bronze
National Gallery of Art, Corcoran Collection, Washington, DC. Museum Purchase. 2014.136.237

[PLATE 4.12]

ALEXANDER PHIMISTER PROCTOR

Indian Warrior (Gorham, detail – underside), ca. 1916

Bronze
Buffalo Bill Center of the West, Cody, Wyoming. Gift of A. Phimister Proctor Museum with special thanks to Sandy and Sally Church. 4.08.2

32   See David B. Dearinger (ed.), *Paintings and Sculptures in the Collection of the National Academy of Design*, vol. 1 (New York: Hudson Hills Press, 2003), 452.

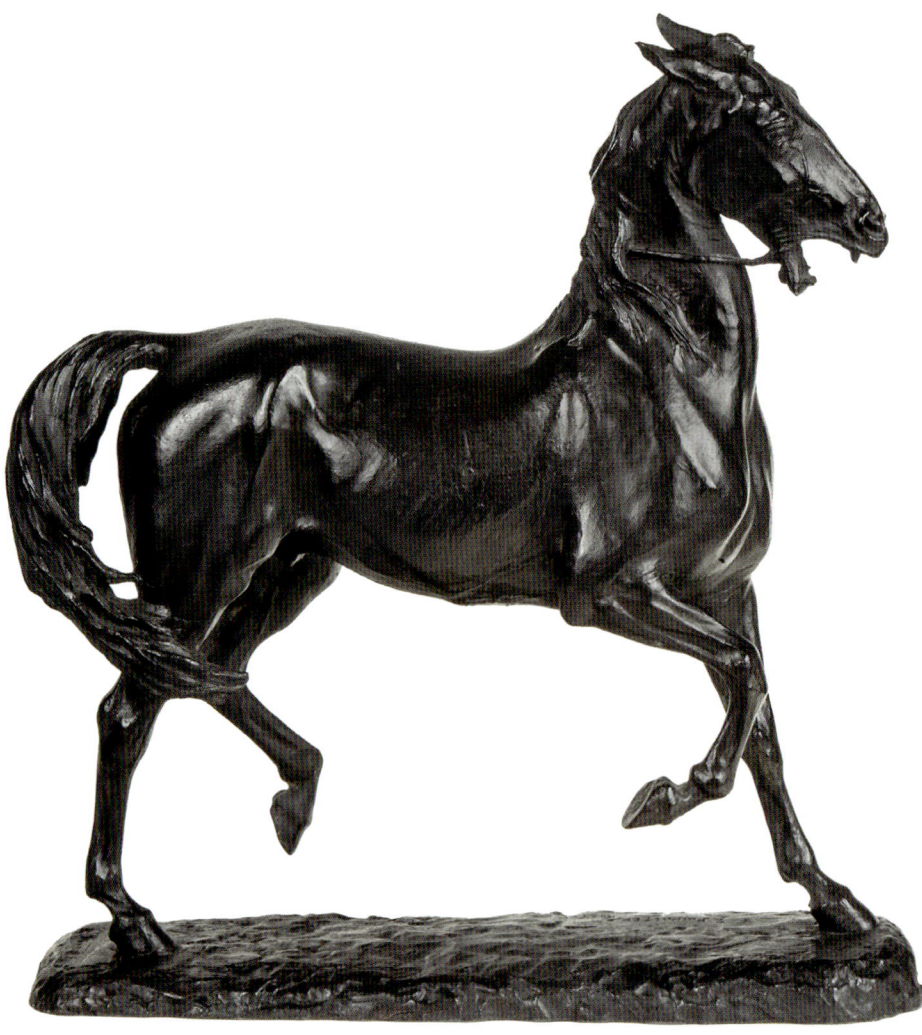

[PLATE 4.13]

ALEXANDER PHIMISTER
PROCTOR

Horse, 1904

Bronze, 16 in. (height)
National Academy Museum, New York,
New York / Bridgeman Images

of 1909 (Museum of Fine Arts, Boston), and James Earl Frasier's later monument, *End of the Trail,* [PLATE 4.15] featured at the Panama-Pacific Exposition in San Francisco in 1915, carried a totally contrary message, that of rejection and downfall. One sculpture critic would write of the former work that it revealed "the pathos of contrast between two cultures, the lower and the higher, the vanishing and the enduring."[33] Both Dallin's work and Frasier's were symbols of universal shame for the way Indians had been treated and the ways America's Native cultures were consequently perceived as overpowered and disappearing. In that context, Proctor's vision was racially nonhierarchical and refreshingly devoid of doomsday prophesies. His message was fundamentally more uplifting for Native people and the nation alike.

33   Adeline Adams, *The Spirit of American Sculpture* (New York: National Sculpture Society, 1923), 140.

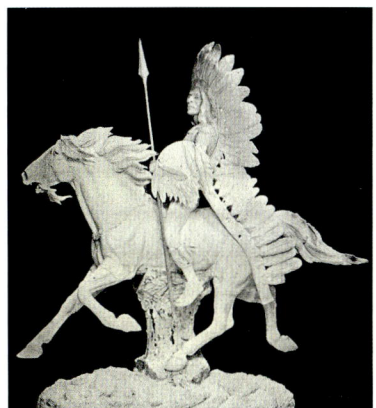

[PLATE 4.14]

UNKNOWN PHOTOGRAPHER

Sioux Indian Chief

(Walter W. Winans)
(b. Russia, 1852 – 1920), 1900
Photograph, b&w
McCracken Research Library, Buffalo Bill Center of the West,
Cody, Wyoming

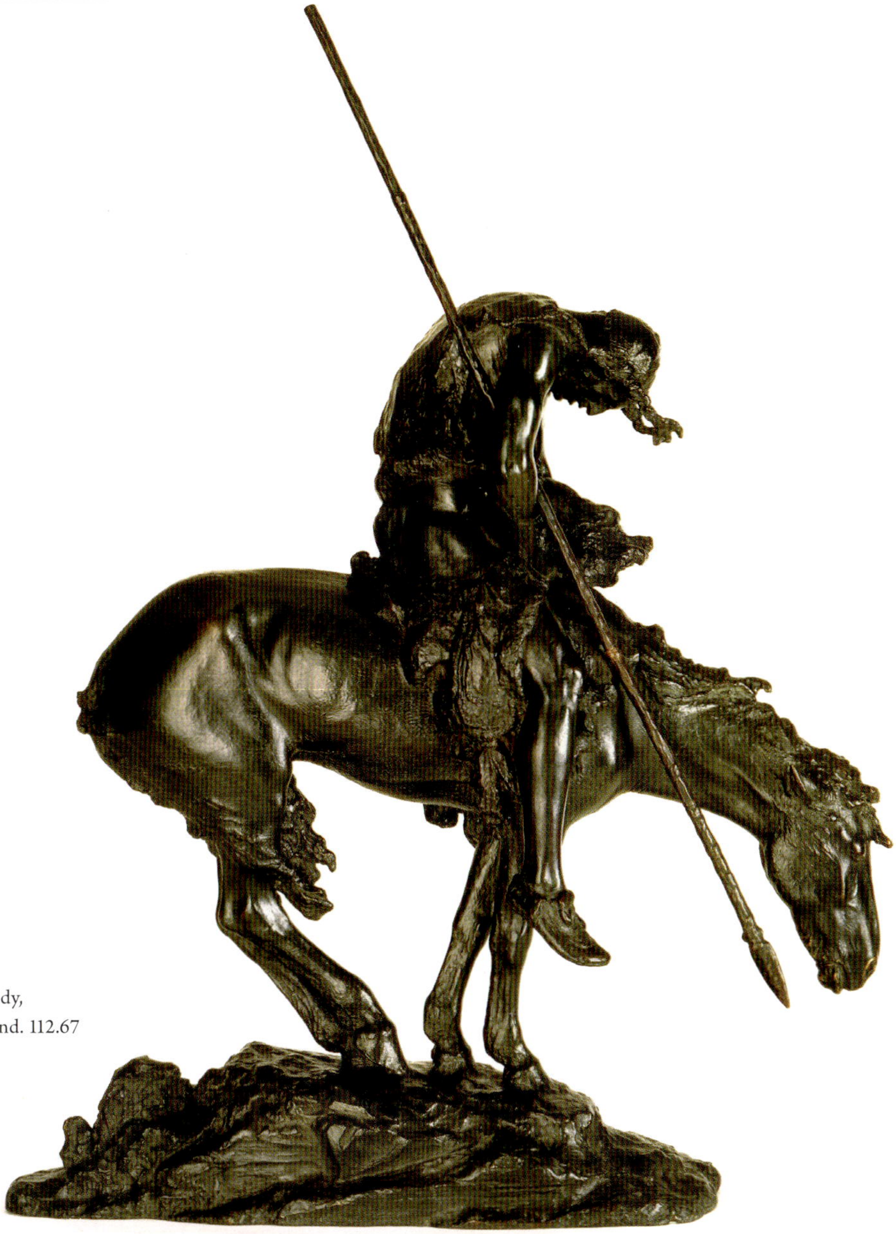

[PLATE 4.15]

JAMES EARLE FRASER

(1876 – 1953)

End of the Trail, ca. 1918

Bronze, 33 ¾ in. (height)
Buffalo Bill Center of the West, Cody,
Wyoming. Clara Peck Purchase Fund. 112.67

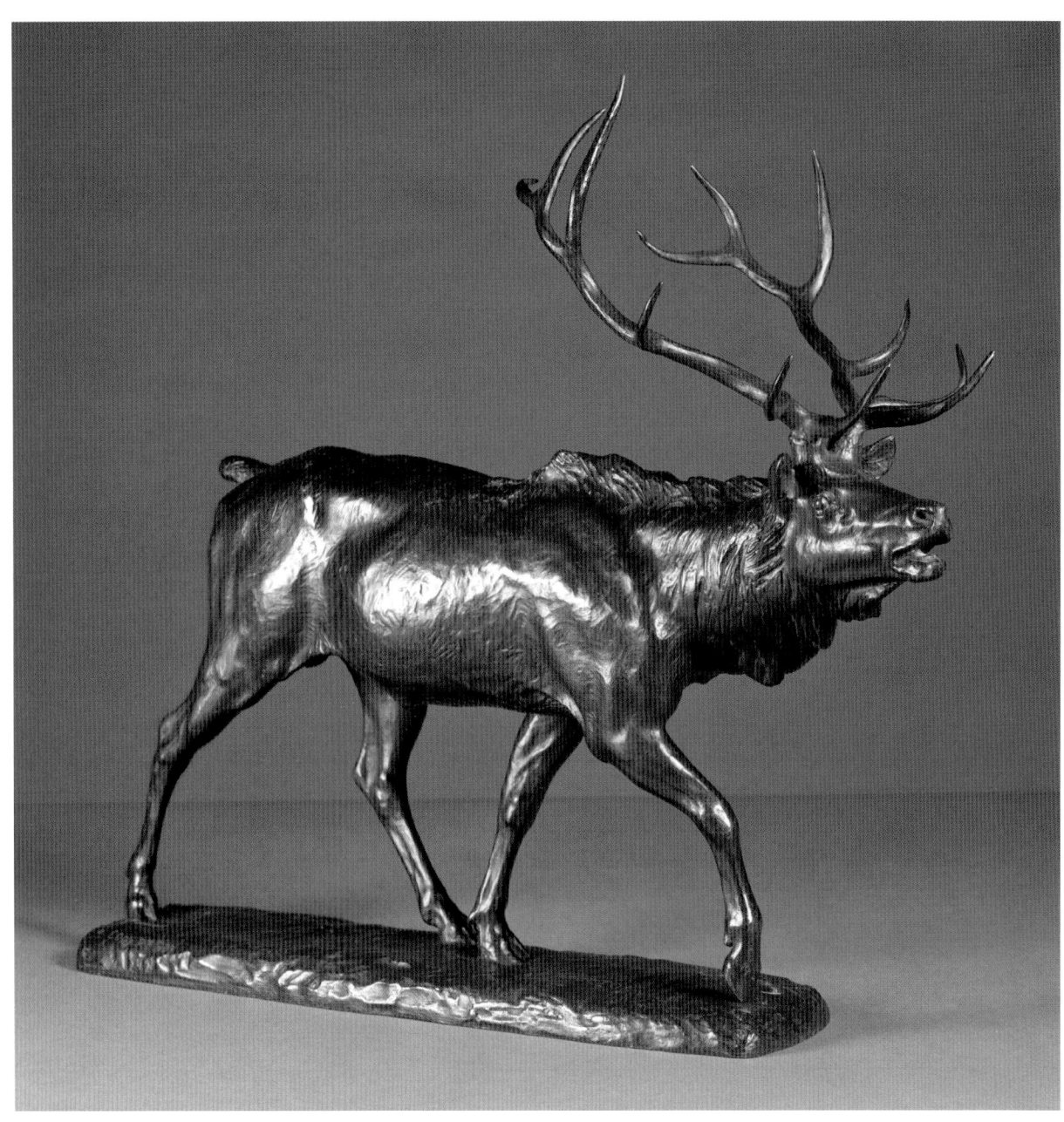

ALEXANDER PHIMISTER PROCTOR, *Elk,* ca. 1899. Bronze, 17 in. (height). Buffalo Bill Center of the West, Cody, Wyoming. Gift of A. Phimister Proctor Museum with special thanks to Sandy and Sally Church. 2.16.1. Photograph by William J. O'Connor

ELK

The Challenge; Elk-Challenge; The Challenge-Elk; American Elk; Elk Challenging; The Challenged Elk

Proctor's *Elk* was first modeled around 1899, probably before he left for his second trip to Paris. American writer Georgia Fraser saw the model for this work in Proctor's Paris studio in early 1900. It was still a plaster, not having been cast in bronze yet, and it had lost its antlers in shipment to France. Even though confronting it in this preliminary and compromised state, Fraser was still impressed. Proctor's "modeling of animals is never at fault," she wrote, and "it speaks volumes for the artist that the beautiful creature has lost none of its dignity by the loss of its horns *en voyage*."[1]

A bronze casting of it was exhibited as *The Challenge—Elk* in the American pavilion at the 1900 Paris Exposition Universelle, as part of an ensemble of eight sculptures that garnered Proctor a gold medal.[2] The elk's authoritative stance and maturity, combined with the aggressive expanded title, mark this work as the absolute antithesis of his bronze of the frail *Young Fawn*, also displayed at the exposition. Here is a full-grown male wapiti asserting his vigor and prowess as a leader of his herd. It was evidence of the breadth of Proctor's themes and the systemic complexity that he saw in nature. The *Elk* pictured an animal that could survive and perpetuate himself even in the face of Proctor's most adversarial wild protagonists, such as his *Stalking Panther*.

Subsequent writers saw the contrast between Proctor's *Young Fawn* and *Elk* as a metaphor for what many people of the era perceived as nature's fundamental construct, the Darwinian notion of survival of the fittest. In 1910, a Toronto critic illustrated a casting of *The Challenge* next to a photograph of Proctor, noting that the artist was uncommonly "able to inspire his figures with the life and spirit of the wilderness." Yet when the critic chose to discuss the *Fawn*, it was with a strong sense of denouement. "The little figure is an exquisite expression of the grace and the shivering timidity of forest life. It contains all the tragedy of its race."[3] Survival seemed not to be in the cards for the baby deer.

---

1 Georgia Fraser, "The Sculptors of the United States Pavilion at the Paris Exposition," *Brush and Pencil*, 5 (February 1900), 234.

2 *Official Illustrated Catalogue: Fine Arts Exhibit, United States of America, Paris Exposition of 1900*, no. 44.

3 "A Successful Canadian Sculptor."

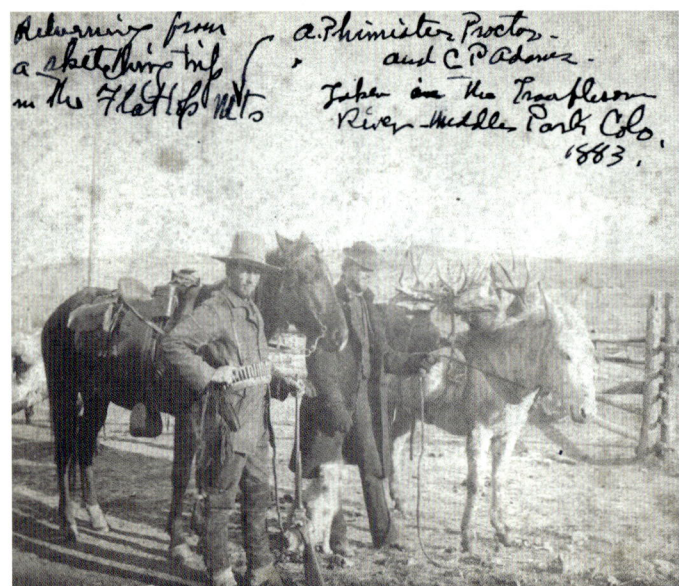

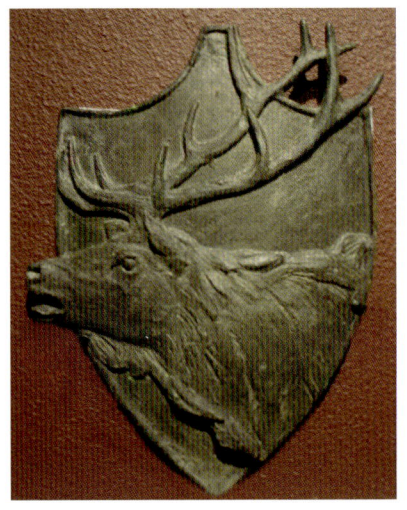

[PLATE 5.1]

UNKNOWN PHOTOGRAPHER

Proctor with bull elk, 1883

Photograph, b&w
Alexander Phimister Proctor Collection,
MS 242, Harold McCracken Research
Library, Buffalo Bill Center of the West,
Cody, Wyoming. P.242.346

[PLATE 5.2]

ALEXANDER PHIMISTER
PROCTOR

Elk, ca. 1912

Painted plaster plaque, 13 ½ in. (height)
Buffalo Bill Center of the West, Cody,
Wyoming. Gift of A. Phimister Proctor
Museum with special thanks to Sandy
and Sally Church. 4.12

In later years, Proctor would write of a life-and-death experience that occurred when he was a boy and, in the Colorado Rockies, shot his first bull elk. When his first shot only wounded the elk, the hunter became the hunted, and Proctor narrowly survived the scrape. On the same day, he killed and was nearly killed by a grizzly bear as well.[4] There was no distance, nor had there ever really been any, between the artist and that "life and spirit of the wilderness" with which the Toronto critic visually and symbolically allied Proctor and his elk sculpture. Nature's raw domain was truly the artist's province. [PLATE 5.1]

Castings of this work are marked on the artist's base with a copyright date of 1899. Records from the copyright files at the Library of Congress, however, suggest that an application for copyright may not have been submitted until a decade later, in 1909. In February of that year Proctor was granted a copyright for what he referred to as "Elk. A small statue."[5] The work was known variously in its exhibition history as *The Challenge* and *The Challenge—Elk.*[6] A high relief plaster plaque of the elk's head was made for a bronze that the artist was thought to have sold to Gifford Pinchot in 1912. [PLATE 5.2] It was copyrighted that year also as "The Challenge" and was defined simply as an "Elk in bronze."[7]

About a third of the half-dozen known castings of *Elk* were made with the lost-wax method by Pompeian Bronze Works in New York before 1913. [PLATE 5.3] In the early 1900s Proctor also used Roman Bronze Works to cast the piece in lost wax. At least as many as four of those appear to have been made, as the one known Roman Bronze Works casting is marked no. 4 and dates from around 1904. Only one Gorham Co. Founders sand-cast version is known to exist, an example of post-1913 manufacture. It served as a metal pattern for subsequent casts and was patinaed later. [PLATE 5.4]

4   Ebner, *Sculptor in Buckskin,* 34–40.

5   Copyright record 28272, filed February 4, 1909, with the Library of Congress.

6   Listed in 1901 under the title *The Challenge,* it was the first bronze he ever exhibited at the National Academy of Design. See Peter Hastings Falk (ed.), *The Annual Exhibition Record of the National Academy of Design, 1901–1950* (Connecticut: Sound View Press, 1990), 426.

7   Copyright record 42236, filed November 21, 1912, with the Library of Congress.

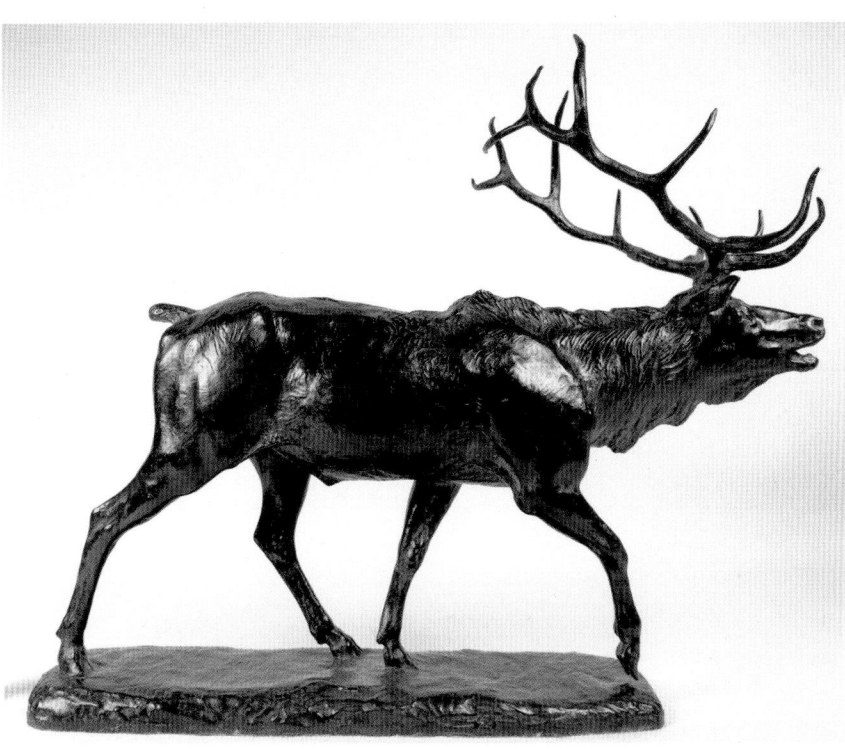

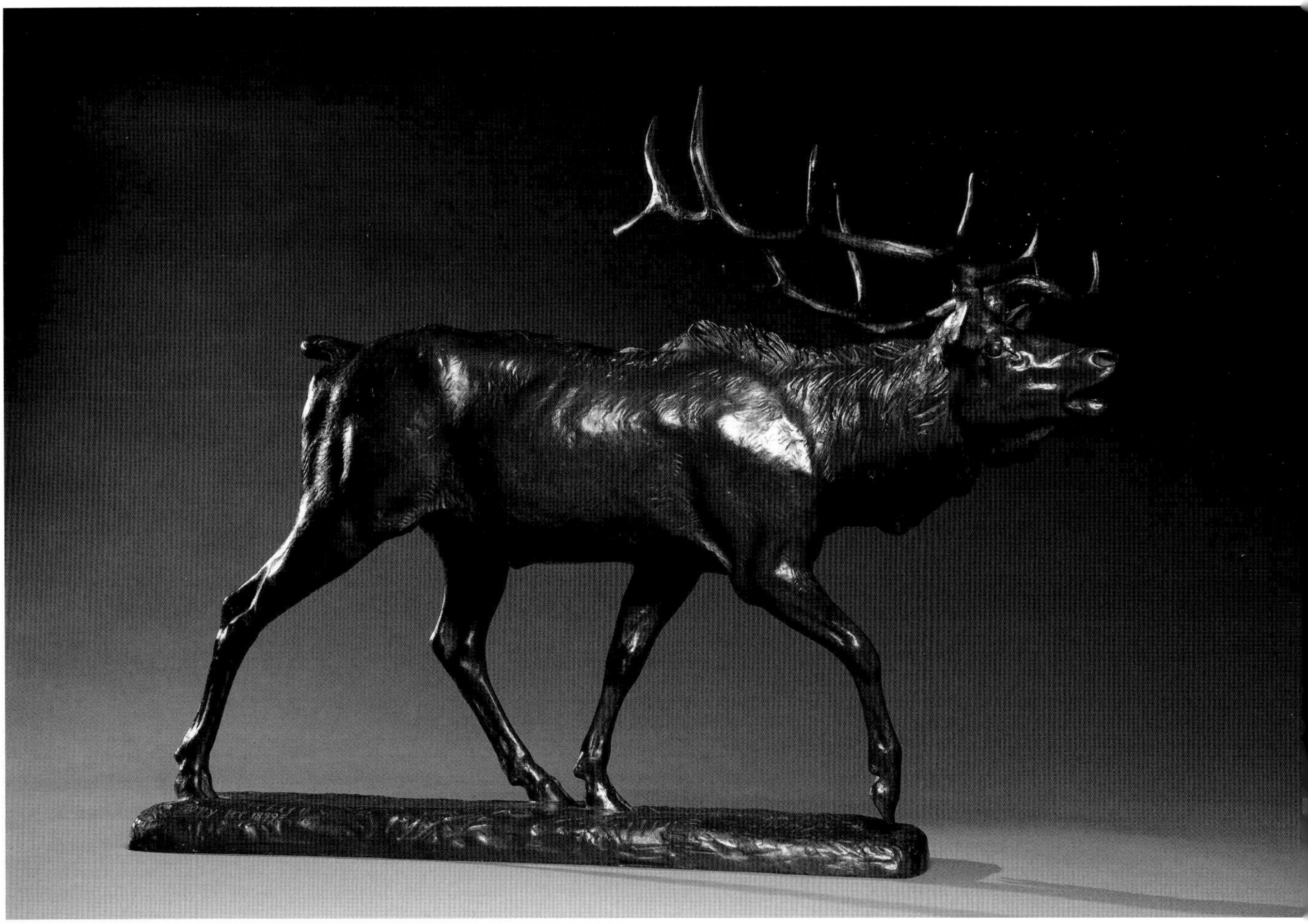

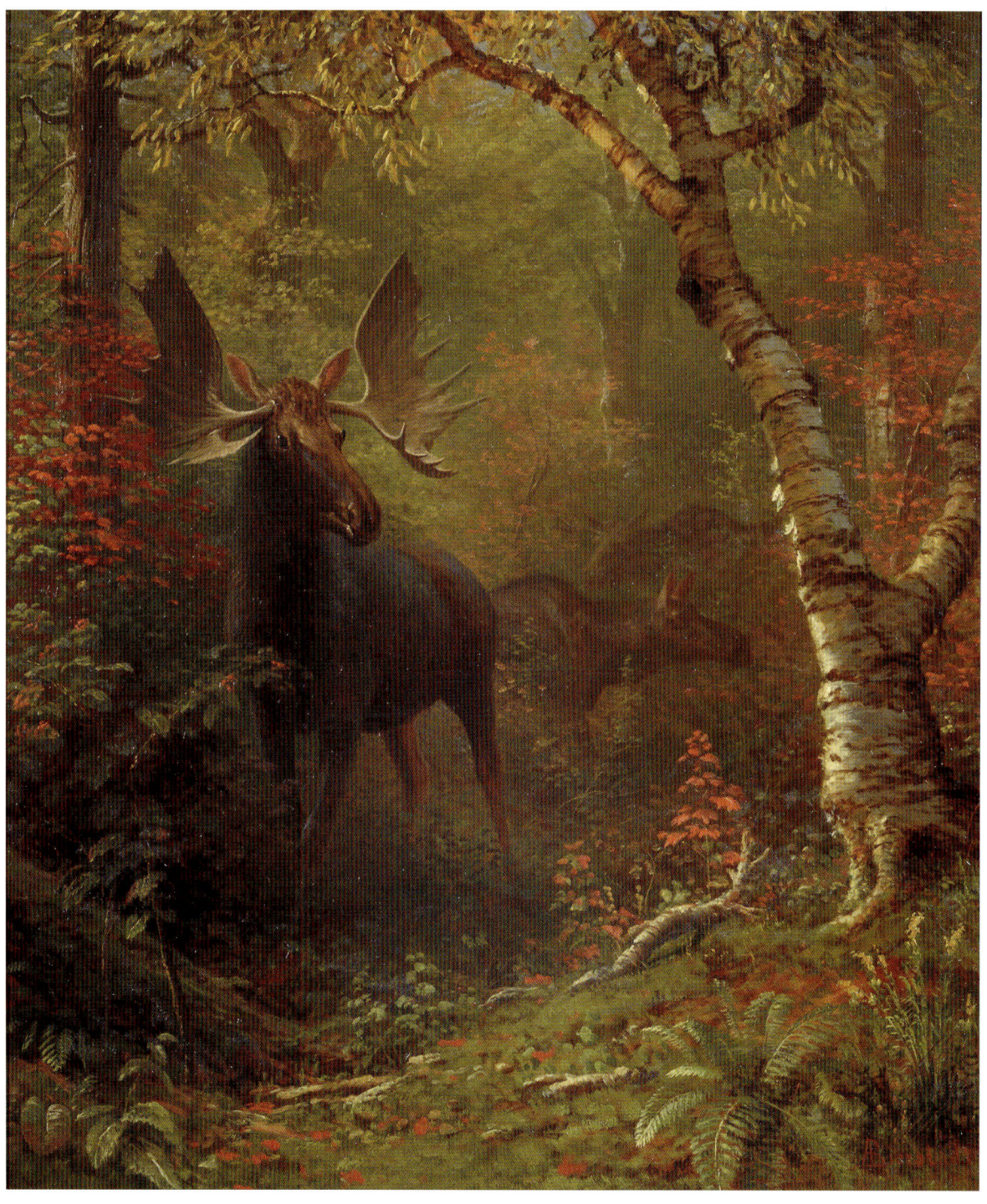

[PLATE 6.2] ALBERT BIERSTADT, (b. Germany, 1830 – 1902), *Moose,* ca. 1883. Oil on canvas, 50 x 43 ⅓ in. The Haggin Museum, Stockton, California. 1931.391.12

MOOSE

Bull Moose

America's first wildlife conservation organization, the Boone and Crockett Club, had among its ranks in the nineteenth century two major American artists, one the grand-manner painter Albert Bierstadt, and the other the animalier sculptor Alexander Phimister Proctor. Bierstadt was a charter member, listed in the minutes of the club's first meeting in 1888. Proctor came to the club five years later, in 1893. They were both invited to join the distinguished and select group because of their prowess as hunters of North American game, and they both remained members for the rest of their lives.

Bierstadt had hunted moose on the New Brunswick–Maine border in 1880 and had returned with a record trophy head. The mount's antlers measured an impressive 64¼ inches across. The artist proudly presented it to the New York Zoological Society.[1] Although Bierstadt's guide, rather than the artist, had actually shot the moose, the mount was well established in the club's literature as the "Bierstadt Head."[2] [PLATE 6.1] So enthralled was the painter with his feat as a sportsman that he produced not one, but at least three important paintings of the subject of his crowning hunting achievement. [PLATE 6.2]

Proctor was an even more zealous hunter of big game than Bierstadt. When Proctor's initial major commission came along—to sculpt in plaster a half-dozen heroic-sized western animals for the bridge abutments at Chicago's Columbian Exposition, moose were

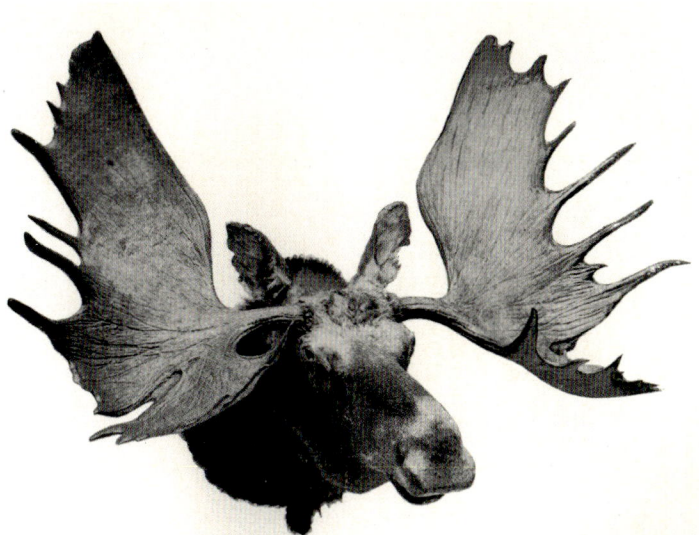

[PLATE 6.1]

UNKNOWN PHOTOGRAPHER

Moose (trophy mount, harvested by Albert Bierstadt)

Illustration in George Bird Grinnell (ed.), *American Big Game in Its Haunts: The Book of the Boone and Crockett Club,* (New York: Forest and Stream Publishing Company, 1904), 385.

---

1 Gordon Hendricks, *Albert Bierstadt: Painter of the American West* (New York: Harry N. Abrams, Inc., 1973), 264–65.

2 On who shot the moose, see Eric W. Nye and Sheri I. Hoem, "Big Game on the Editor's Desk: Roosevelt and Bierstadt's Tale of the Hunt," *New England Quarterly*, 60 (September 1987). The mounted head is illustrated in one of the club's early histories: George Bird Grinnell (ed.), *American Big Game in Its Haunts: The Book of the Boone and Crockett Club* (New York: Forest and Stream Publishing Company, 1904), 384.

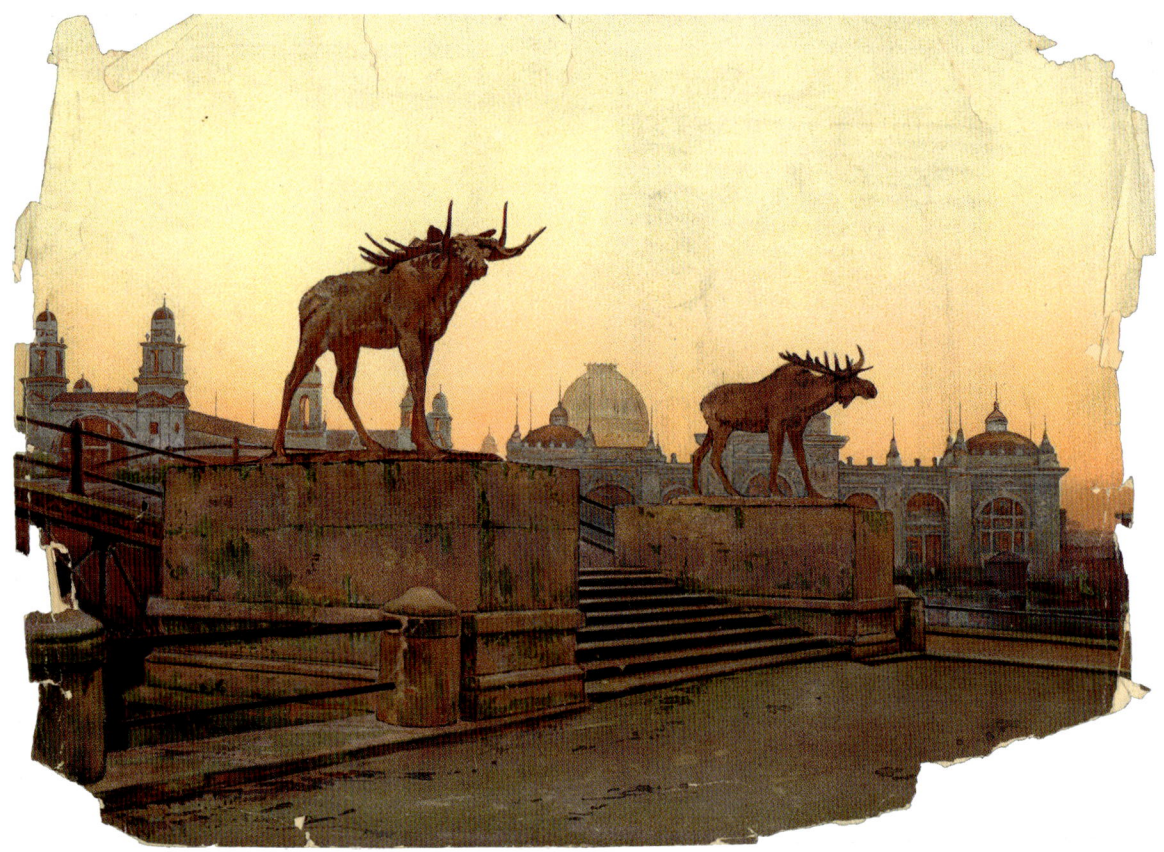

[PLATE 6.3]

an important part of his submission. His monumental moose seemed a bit weighed down by the heft of their antlers, but the public and critics nonetheless responded favorably with such comments as "Few things in the entire exposition were more interesting or impressive than those great motionless creatures."[3] [PLATE 6.3]

Proctor revisited the moose theme after he joined the ranks of Bierstadt by harvesting a trophy-sized bull of his own in 1902. His prize came from the Canadian Northwest. When he shipped the rack home, it was claimed to be "the biggest moose ever brought to New York, and . . . probably the largest ever killed."[4] The antlers, though measuring only 40½ inches across, [PLATE 6.4] were nonetheless loaned to the American Museum of Natural History. The moose was of such magnitude that Proctor's friend and fellow Boone and Crockett Club member Gifford Pinchot began to pressure the artist for a sculptured version of the beast. They decided on a large bas-relief bronze overmantel picturing not only Proctor's bull but a whole family of moose. Proctor completed two castings of what he called *Moose Family* [PLATE 6.5] in 1906, after much fussing with the composition and special problems with patination and the positioning of the calf on the right.[5]

---

3   Lorado Taft, quoted in "Portland's Art Tastes Commended by One of Great Animal Sculptors."

4   "Largest Bull Moose Killed in Canada by a Sculptor," *New York World* (May 26, 1902).

5   Hassrick, *Wildlife and Western Heroes*, 137.

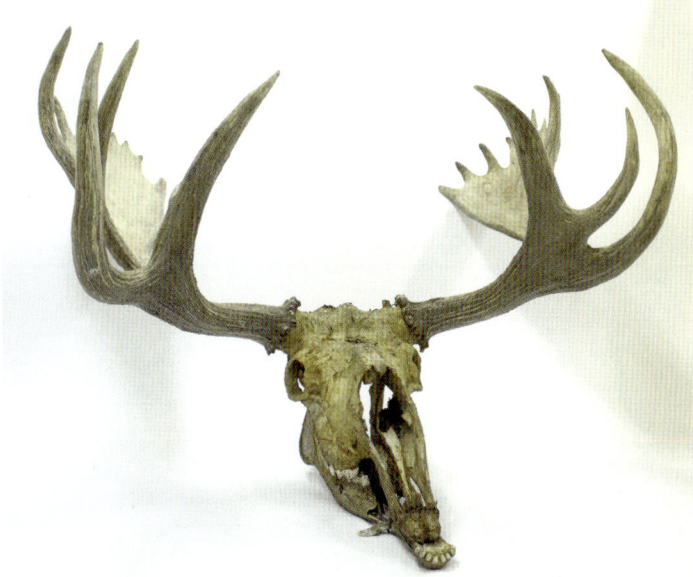

[PLATE 6.4]

KIM ZIERLEIN,
PHOTOGRAPHER

Bull Moose trophy (harvested by
Alexander Phimister Proctor,
1902)

Bone, 45 in. (spread)
Buffalo Bill Center of the West, Cody,
Wyoming. Gift of A. Phimister Proctor
Museum with special thanks to Sandy
and Sally Church. 11.06.738

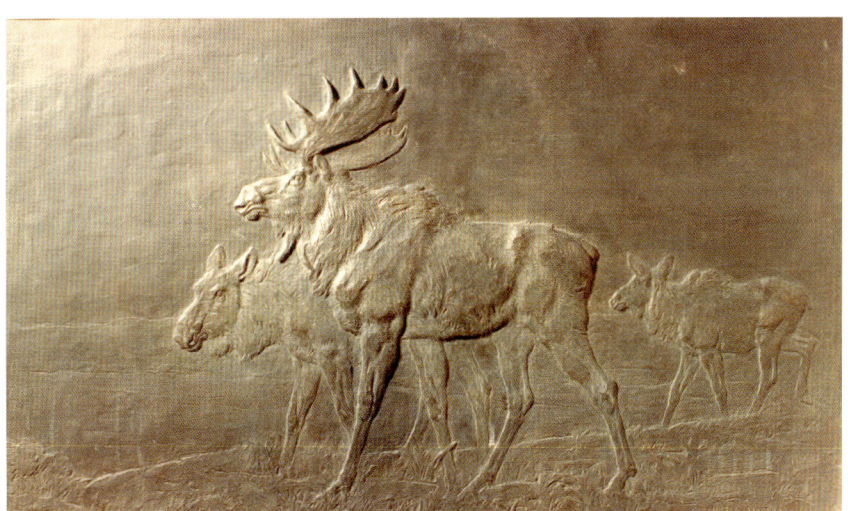

[PLATE 6.5]

ALEXANDER PHIMISTER
PROCTOR

Moose Family, 1906

Bronze bas relief, 5 ft. (height)
Grey Towers National Historic
Landmark, Milford, Pennsylvania

In the course of developing Pinchot's *Moose Family*, and possibly as
part of the process, Proctor began to conceive a three-dimensional portrait
of his bull moose. By 1907 he had copyrighted and probably cast a bronze
or two of what he titled simply *Moose*. [PLATE 6.6] The beast is alert and
majestic, though a little inert in its pose. The animal's antlers, unlike those
in the similarly posed Columbian Exposition plaster monuments, are
substantially uplifted, almost perky, and are so impressive that they nearly
dwarf their host.

Relatively few castings of Proctor's *Moose* are identified today. Only
four lifetime bronzes and one pattern are known. Fellow animalier artist
Carl Rungius successfully hunted moose in New Brunswick around 1905

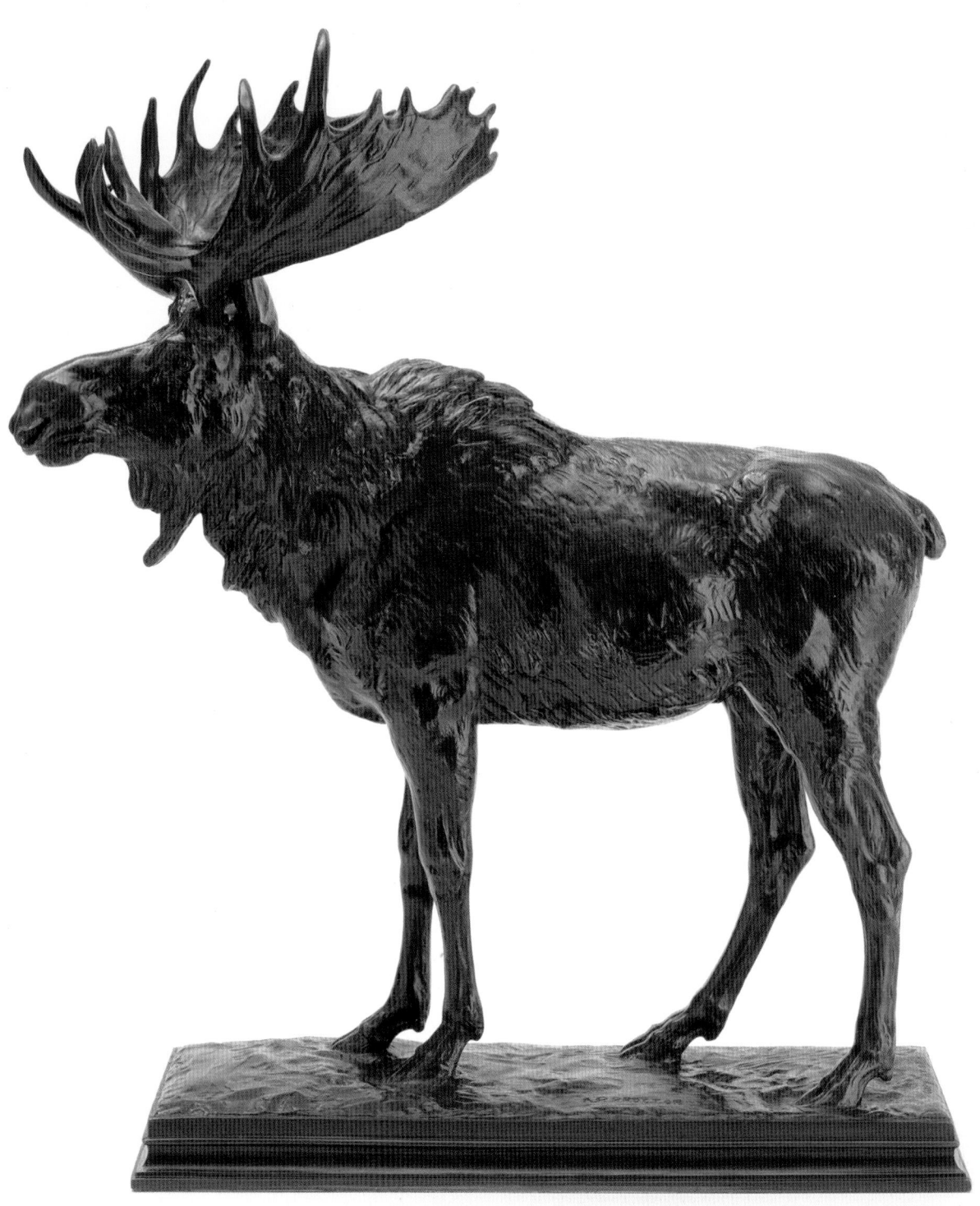

[PLATE 6.6]

ALEXANDER PHIMISTER PROCTOR

Moose, 1907

Bronze, 19 ½ in. (height)
Buffalo Bill Center of the West, Cody, Wyoming. 53.61

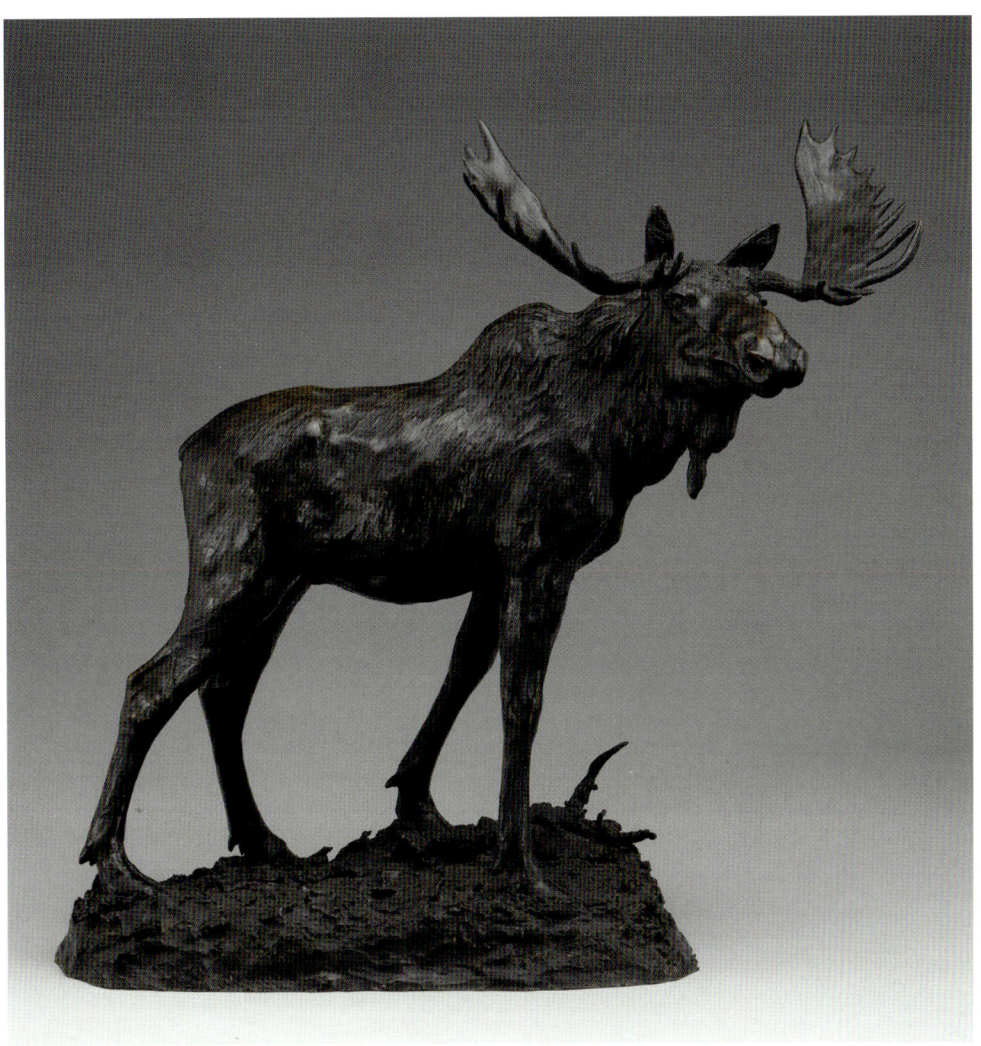

and produced at that time a sculptural portrait of the animal in bronze with Roman Bronze Works. It was titled *Alert* and, despite Theodore Roosevelt's purchase of a casting (Sagamore Hill, National Historic Site), the work was not commercially viable.[6] Henry Mervin Shrady, whose *Bull Moose* [PLATE 6.7] had been quite successful early in the decade and had even found its way onto the grounds of the Pan-American Exposition in Buffalo, New York, in 1901 as a monumental plaster decoration, perhaps saturated the market. It was uncannily close in pose and portrayal to Proctor's 1893 *Moose* monuments from the Columbian Exposition. All three artists, Proctor, Rungius, and Shrady, irrespective of their artistic inspiration, motivation, and popularity, were responding to cautionary claims that the moose was about to become extinct.[7] Such sentiments generally seemed to help sell art, but the results in this case were uneven.

[PLATE 6.7]

HENRY MERVIN SHRADY

(1871 – 1922)

Bull Moose, 1900

Bronze, 19 in. (height)
The Metropolitan Museum of Art, New York, New York. Bequest of George D. Pratt. 48.149.25. Art Resource, NY

6 Jon Whyte and E. J. Hart, *Carl Rungius: Painter of the Western Wilds* (Calgary: Glenbow-Alberta Institute, 1985), 62–63.
7 See Thayer Tolles and Thomas Brent Smith, *The American West in Bronze* (New York: Metropolitan Museum of Art, 2013), 71–72.

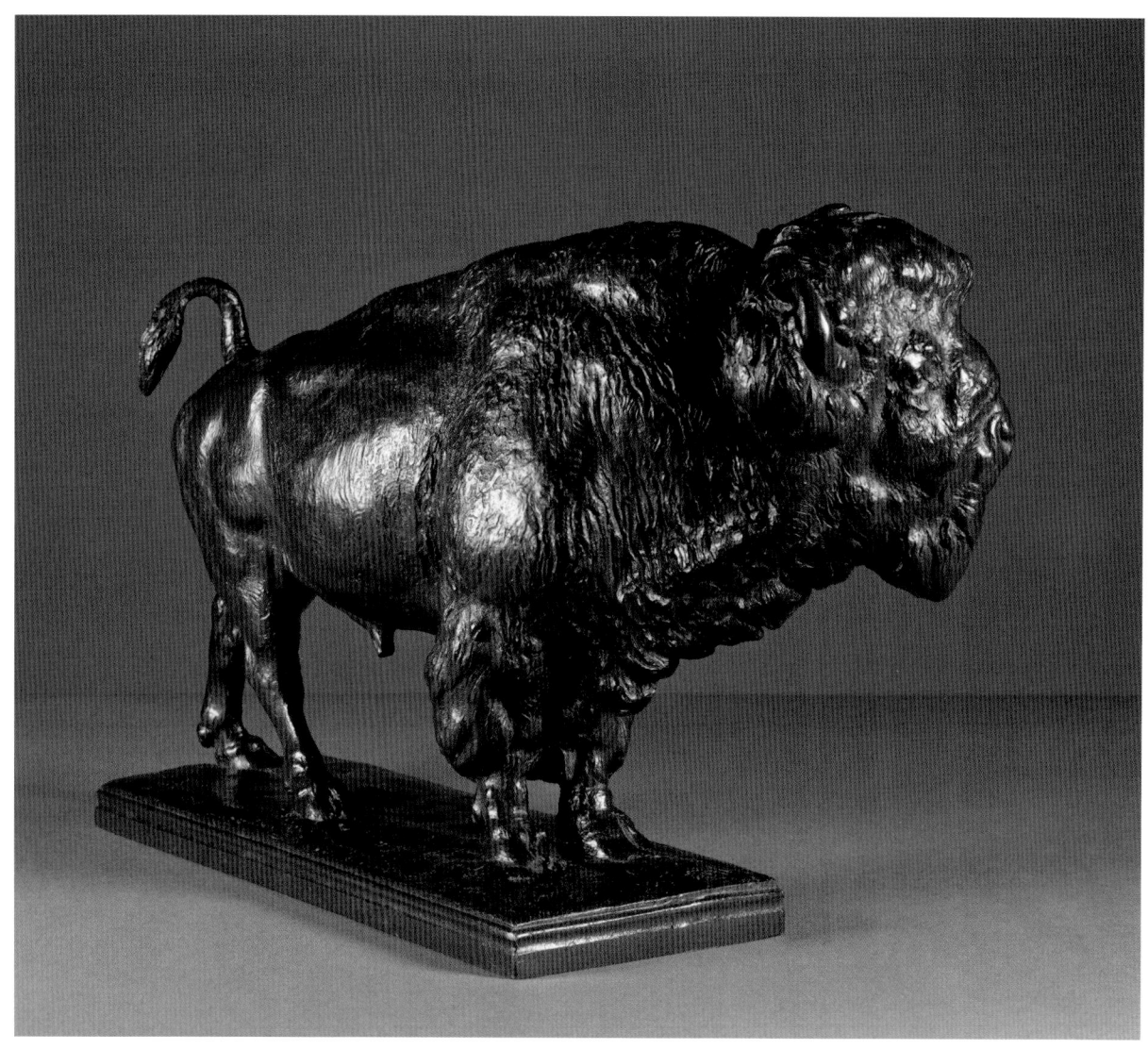

ALEXANDER PHIMISTER PROCTOR, *Q Street Buffalo,* 1912. Bronze, 13 ¼ in. (height). Buffalo Bill Center of the West, Cody, Wyoming. Gift of A. Phimister Proctor Museum with special thanks to Sandy and Sally Church. 2.16.2. Photograph by William J. O'Connor

BUFFALO

Model of Buffalo for Q Street Bridge; Bison. Model for Q Street Bridge; Q Street Buffalo; Standing Buffalo

During the first decade of the twentieth century, myriad appeals reached the press calling for Americans to take heed of a desperate situation in the West. The region's symbol (some regarded it as a national symbol), the buffalo, was about to become extinct. Yellowstone National Park and the world's first conservation organization, the Boone and Crockett Club, had, starting in the late 1880s, pushed for governmental action to stem the slaughter by poachers in the park. The result was the National Park Protective Act of 1894 (commonly known as the Lacey Act), which made poaching buffalo in Yellowstone punishable by law. At that time there were about 250 of the shaggy beasts left in the park. By 1908, despite strict new, legally enforceable regulations, that number had dwindled to about twenty.[1]

A more substantial herd resided in private hands on a ranch in the Flathead Reservation of Montana, north of the park. Owned by a rancher named Michael Pablo, the herd contained around seven hundred purebred prairie buffalo, and they were for sale for $200 apiece. The U.S. government ironically expressed no interest in acquiring them, so Pablo turned north and sold most of the herd to the Canadian government between 1907 and 1909. Montana artist Charles M. Russell spent several weeks in 1908 and 1909 watching and recording the so-called Pablo roundup and promoted the thrill of the event in spirited paintings such as *Pablo's Buffalo Hunt.* [PLATE 7.1]

Buffalo were much on Proctor's mind in 1909. He had been invited by President Theodore Roosevelt that year to modify the fireplace in the State Dining Room of the White House. The artist was to sculpt two high-relief buffalo heads on the mantel posts. The president, an

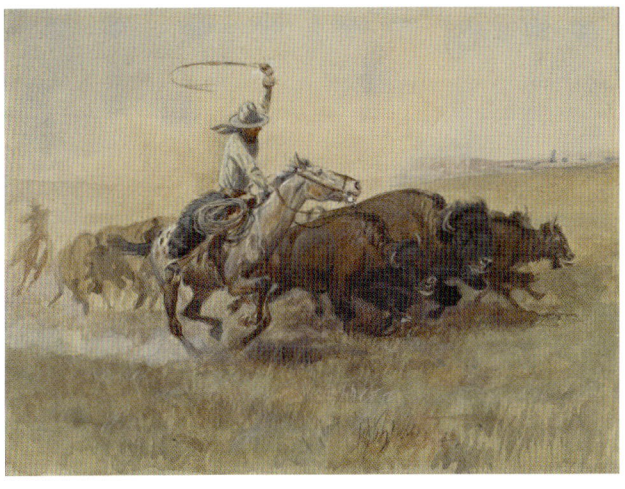

[PLATE 7.1]

CHARLES MARION RUSSELL

(1864 – 1926)

Pablo's Buffalo Hunt, ca. 1909

Watercolor on cardboard, 8 ¾ x 11 ¾ in. C. M. Russell Museum, Great Falls, Montana

---

1   Ernest Harold Lawson, "The Fight to Save the Buffalo," *Country Life in America* 3 (January 1908), 348. Proctor had become a member of the Boone and Crockett Club in 1893 at the invitation of Theodore Roosevelt, the organization's founding president.

[PLATE 7.2]

ALEXANDER PHIMISTER
PROCTOR

Buffalo (Prairie Monarch), 1911

Bronze, 35 in. (height)
National Museum of Wildlife Art,
Jackson, Wyoming. JKM Collection

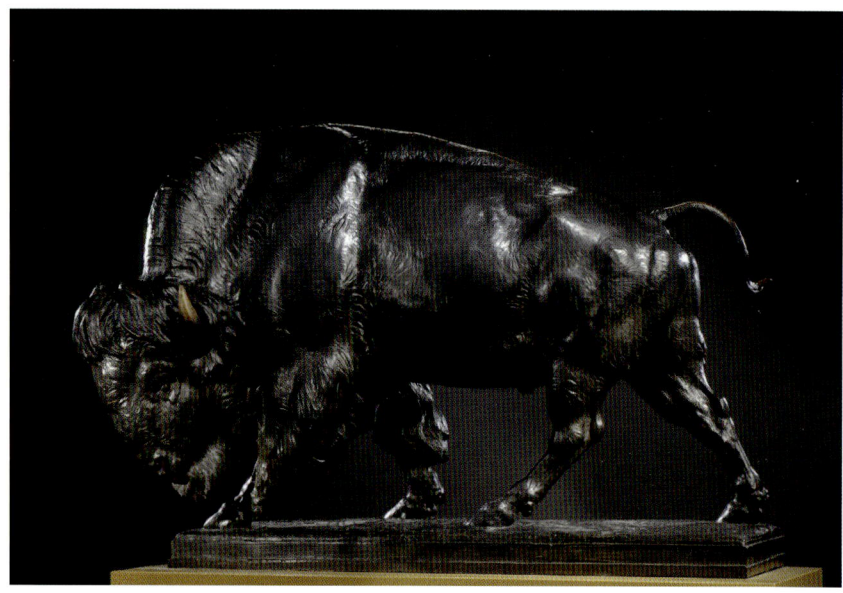

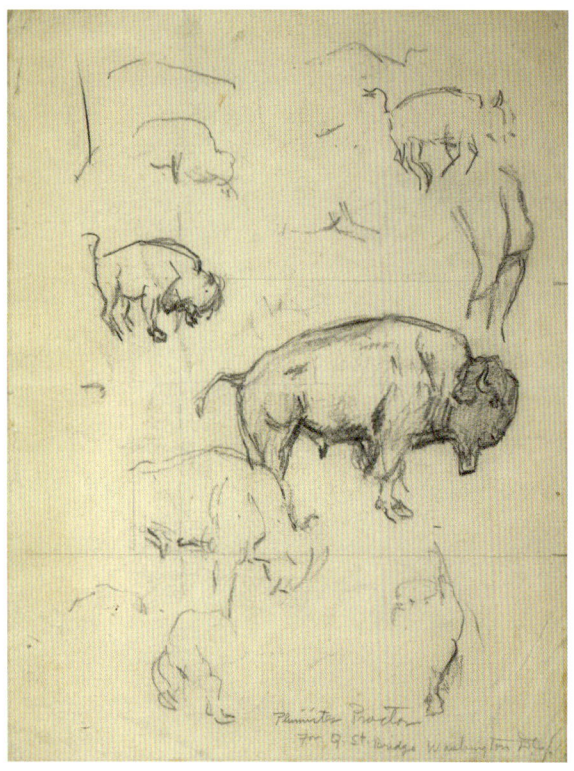

[PLATE 7.3]

ALEXANDER PHIMISTER
PROCTOR

*Buffalo, (study for Q Street
Buffalo)*, ca. 1911

Graphite on paper, 11 x 8 ⅜ in.
The Metropolitan Museum of Art,
New York, New York. Gift of Gifford
MacGregor Proctor. 1993.80. Art
Resource, NY

honorary member of the American Bison Society,
saw the buffalo as "the most distinctive game animal
on this continent" and worthy of "all good citizens'
. . . efforts for its preservation."[2] It was an emblem of
America's wildlife and of his conservation work as
leader of the nation.

In 1911, Proctor completed an enlarged version
of his first Buffalo sculpture, from 1897.[3] The new
variation was cast singularly in a four-foot bronze
and sold to Herbert L. Pratt for his Glen Cove, New
York, estate. As with its predecessor, the bull's head is
lowered, and its pose suggests that the bull is moving
forward with a powerful stride. [PLATE 7.2]

Proctor was looking for a fresh model when,
around 1910, he received a lucrative commission
for four monumental buffalo to decorate a new
transportation link between Georgetown and
Washington, D.C., the elegantly curved Q Street
Bridge. No doubt fully aware of the Pablo herd
and the Canadian acquisition, he decided to go in
search of a real western-prairie buffalo, given that
his first bison sculpture, of a wood buffalo, had been
sketched in a Paris zoo. The Canadians had settled the Pablo herd on
the prairies of their recently created Buffalo National Park, a 200,000-
acre game preserve near the town of Wainwright in east-central Alberta.
Proctor showed up there in the fall of 1911 to make studies of a few noble
bulls for his proposed sculptures. [PLATE 7.3]

2   Ibid, 295.
3   See Hassrick, *Wildlife and Western Heroes*, 130–31.

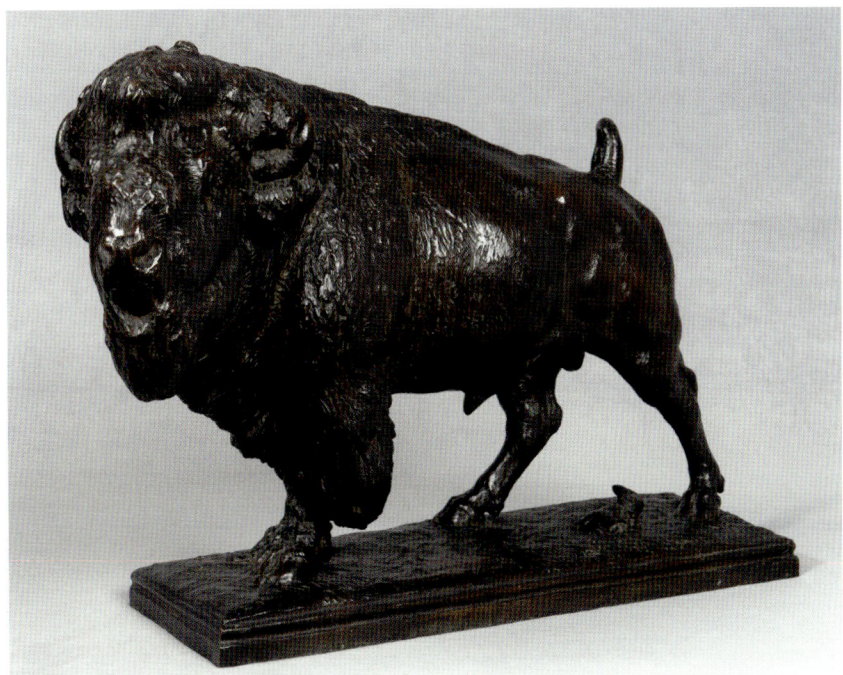

[PLATE 7.4]

ALEXANDER PHIMISTER
PROCTOR

Buffalo, 1913

Bronze, 13 ⅜ in. (height)
Brooklyn Museum, Brooklyn, New York.
Gift of George D. Pratt. 14.565

The resulting four colossal bronze buffalo were put in place in 1914.[4] Their heads were erect and their stance one of alert, staid reserve. The two that faced to the left were called *Buffalo I*, and the two that faced to the right got the titles of *Buffalo II*. Using the 13-inch maquette for *Buffalo I*, which Proctor copyrighted in 1912, the artist had Roman Bronze Works start making tabletop-sized bronzes. The earliest known casting of the Roman Bronze Works production came out of the foundry in 1913, an order from Proctor's patron George D. Pratt, who donated it to the Brooklyn Museum in 1914. [PLATE 7.4] It has several peculiarities, including a misspelling of the artist's last name, but most important is a detail on the top of the artist's base. There, emerging from the earth between the beast's hind legs, are the remnants of a buffalo skull. [PLATE 7.5] This element, which does not appear in other known castings of the work, including the monuments, suggests that Proctor recognized the importance of the preservation efforts that were under way. He was living at the time in New Rochelle, New York, just above the city and no doubt read about them in the *New York Times*, and even possibly visited Charles Russell's exhibition *The West That Has Passed* at the Folsom Galleries

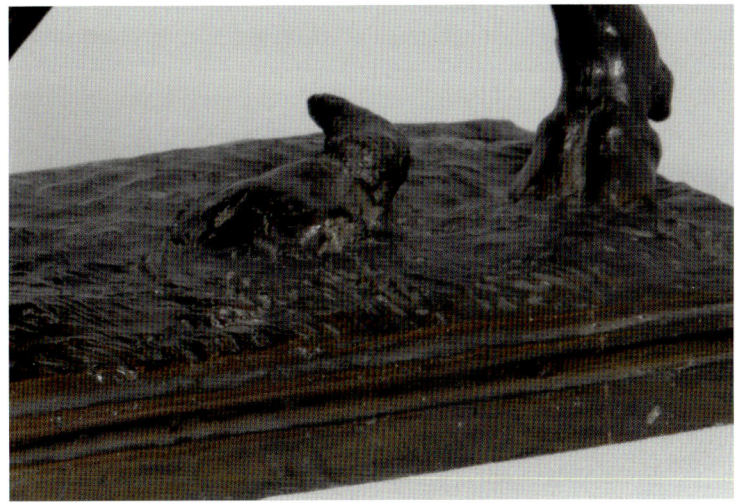

[PLATE 7.5]

ALEXANDER PHIMISTER
PROCTOR

Buffalo (detail – base), 1913

Bronze
Brooklyn Museum, Brooklyn, New York. Gift of George D. Pratt. 14.565

4 Ibid, 169.

in New York in 1911, during the spring and summer before Proctor's trip to the Canadian West.[5] He would have seen Russell's bronze *Nature's Cattle,* [PLATE 7.6] freshly minted by Roman Bronze Works that spring. *Nature's Cattle* carries the message of promise for the beleaguered buffalo, showing a healthy family group crossing the prairies. While sentimental, *Nature's Cattle* is also prescient, providing a testament of hope for the

[PLATE 7.6]

CHARLES MARION RUSSELL
(1864 – 1926)

Nature's Cattle, 1911

Bronze, 4 ¾ in. (height)
Buffalo Bill Center of the West, Cody,
Wyoming. Gift of Mr. and Mrs. W.D.
Weiss. 27.97.7

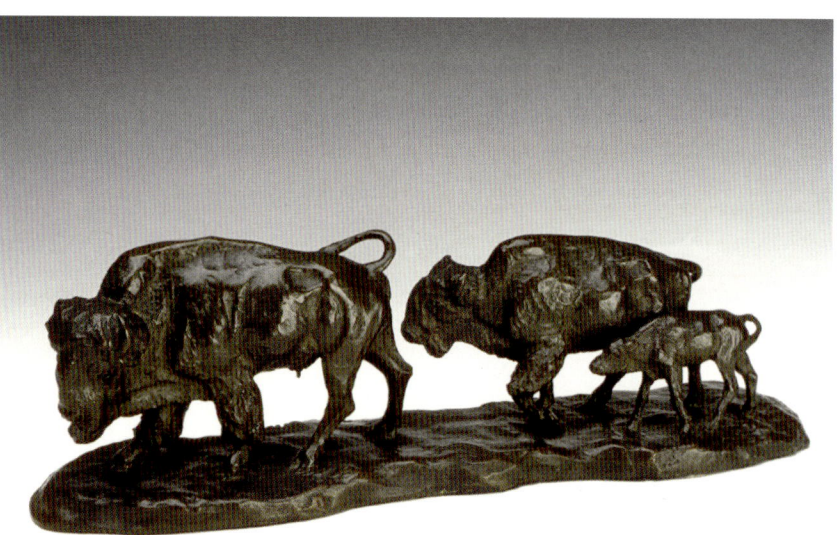

buffalo's future. Proctor's new *Buffalo,* standing astride the skull, a token of a diminished past, evokes the same affirming message: that the buffalo is proud, commanding, and resilient when provided proper stewardship, and that it represented a national symbol worthy of the artist's finest work.

Subsequent castings of the work, whether produced by the Roman Bronze Works, Gorham Co. Founders [PLATE 7.7], or Verbeyst Foundeur in Brussels, have bases that are essentially flat and completely devoid of the skull. Nothing in the artist's records explains why the change was made. Perhaps viewers found it difficult to determine what the skull was and, to simplify the matter, it was removed. With its elimination, however, some of the poignancy of the piece was lost.

Proctor began exhibiting what he called *Bison, Model for Q Street Bridge,* at the Canadian Art Club in early 1913.[6] Later that year it appeared as a featured piece in his show in the new galleries of the Gorham Co. Founders in New York.[7] It went on to see a long history of showings whenever Proctor exhibited large samplings of his work. More than a dozen lifetime castings are known to survive today, including a founder's master model or pattern at the University Museums, University of Delaware.

5   Arthur Hoeber, "Cowboy Vividly Paints the Passing Life of the Plains," *New York Times* (March 19, 1911).

6   Canadian Art Club, *Sixth Annual Exhibition* (Toronto, 1913), no. 75.

7   *Exhibition of Bronzes and Plaster Models by A. Phimister Proctor,* no. 14.

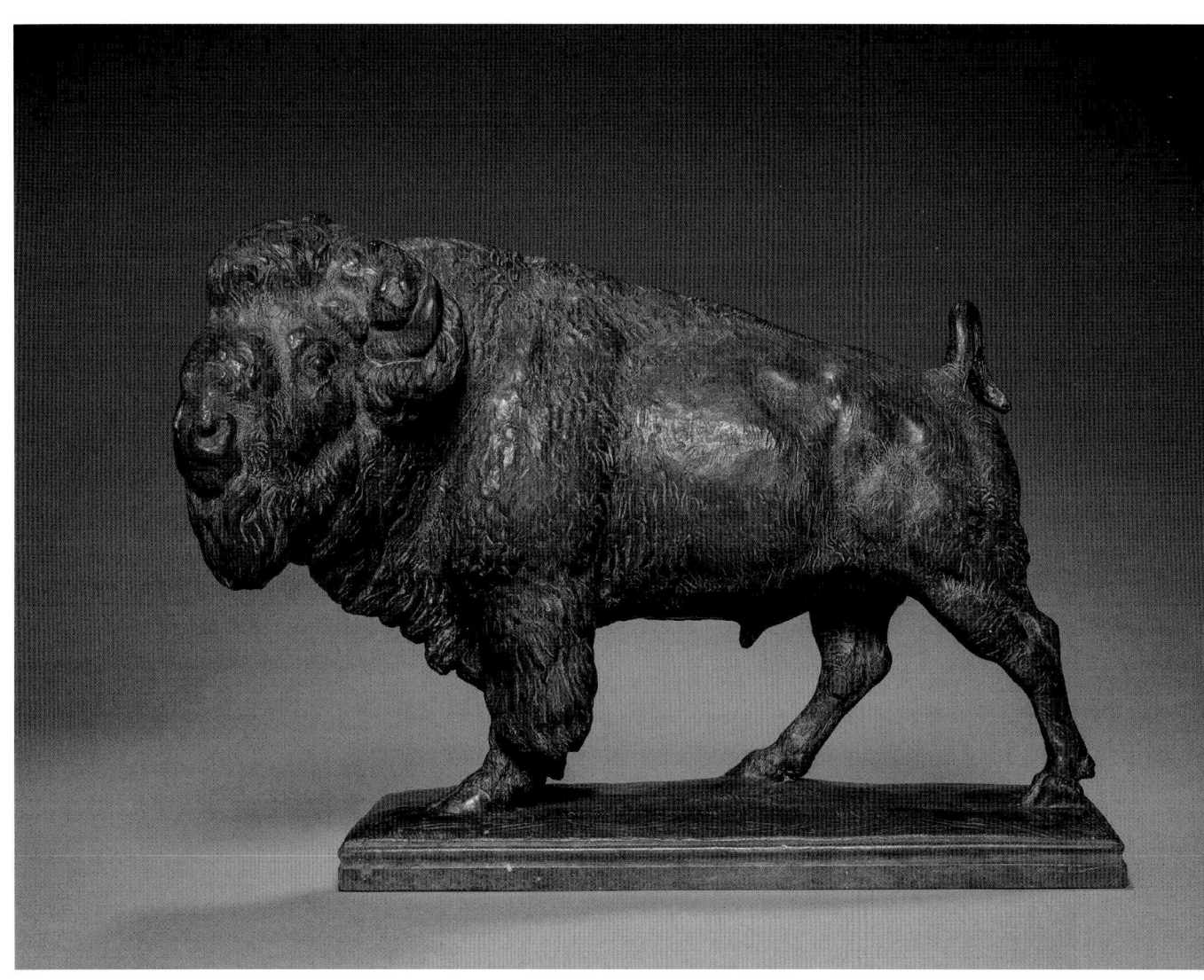

[PLATE 7.7]

ALEXANDER PHIMISTER PROCTOR

Buffalo, (model for *Q Street Buffalo*), ca. 1927

Bronze, 13 ¼ in. (height)
The Cleveland Museum of Art, Gift of George D. Pratt. 1927.291

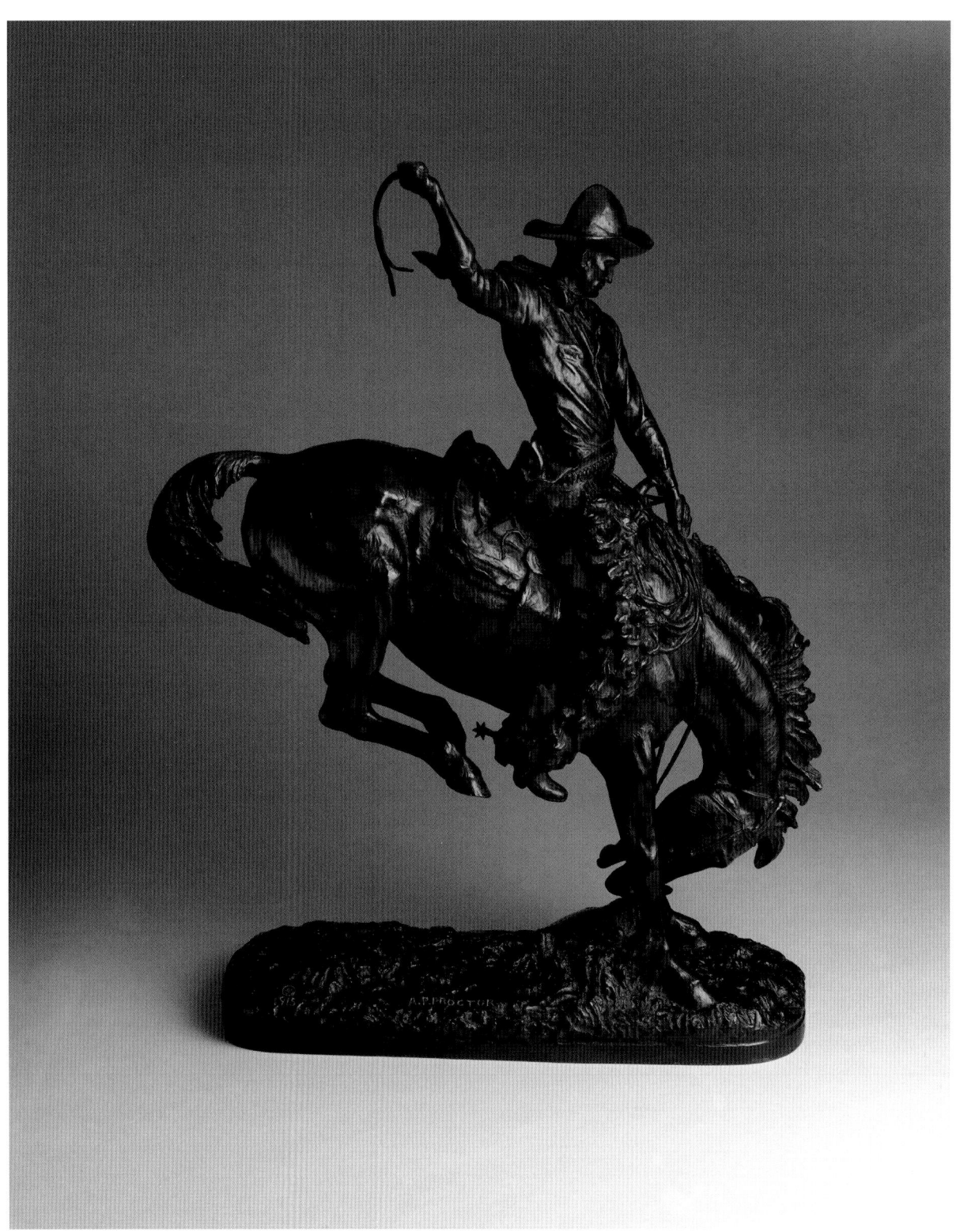

ALEXANDER PHIMISTER PROCTOR, *Buckaroo*, ca. 1915. Bronze, 26 ¼ in. (height). Denver Art Museum Collection: Funds from William Sr. and Dorothy Harmsen Collection by exchange, 2005.12. Photography © Denver Art Museum

BUCKAROO

In the winter of 1913–14, the National Academy of Design hosted its annual winter exhibition, which included 119 representative works by American sculptors. Proctor exhibited one bronze, a small cast of *Buffalo* for the Q Street Bridge in Washington, D.C.[1] For this he received the praise of art critic William Walton in *Scribner's Magazine* for having contributed one of the truly "modern additions to the repertory of art."[2] The *Buffalo* (see plate 7.4) was perhaps the artist's prime achievement as a sculptor of animals. Its powerful simplicity was indeed a modern statement, and the vibrant majesty and monumental proportions of even this small version proved how far Proctor had come since his first sentimental efforts with his two versions of the *Fawn* (see plate 1.2) twenty years earlier.

Yet when Proctor visited the National Academy show and later read the Walton review, he must have been drawn to an especially vital western bronze by California artist and fellow academician Joseph Mora. Titled *Fanning a Twister,* [PLATE 8.1] the work embodied something his *Buffalo* lacked in profound measure. Mora's work was all action and spirit, all energy and dynamism. Unlike Proctor's *Buffalo* with its static grandeur, Mora's little bronze brimmed with ebullience. Proctor must have wondered what it would be like to return to the West, as he had so often done over the years, but this time with the intent not of hunting wild animals, but of bringing the contemporary *human* elements of the western scene to life through his art. The cowboy—having been celebrated in sculpture since 1893 with Proctor's plaster monument *Cowboy* at the World's Columbian Exposition, and in 1895 with Frederic Remington's masterpiece *The Broncho Buster*—was the perfect theme. Proctor had no doubt seen the latter work in the New York showroom windows at Tiffany's and probably even knew of Charles M. Russell's explosive 1911 sculpture of the same subject, *A Bronc Twister,* which was displayed in the shop of Theodore Starr on Fifth Avenue. But neither of these sculptors was currently showing at the National Academy. Mora was likely the most logical inspiration for Proctor. Now, Proctor surely concluded, the

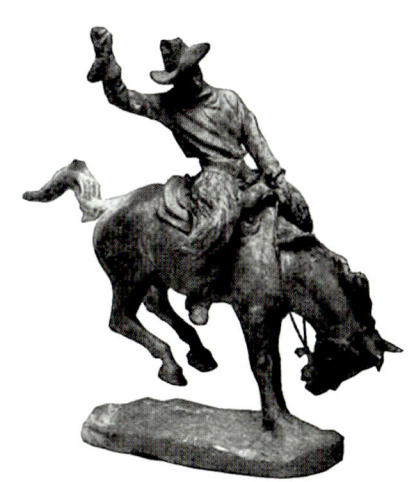

[PLATE 8.1]

JOSEPH JACINTO MORA

(b. Uruguay, 1876 – 1947)

Fanning a Twister, 1913

Bronze
Illustration in *Scribner's Magazine* 55, (January – June, 1914), 665.
Buffalo Bill Center of the West, Cody, Wyoming

1   *National Academy of Design: Winter Exhibition* (New York: National Academy of Design, 1913), 16.
2   William Walton, "The Field of Art," *Scribner's Magazine* 55 (May 1914), 666.

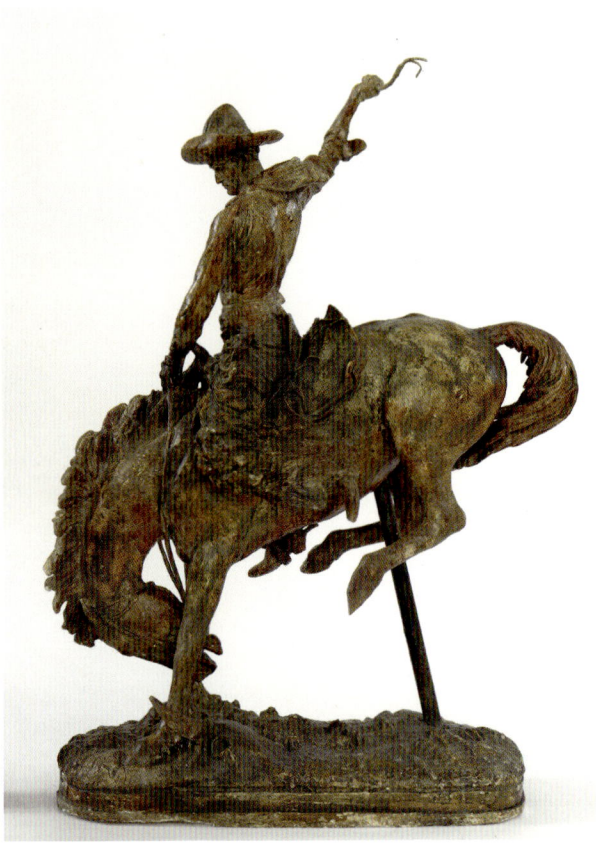

[PLATE 8.2]

ALEXANDER PHIMISTER
PROCTOR

Buckaroo, ca. 1914 – 1915

Plaster, 28 in. (height)
Buffalo Bill Center of the West, Cody,
Wyoming. Gift of A. Phimister Proctor
Museum with special thanks to Sandy
and Sally Church. 11.06.698

subject as well as Mora's pose needed his touch. Somehow he would have to find a way to lend his hand afresh to the cowboy's interpretation

By the next time he saw another of Mora's bronco sculptures, one called *Scratching a Twister* in the Fine Arts Pavilion of the 1915 Panama-Pacific International Exposition in San Francisco, Proctor had fulfilled his wish and produced his own bucking horse and rider.[3] During a visit to Oregon's Pendleton Roundup the previous summer, Proctor had embarked on a bucking-horse sculpture with his own mix of powerful aesthetic design and stylistic restraint. It was elegant, graceful, and controlled, yet at the same time spirited. He had suffered some false starts that fall and even a studio fire that destroyed the first of his cowboy models, but with perseverance, he was back in the Northwest the following summer with what local newspapers referred to as six bronze castings (though they were probably plasters) of western subjects, including one that he had copyrighted under the title *Buckaroo.*[4] The first showing appeared in Seattle at the Washington State Art Association galleries.[5] Proctor then displayed the works in the private residence of Mr. and Mrs. John G. Edwards of Portland, where his cowboy sculpture was singled out as an exceptional tour de force and the representation of a national icon. The sculpture was "full of verve and action, both horse and man typically American, typically Western," wrote the *Morning Oregonian.* Yet even as the sculptor demonstrated a primary interest in the "expression of action," the reporter continued, "he never loses the rare sense of decorative beauty which is characteristic of his more monumental works."[6] When a plaster cast of the piece [PLATE 8.2] was sent to Pendleton in late July 1915, a local newspaper boasted that it would soon be converted into a monument for that city.[7] Unfortunately, that honor was not to be, but according to one of the local papers, the plaster model that had "created a furore [*sic*] in art

3   The *Official Catalogue of the Department of Fine Arts, Panama-Pacific International Exposition* (1915) lists and illustrates Mora's bronze.

4   For reference to the studio fire, see "Sculpture on Exhibit," *East Oregonian* (November 16, 1914). The copyright was filed from New York on July 8, 1815. Images of the works that were illustrated in the newspapers at the time appear to be depictions of plasters, not bronzes. See, for example, "Sculptor Is Guest," *Portland Morning Oregonian* (July 23, 1915).

5   "Noted Sculptor Exhibiting in Seattle," *Seattle Post-Intelligencer* (July 21, 1915).

6   "Sculptor Is Guest."

7   "Famous Statue to Be Exhibited Today," *Pendleton East Oregonian* (July 29, 1915). The sculpture, referred to clearly as a plaster cast, was shown at the Frazier Book Store in Pendleton. The city's other newspaper referred to the work as a plaster also. "To Exhibit 'Buckaroo,'" *Pendleton Tribune* (July 29, 1915).

circles" in Seattle and Portland had been well enough received to encourage the artist to send the plaster east to be cast in bronze.[8]

It is thought that the plaster was shipped in August to the Gorham Co. Founders in Providence, Rhode Island. There, according to the company's records, a singular sand-cast bronze was completed by mid-September.[9] What is thought to be this initial bronze, or one much like it, is marked with a set of letters, QACQ , and the boxed-in symbol "G/she wolf symbol/C" [PLATE 8.3 and PLATE 8.4], which denotes an early cast. It was sent back to Oregon in early November, where, with great fanfare, the first *Buckaroo* bronze was exhibited in Pendleton.[10] The statue did not rest on its pedestal for long, however. Such was the enthusiasm for this bronze masterpiece that locals and supporters from across the state pressured Proctor to forward it immediately to San Francisco to adorn the galleries of the Oregon Pavilion of the Panama-Pacific International Exposition. Contending in a headline that it "Typifies Possibilities of Western Art," the *Portland Oregonian* reported that the *Buckaroo* bronze had on November 12 been "unveiled in the art room" of the Oregon Pavilion. It proved, for Proctor at least, that the West held fresh possibilities for his art. He was present to watch the bronze emerge from beneath the drape of an American flag, and he then offered complimentary remarks about how Oregon had served him as muse. It was, he said, "an artist's country. It is the natural haunt of creators."[11] With this comment, Proctor positioned himself as a true creative son of the West. No subject could have done this more effectively than a bronze rider of wild horse flesh.

The records of the Gorham Co. Founders suggest that the plaster for *Buckaroo* was returned from Providence to New York City, either to the Gorham showroom there or to Proctor's East 51st Street studio. In the meantime, using his clay model, Proctor evidently responded to what he foresaw as a stirring demand and produced a second plaster to be used by the Roman Bronze Works in Queens, New York. The resulting new

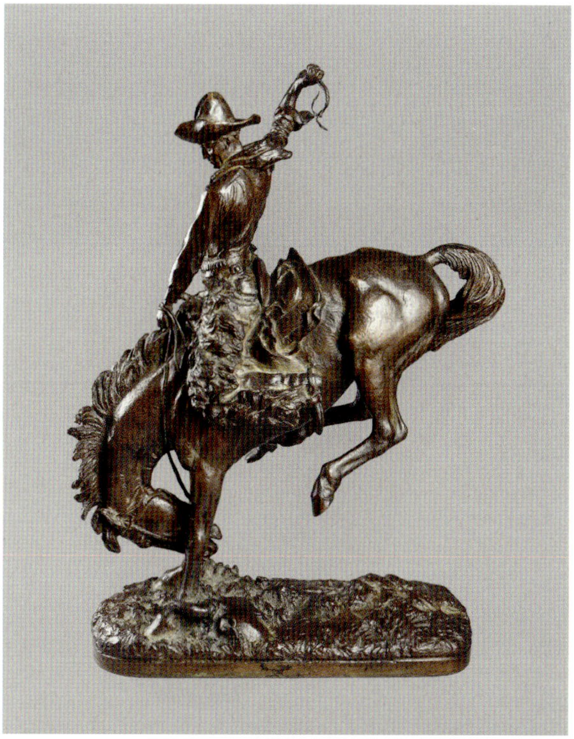

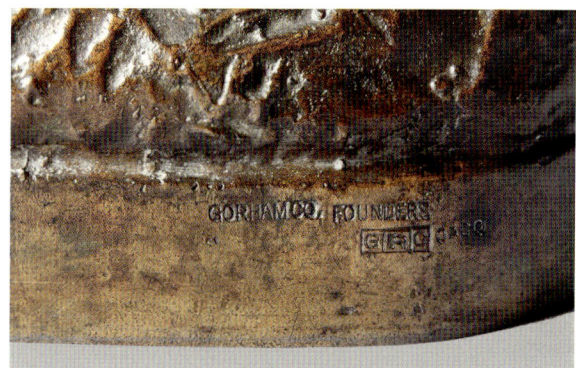

[PLATE 8.3]

ALEXANDER PHIMISTER
PROCTOR

Buckaroo, ca. 1915

Bronze
Private Collection

[PLATE 8.4]

ALEXANDER PHIMISTER
PROCTOR

Buckaroo (Gorham, detail –
foundry mark), ca. 1915

Bronze
Private Collection

---

8   "To Exhibit 'Buckaroo.'"

9   Samuel Hough, "Report on Gorham Foundry Casting QACQ: A. Phimister Proctor's 'Buckaroo,'" undated record for *Buckaroo*, no. 8.2.1, Proctor Archives, McCracken Research Library, Buffalo Bill Center of the West (hereafter cited as Proctor Archives).

10   "'Buckaroo' on Exposition," *East Oregonian* (November 2, 1915).

11   "Oregon Sculpture Is Seen by Public," *Portland Oregonian* (November 12, 1915).

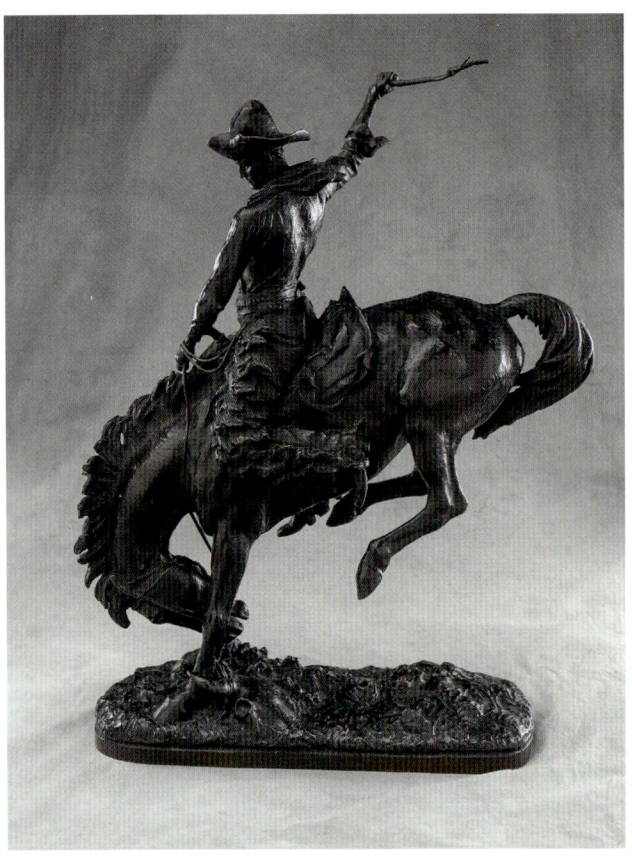

[PLATE 8.5]

ALEXANDER PHIMISTER
PROCTOR

Buckaroo, ca. 1916

Bronze, 27 ½ in. (height)
Oregon Historical Society, Portland,
Oregon

castings were slightly different from the Gorham piece. In the Roman Bronze Works castings, the rider's left hand is generally free from the horse's mane, there is a hole visible in the mane, and the tail does not connect with the animal's rump (see plates 8.5 and 8.7). The Roman Bronze Works ledgers record that in 1916 and 1917, no fewer than seven castings were made.[12]

One of those early Roman Bronze Works castings—all produced using the lost-wax, rather than the sand-cast, method—was ordered as a special presentation piece from the artist to his old Portland friend and promoter John G. Edwards (Beinecke Rare Book and Manuscript Library, Yale University, New Haven, Connecticut). Edwards had been a legendary cattleman and sheep rancher in Wyoming and eastern Oregon and, in his later years, was himself devoted to painting and sculpting. The Proctor bronze reflected Edwards's love of art and his self-image as an adventuresome man of the West.[13] Another early lost-wax casting was made for a group of citizens from Pendleton who considered the *Buckaroo* [PLATE 8.5] the quintessential symbol of their city and the West. For that reason they chose to make a gift of it to one of the city's heroes, Charles Samuel Jackson, a pioneer newspaper man from Pendleton who had served as publisher of the *Eastern Oregonian* for twenty years before moving to Portland in 1902 to found the *Oregon Journal*. The presentation was made in January 1917. In gratitude, Jackson wrote that the city representatives "could not have selected a finer implement with which to emblazon upon my heart the good will of Pendleton."[14]

It is not known which foundry's casting Proctor took with him to Denver in 1917 when he attended William F. Cody's funeral and, through the artist's wife, fortuitously connected with the city's mayor, Robert Walter Speer.[15] What is known is that Speer commissioned Proctor to turn the *Buckaroo* into a heroic-sized bronze monument for Denver's new Civic Center and that the artist chose to enlarge the Gorham model and use Gorham Co. Founders for casting the monument. It was titled

12   Ledger 2, p. 67, and ledger 5, p. 308, Roman Bronze Works Archives, Amon Carter Museum, Fort Worth, TX.

13   A biographical sketch appeared in K. W. Fitzgerald, "Sheep King: John Edwards Wills Wool Fortune to Oregon," *Portland Oregonian* (April 7, 1946).

14   "C.S. Jackson Gives Characteristic Thanks for Present of 'Buckaroo,'" *Eastern Oregonian* (January 22, 1917).

15   Hassrick, *Wildlife and Western Heroes*, 192–93.

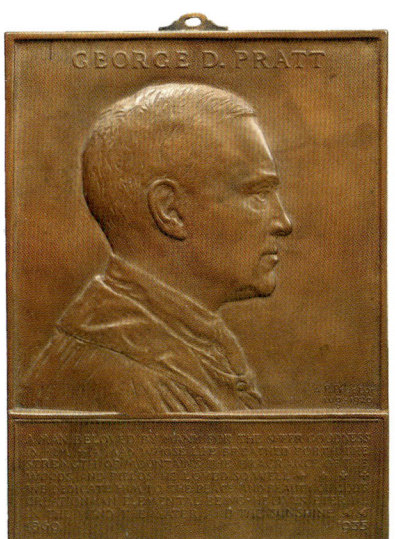

Broncho Buster and dedicated in 1920. To illustrate how open Proctor was with regard to his selection of foundries and how he liked to spread the work around, yet still obtain the most affordable castings possible, the production for the companion Denver monument, *On the War Trail*, was assigned to the Roman Bronze Works foundry in Queens. It was dedicated in 1922.

The *Buckaroo* was a favorite piece for one of Proctor's major patrons, a frequent hunting companion from the early 1910s and Standard Oil Company's president, George DuPont Pratt. [PLATE 8.6] Between 1916 and 1932 Pratt commissioned at least three bronze castings of the *Buckaroo* from Proctor, two of them from Roman Bronze Works and one or more from Gorham. An early Roman Bronze Works casting, now in the collections of the Metropolitan Museum of Art in New York, is specially marked, on the base, "CAST FOR GEO. D. PRATT / BY A.P.P." [PLATE 8.7] One other Roman Bronze Works bronze of the *Buckaroo*, ordered by Pratt for the Boy Scouts of America, is in the collections of the R. W. Norton Art Gallery in Shreveport, Louisiana.

Pratt ordered more of these castings from Proctor to be manufactured by Gorham, as indicated by a surviving plaster model marked on one side of the base, "CAST FOR GEO. D. PRATT / A.P.P." (Buffalo Bill Center of the West; see plate 8.2). Pratt also purchased at least one other casting from the Gorham Co. Founders, which he donated in 1932 to his alma mater, Amherst College, and is now in the collection of the Mead Art Museum. [PLATE 8.8] It was cast in lost wax under subcontract by Eugene Gargani & Sons.[16] The arrangement with Gorham lasted until 1934, and at least one other casting, now located

[PLATE 8.6]

ALEXANDER PHIMISTER PROCTOR

George D. Pratt, 1935

Bronze, 7 ¼ in. (height)
Amherst Library, New York, New York.
Gift of the estate of Herbert L. Pratt /
Bridgeman Images

[PLATE 8.7]

ALEXANDER PHIMISTER PROCTOR

Buckaroo, ca. 1917

Bronze, 28 ½ in. (height)
The Metropolitan Museum of Art, New York, New York. Bequest of George D. Pratt. 48.149.26. Art Resource, NY

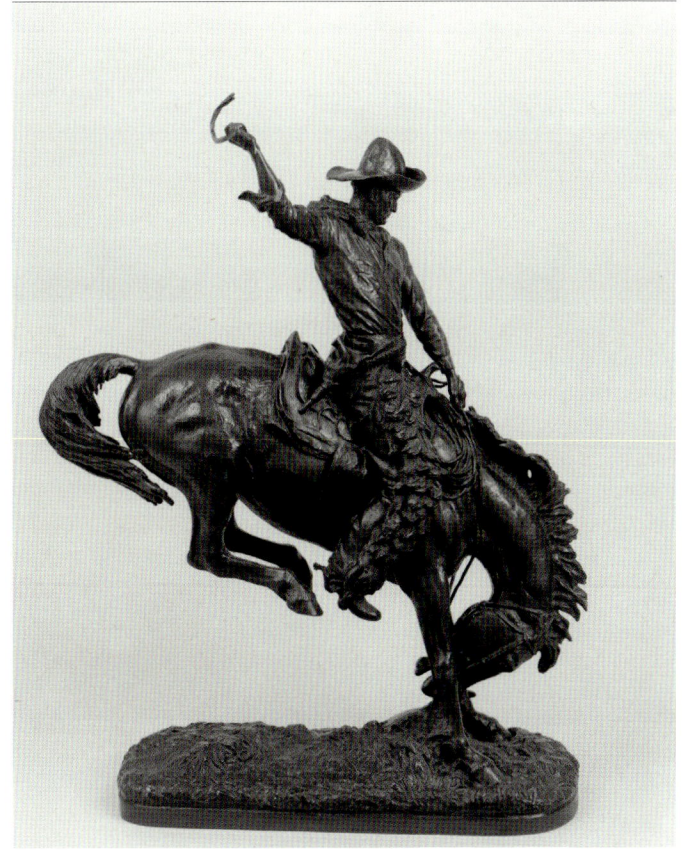

---

16   See Janis Conner, "After the Model: Bessie Potter Vonnoh's Early Bronzes and Founders," in Julie Aronson (ed.), *Bessie Potter Vonnoh: Sculptor of Women* (Athens: Ohio University Press, 2008), 244.

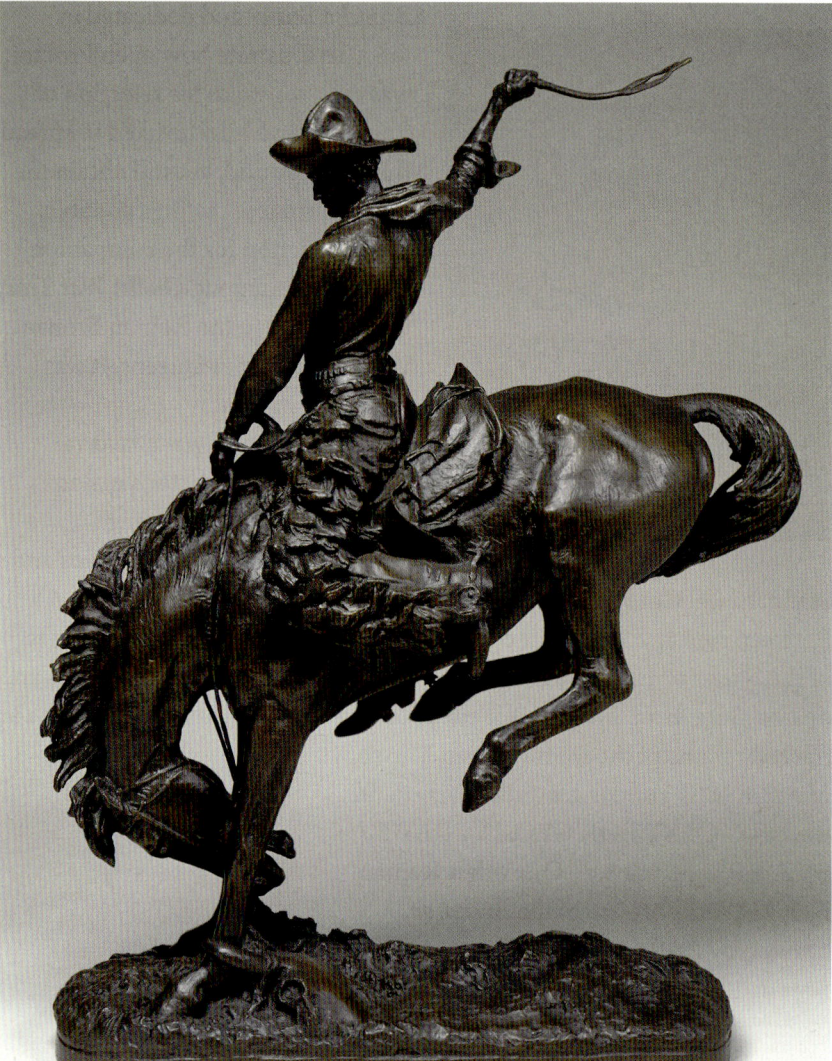

[PLATE 8.8]

ALEXANDER PHIMISTER
PROCTOR

Buckaroo, 1932

Bronze, 26 ½ in. (height)
Mead Art Museum, Amherst College,
Amherst, Massachusetts. Gift of George
D. Pratt / Bridgeman Images

[PLATE 8.9]

ALEXANDER PHIMISTER
PROCTOR

Buckaroo, (Gorham / Gargani,
detail – foundry mark), ca. 1915

Bronze
Denver Art Museum Collection: Funds
from William Sr. and Dorothy Harmsen
Collection by exchange, 2005.12.
Photography © Denver Art Museum

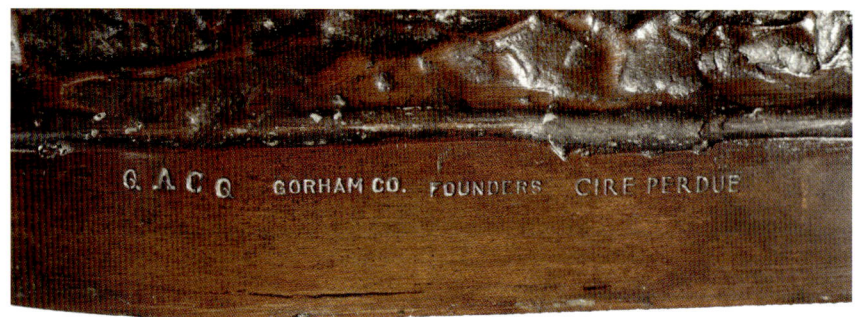

at the Denver Art Museum, is thought to have been the result of that
agreement. [PLATE 8.9]

In 1935 Proctor placed an order for another *Buckaroo* from
Roman Bronze Works for a Christmas present to the art collector and
philanthropist Ernest E. Quantrell of Bronxville, New York, from his family

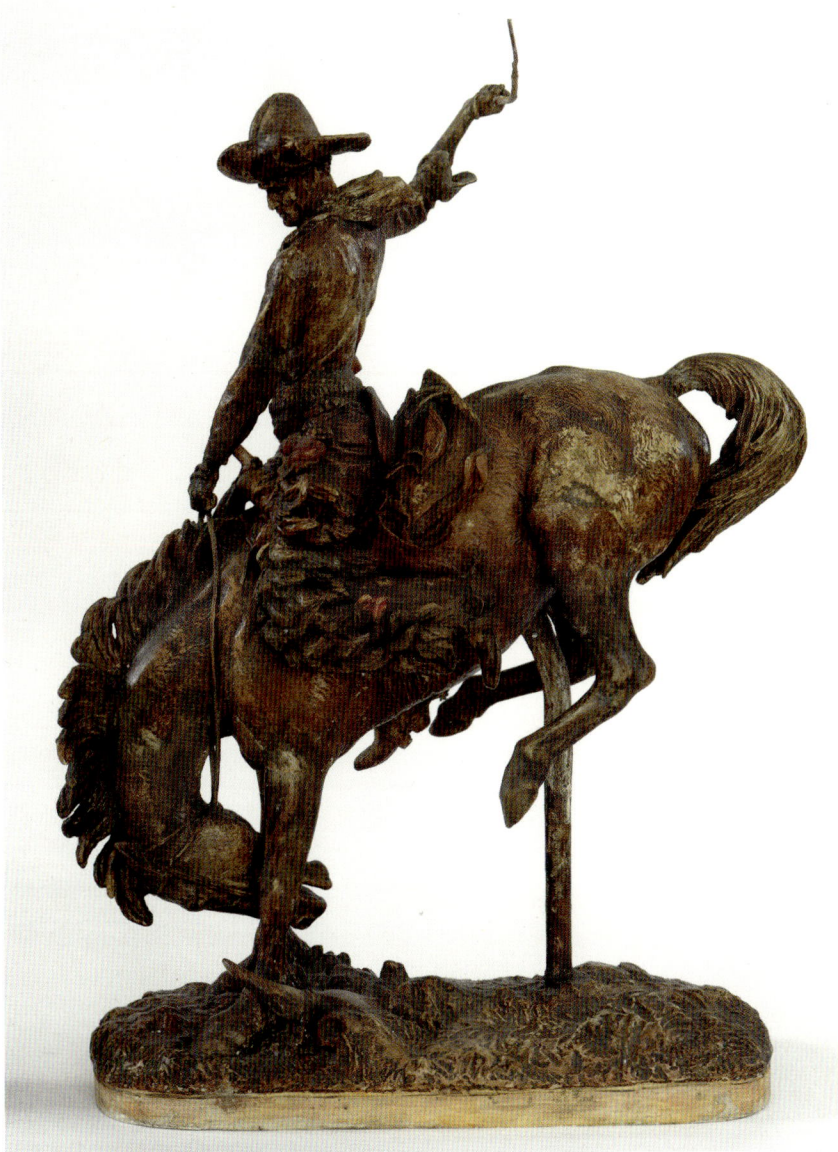

[PLATE 8.10]

ALEXANDER PHIMISTER
PROCTOR

Buckaroo, ca. 1918 – 1920

Plaster, 28 in. (height)
Buffalo Bill Center of the West, Cody,
Wyoming. Gift of A. Phimister Proctor
Museum with special thanks to Sandy
and Sally Church. 11.06.697

(Rees-Jones Collection, Dallas, Texas). The casting of this latter bronze
cost Proctor $210. In this case and that of Pratt's Gorham casting, the "sale
price" was listed as $475, though Pratt's casting was discounted to $332.50
while the Quantrells' bronze cost his family $400.[17] Pratt was a sufficiently
loyal patron to garner a somewhat deeper discount.

A second, undated plaster model for this bronze exists [PLATE 8.10]
that is thought to have come from the Roman Bronze Foundry. In it, the
horse's rump is an inch or more higher than in earlier castings, and the
reins are oddly connected to the bridle near the throat of the horse rather
than at the mouth. No lifetime bronze castings from this plaster are known
to exist today.

---

17   Figures from Proctor's Account Book, 1930s, Proctor Archives.

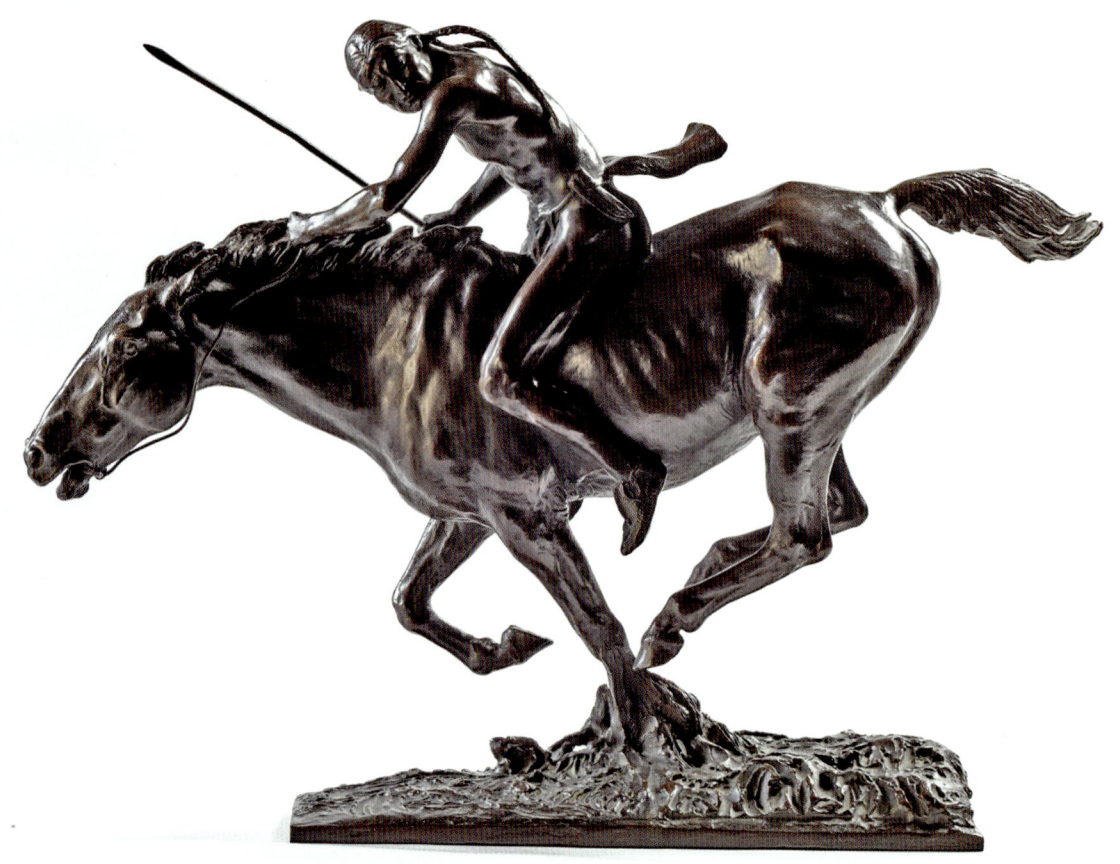

ALEXANDER PHIMISTER PROCTOR, *Pursued,* 1914. Bronze, 16 ½ in. (height). Tacoma Art Museum, Tacoma, Washington. Gift of Erivan and Helga Haub. 2014.6.95

PURSUED

Indian Pursued; Pursued: Cheyenne Indian; The Pursuit

In 1900, while Proctor was focused on his remarkable creations as an animalier sculptor, his contemporary, the western painter and sculptor Frederic Remington, embarked on a series of works in several media devoted to some of the most acclaimed residents of the northern plains, the Cheyenne Indians. He first published a set of eight dramatic pastel drawings known as *A Bunch of Buckskins,* one of the highlights of which he titled *A Cheyenne Buck.* [PLATE 9.1] It somewhat resembled the idealized and majestic pose that Proctor had chosen for his *Indian Warrior* a few years earlier.

Another Remington interpretation of the Cheyenne people appeared as a bronze in 1902, *The Cheyenne.* [PLATE 9.2] As opposed to an idealized representation, however, this rendition presented a Cheyenne warrior as animated and defiant. Every movement of man and horse in the sculpture reinforced the expression on the warrior's face, a rebellious grimace charged with emotional symbolism that cried out for cultural survival. He was the exemplar of resistance, an emblem of male pride and bellicosity. A couple of years earlier, Remington had written his last major piece of fiction, a novel about a Cheyenne family that he titled *The Way of an Indian.* Not published until 1906, it bore the same message of cultural conflict and struggle.[1] In it, Remington strove to present what he saw at the time as the true Indian story. It was a heartbreaking tale of primal man against pernicious civilization, of tragic human loss and the dissolution of generations of cultural legacy. Remington's friend and admirer President Theodore Roosevelt praised the author for revealing a convincing "understanding" of the Indian in the book's pages.[2]

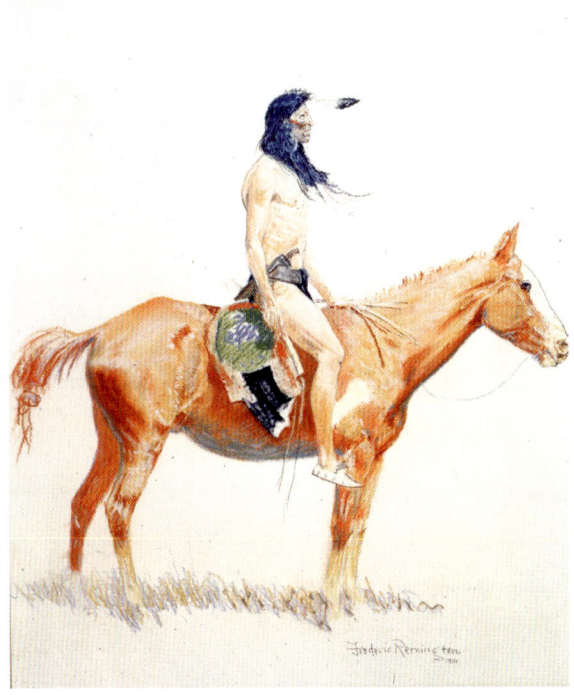

[PLATE 9.1]

FREDERIC REMINGTON

(1861 – 1909)

A Cheyenne Buck, 1901

Pastel on academy board, 33 x 24 ¼ in.
National Cowboy & Western Heritage
Museum, Oklahoma City, Oklahoma. A.90.2

1   The book was published initially in serial form in *The Cosmopolitan* 40 (November 1905–March 1906). The book followed; *The Way of an Indian* (New York: Fox Duffield & Company, 1906).

2   Roosevelt to Remington, February 20, 1906, quoted in Allen P. and Marilyn D. Splete (eds.), *Frederic Remington—Selected Letters* (New York, Abbeville Press, 1988), 359.

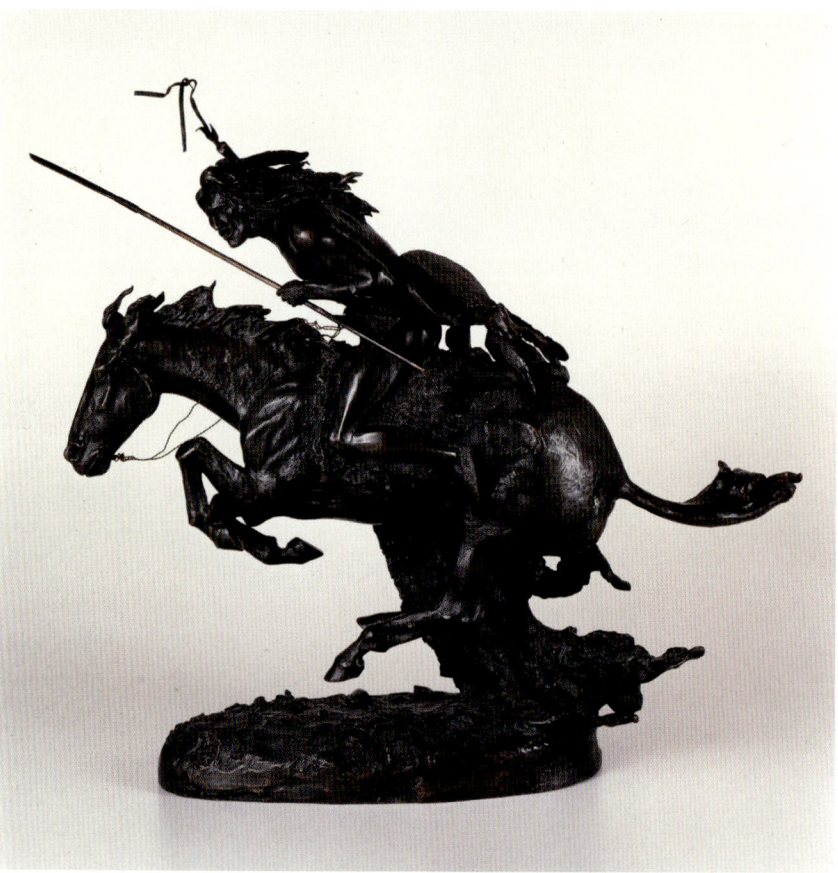

[PLATE 9.2]

FREDERIC REMINGTON

(1861 – 1909)

The Cheyenne, ca. 1905

Bronze, 22 ½ in. (height)
Buffalo Bill Center of the West, Cody,
Wyoming. Gift of Mrs. Henry H.R. Coe.
17.71

Another writer of the time, Proctor and Roosevelt's friend and fellow Boone and Crockett Club member George Bird Grinnell, gained fame for his informed and sympathetic treatise on the Cheyenne people that would appear in print as *The Fighting Cheyennes* [PLATE 9.3] in 1915.[3] In that volume, Grinnell believed he could expose the true nature and history of the venerated Plains tribe by basing his research on direct Cheyenne interviews. He eschewed the standard U.S. military's accounts of the Anglo-Indian encounters in the West and relied instead on the Indian perspective.

One of the Cheyenne leaders who played a primary role in Grinnell's book was a warrior chief named Little Wolf. Grinnell devoted one whole chapter to Little Wolf's leadership in the arduous and powerfully symbolic 1879 venture of moving his people from Indian Territory, Oklahoma, where they had been forcibly relocated, back to their ancestral home in the Powder River country of Montana. He and his band literally fought their way north, battling multiple U.S. military forces along the way and ultimately surrendering to Captain W. P. Clark, an old friend of Little Wolf and an emissary of General Nelson Miles. Little Wolf and his people ended up on the Cheyenne Reservation near Lame Deer, Montana, making the trip's travails worth the effort. Though diminished in strength and numbers, they were home at last.

---

3   George Bird Grinnell, *The Fighting Cheyennes* (New York: Charles Scribner's Sons, 1915).

Little Wolf died in 1904, but Grinnell's telling of his life, as one of the truly great men of Plains Indian history, sustained his legendary reputation.[4] There is no specific evidence that Grinnell and Proctor discussed Little Wolf or even the Cheyenne Indians. Yet the fact that Proctor decided in 1915 to venture west in search of worthy human subjects and found his inspiration on the Cheyenne Reservation with the chief's nephew, Laban Little Wolf, suggests that the author and the artist had probably conversed about the matter. Laban's son, Robert, became the primary model for Proctor's sculpture *Pursued*, a work invested with a sense of destiny and flight that mirrors the plight of the Northern Cheyenne people and the dramatic tale of the model's great uncle. *Pursued* can be presumed to be a metaphor for the Cheyenne Indians in their worthy yet perilous quest to find a well-deserved, compatible, and historically resonant homeland.

Proctor had known Grinnell at least since 1893 in Chicago, when the artist was inducted into the Boone and Crockett Club, and probably connected with him again in 1895 in Montana.[5] They had much in common, both with the historic conservation organization and with Indians. Grinnell was working in 1895 on the establishment of Glacier National Park but, as a student of the Blackfeet Indians, was in Montana also to visit the native people of the region. Proctor was on a hunting trip just outside the park's future boundaries with his lawyer friend and another fellow Boone and Crockett Club member Henry L. Stimson. Proctor set aside time during his trip to visit the Blackfeet Reservation and search for a model for his first major work, *Indian Warrior* (see plate 4.5).

In 1908, Proctor provided the Boone and Crockett Club with its emblem, his *Head of a Brown Bear*. Members at that year's annual dinner in New York were each given, as a favor, a plaster casting of the piece by the artist. Grinnell attended the dinner and, as chairman of the nominating committee, was an officer of the club. Their friendship would no doubt have been further cemented by Proctor's generous gesture toward the club and his fellow wildlife conservationists.

Many years later, in his autobiography, Proctor referred to his intentions with *Pursued*. He said that he wanted to create an equestrian Indian being chased "by an unseen enemy."[6] Robert looks over his left shoulder, just as his great uncle had done many times in his attempts

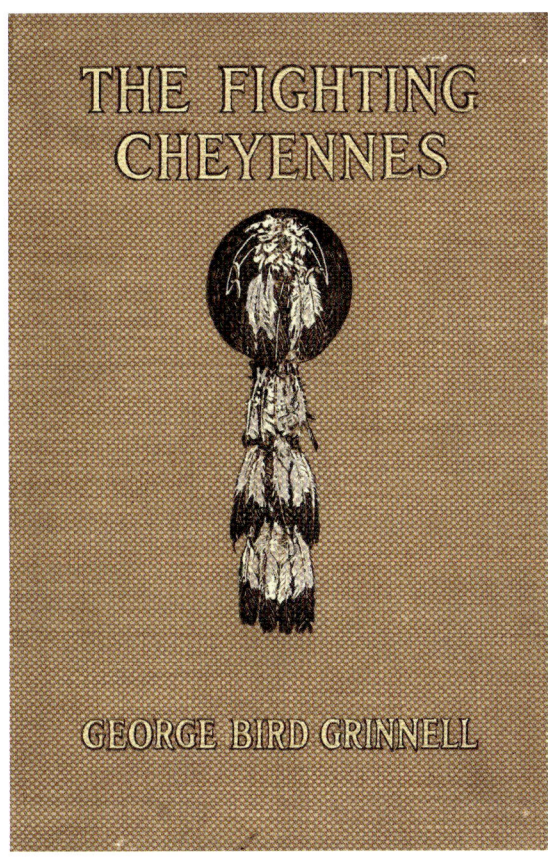

[PLATE 9.3]

GEORGE BIRD GRINNELL
(1849 – 1938)
The Fighting Cheyennes, 1915
Front cover of book
Harold McCracken Research Library,
Buffalo Bill Center of the West, Cody,
Wyoming. E99.C53 G8 1915

---

4 Ibid., 427.

5 Proctor mentions meeting Grinnell at the annual Boone and Crockett dinner in 1893.
See Ebner, *Sculptor in Buckskin*, 111, 127.

6 Ibid., 158.

to escape from the U.S. Army. To add an extra element of peril, Proctor wanted his subject to appear to be running downhill, hence the elevated rump of the horse even though the ground seems only slightly sloped.[7] The work is drama in action, giving a real sense of fright and desperation. It is the antithesis of Remington's *The Cheyenne*, in which the warrior is aggressive and frightful in his own right. Proctor's work is fearful, while Remington's is adversarial. Proctor's seems to project the Indian perspective much as Grinnell had, while Remington's, given its vengeful countenance, rather justified the Anglo and military viewpoint that the Indian was a worthy adversary, but an adversary nonetheless.

Another perspective might be considered as well when comparing Remington's *The Cheyenne* and Proctor's *Pursued*, one that involves the level of sculptural decorum that each represented. Both works were assessed in 1915, and the critical perceptions were strikingly disparate. Remington's bronze was viewed as daring, rough, and controversial even six years after his death. A casting of *The Cheyenne* was exhibited posthumously at the Panama-Pacific International Exposition in 1915 and was considered by one critic, Eugen Neuhaus, as "lacking in repose" and "wild and ill-mannered" when compared with other works in the vast San Francisco display.[8] At exactly the same time, Proctor's Indian sculpture was regarded as the opposite. Canadian critic W. H. de B. Nelson wrote that "Proctor never wanders out of his way to compose some striking effect calculated to cause a sensation," but rather stays within the "accepted canons of sculptural taste."[9] Proctor countered Remington's brashness with propriety. As the *Los Angeles Times* would say a few years later, "Strength and delicacy, power and refinement, classic poise with modern freedom— these are the qualities of the sculptures of A. Phimister Proctor."[10]

In his short lifetime, Remington produced as many as twenty casts of *The Cheyenne*. Proctor, over many more years and with two variations, cast somewhere close to the same number of *Pursued* (sixteen are known today). There appeared to have been a modestly healthy appetite then for both versions of the Cheyenne rider.

Actually there was more than one rider involved in the conceptualization of Proctor's *Pursued*. Robert Little Wolf, the grand-nephew of the great chief of the same name, modeled through much of the summer of 1914. When Robert had to return to ranching obligations, Proctor was forced to find another young Cheyenne to pose. J. R. Eddy was the primary agent of the Cheyenne Reservation. It was Eddy who introduced Proctor to the Little Wolf family, and it was probably Eddy who found a substitute, a young graduate of Carlisle Indian School, Rutherford

7   Ibid., 159.

8   Eugen Neuhaus, *The Galleries of the Exposition* (San Francisco: Paul Elder & Company, 1915), 56.

9   W. H. de B. Nelson, "Phimister Proctor: Canadian Sculptor," *Canadian Magazine* 44 (April 1915), 500.

10   "Proctor, A Sculptor of Unusual Power."

Rolling Bull. Proctor commented that, like Robert, Rutherford "was willing to pose in a G-string and braids." Rutherford persevered into the fall of the year, despite the "onset of cold weather," and until the plaster was completed and sent from Montana to New York to be cast.[11]

Proctor probably produced that first bronze cast in late 1914. It was exhibited initially with five other bronzes in Seattle in the galleries of the Washington State Art Association the following July, and then traveled on a whirlwind tour to a private residence display in Portland, Oregon, and finally the public library in Pendleton.[12]

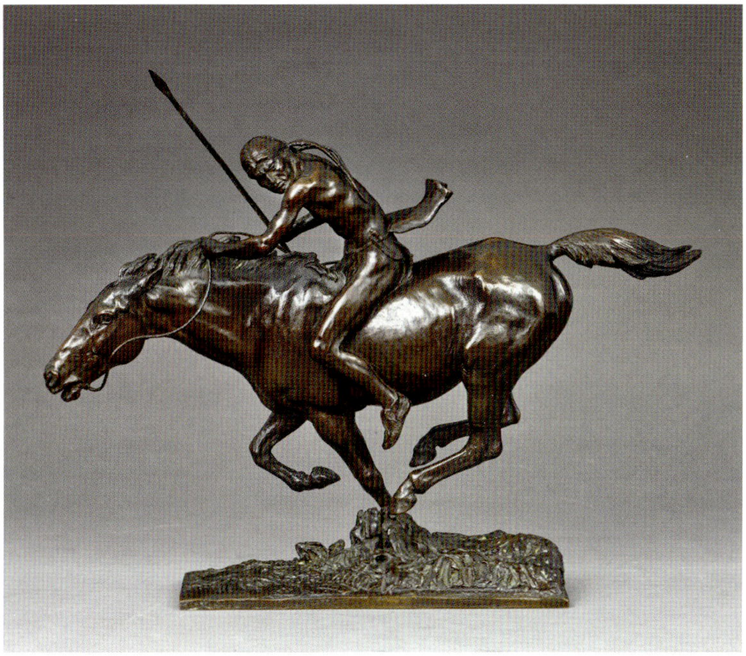

There were two different versions of this work. The first resulted directly from the artist's experience with the models, Robert Little Wolf and Rutherford Rolling Bull. He had the models race down a hill past him until he was able to grasp the essence of interaction between horse and rider, and capture the speed and flow of the group. That version portrays the horse suspended on only one hoof galloping from right to left with the rider holding a spear and looking over his left shoulder. The horse's rump is elevated, and the base extends beneath five-eighths of the length of the horse. The rear of the base is slightly raised, suggesting a lift in the ground that mirrors the heightened hindquarter of the horse, or an object over which the horse has just jumped. As is normal with Proctor's work, the figures are animated but graceful. Of the ten known castings of the first version, made between 1915 and 1928, all but two were cast by Roman Bronze Works in lost wax. [PLATE 9.4] The two exceptions are sand castings from Gorham Co. Founders. Proctor's old friend Henry Stimson, secretary of war in the Taft administration, purchased one of the Gorham casts as a gift for his aide de camp, Henry Regnier.

The second version of *Pursued* was initially modeled in Brussels over the winter of 1927–28. The Proctors had settled in Brussels after several years in Rome. Mussolini was inciting riots in Italy, and the artist made a strategic retreat to Belgium before the situation became too volatile. Proctor moved into a comfortable studio there and, among other things, began reworking his Cheyenne rider sculpture. The first casting was

[PLATE 9.4]

ALEXANDER PHIMISTER PROCTOR

Pursued, ca. 1914–1922

Bronze, 18 ½ in. (height)
The Rees-Jones Collection, Dallas, Texas

---

11 Ebner, *Sculptor in Buckskin,* 162.

12 See "Sculptor to Exhibit Small Bronzes Here," *Seattle Post-Intelligencer* (July 16, 1915), and Lilian Tingle, "Noted Sculptor, Now in Portland, Is Putting Cowboy on 'Art Map,'" *Portland Oregonian* (July 25, 1915) and *Pendleton Evening Tribune* (September 17, 1915).

[PLATE 9.5]

ALEXANDER PHIMISTER
PROCTOR

Pursued, 1928

Bronze, 17 in. (height)
Smithsonian American Art Museum,
Washington, DC. Museum purchase.
1992.3

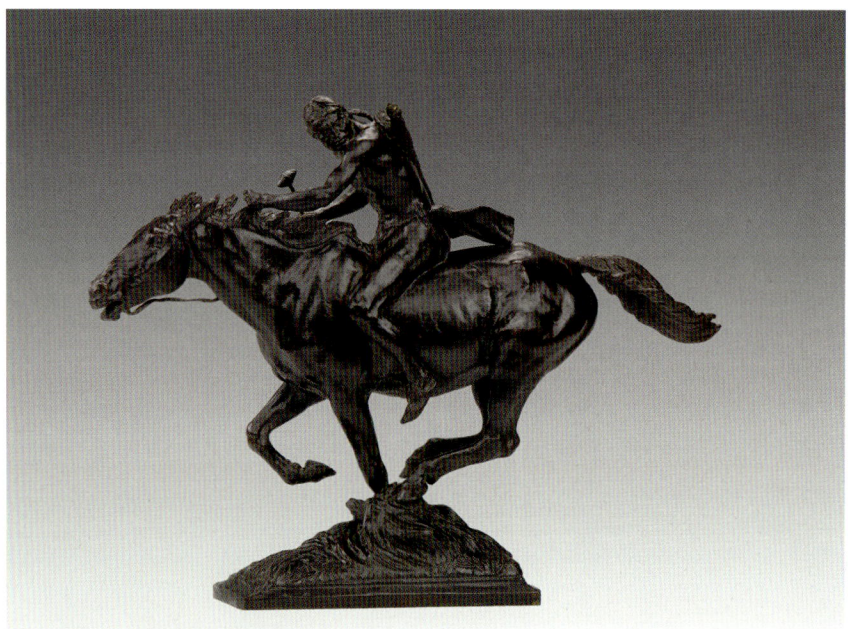

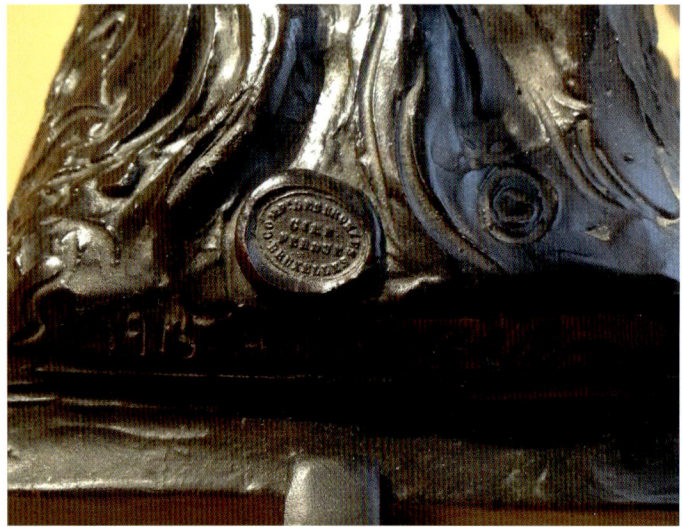

[PLATE 9.6]

ALEXANDER PHIMISTER
PROCTOR

Pursued (Comp. De Bronzes,
detail – foundry mark), 1928

Bronze
Smithsonian American Art Museum,
Washington, DC. Museum purchase.
1992.3

produced in Belgium by the Comp.
De Bronzes foundry in lost wax.
[PLATE 9.5 and PLATE 9.6]

It showed a set of remarkable
revisions that included a replacement of
the spear with a war club, a quiver over
the warrior's shoulder, a lowering of the
rider's breechcloth and the horse's rump, a
shortening and reconfiguration of the base,
and the addition of inclusive dates "1915
and 1928." It appears that, when Proctor
and his family returned to the United
States, he sent the new model to Gorham.
By that date, Gorham was promoting its
new use of the lost-wax process. One of the
former employees of the Roman Bronze Works, Eugene Gargani, started
subcontracting work for Gorham in 1928, just in time to accommodate
Proctor and his newest sculpture. Gargani's cast number 1, in *cire perdue*
and carrying a Gorham Co. Founders mark, was probably produced that
year under the Eugene Gargani & Sons contract. [PLATE 9.7 and PLATE
9.8] One of these late Gorham castings, a bronze that sold to Proctor's
friend the oil magnate George Dupont Pratt and that is now in the
collection of the Mead Art Museum, came at a cost of $155 in 1932.[13]

13   Proctor's Ledger Book, Proctor Papers, McCracken Research Library, Buffalo Bill Center
     of the West.

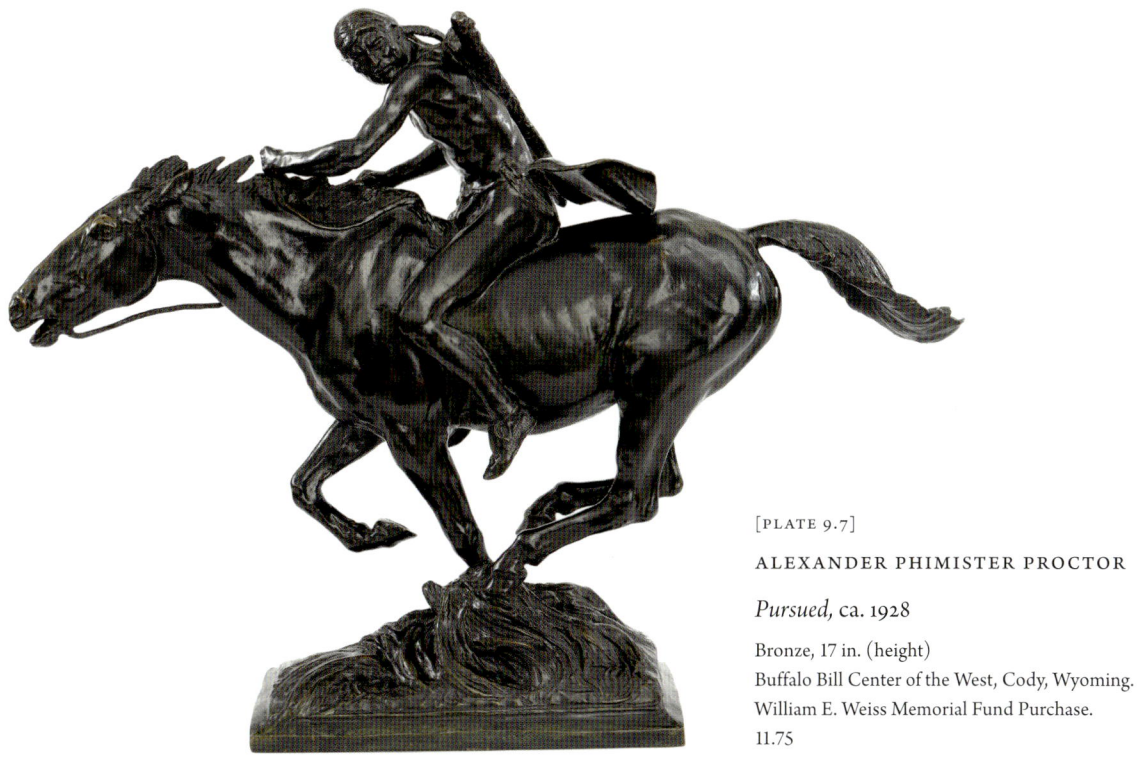

[PLATE 9.7]

ALEXANDER PHIMISTER PROCTOR

Pursued, ca. 1928

Bronze, 17 in. (height)
Buffalo Bill Center of the West, Cody, Wyoming.
William E. Weiss Memorial Fund Purchase.
11.75

[PLATE 9.8]

ALEXANDER PHIMISTER
PROCTOR

Pursued (Gorham / Gargani,
detail – foundry mark), ca. 1928

Bronze
Buffalo Bill Center of the West, Cody,
Wyoming. William E. Weiss Memorial Fund
Purchase. 11.75

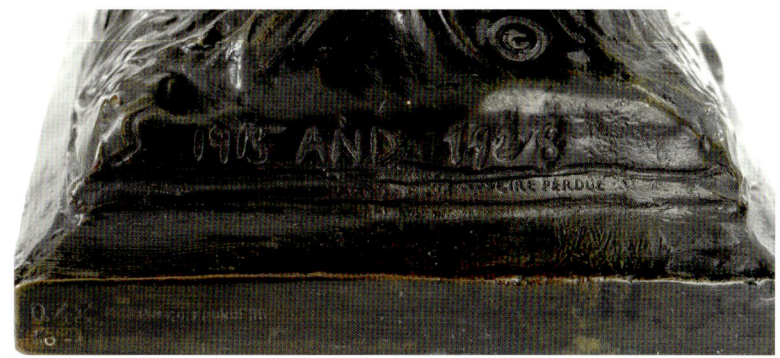

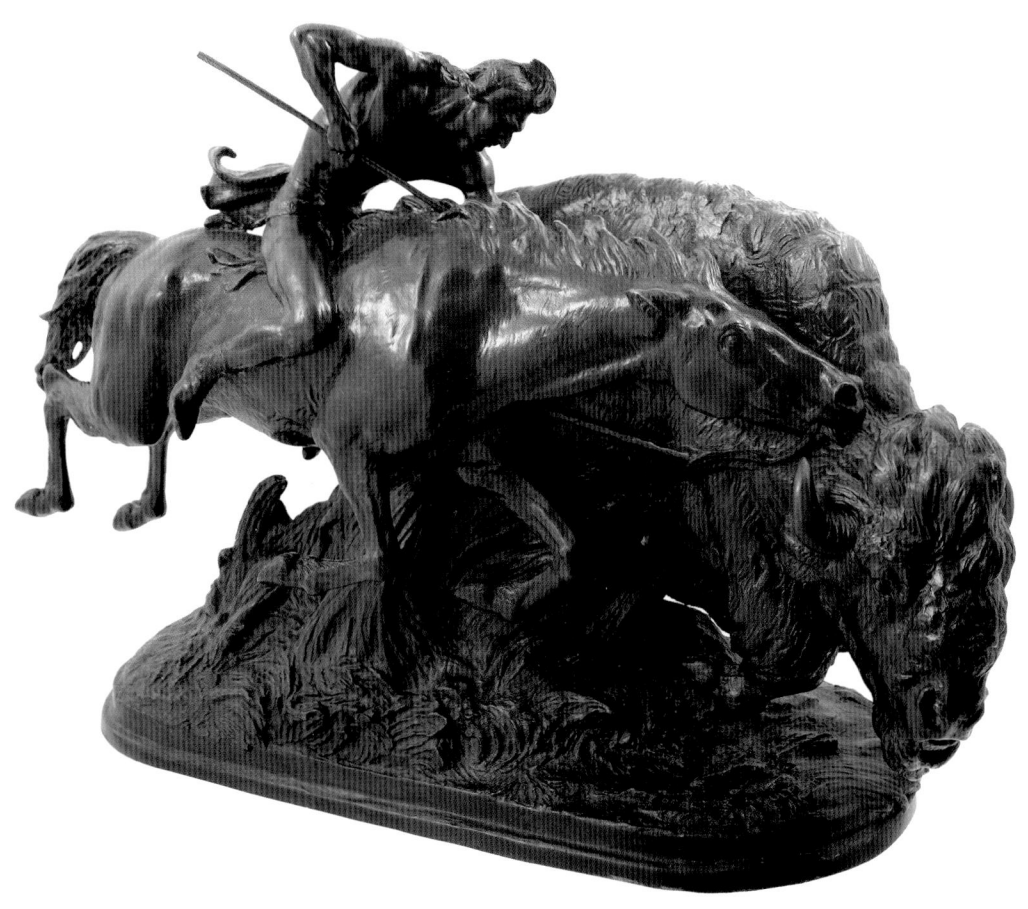

ALEXANDER PHIMISTER PROCTOR, *Buffalo Hunt,* 1917. Bronze, 18 ¼ in. (height). Buffalo Bill Center of the West, Cody, Wyoming. Gift of A. Phimister Proctor Museum with special thanks to Sandy and Sally Church. 4.08.3

THE BUFFALO HUNT

*Death of the King of the Herd; Indian Pursuing Buffalo;
Indian and Buffalo Group; The Chase*

For Proctor's singular portrayal of a buffalo hunt, he selected a set of heroic characters that would perform the chase in as dramatic a way as possible. The artist had neither seen nor participated in such a pursuit, so the piece was informed totally by his larger-than-life view of what hunting was all about—a grand and mortal contest between man and nature. To magnify the human element in the scene, he selected none other than one of the survivors of the Nez Perce War, Chief Joseph's nephew Jackson Sundown. Also, as a means of building credibility for his personal creative endeavor, Proctor moved himself and his family for a summer into a teepee owned by Sundown on the Fort Lapwal Reservation near Lewiston, Idaho. And to reflect his own identity as an intrepid hunter of trophy animals, he selected an epic-sized buffalo bull as the quarry. These ideal elements were all connected at close quarters by a spear that, thrust by one of the actors in the drama, was intended to complete the sculptural narrative. It was an allegory to native vibrancy, nature's revolving saga of life and death, and the incredible energy that Proctor saw embodied in the West.

The pieces of this sculptural amalgam are more complex than they might appear. The bronze does celebrate the Plain Indians' dependence on the buffalo for survival and Native people's powerful link with their primary means of sustenance. The model the artist chose, Jackson Sundown [PLATE 10.1], however, was famed not as a hunter, but rather as one of the most celebrated champion rodeo bronc riders of his day. In a reversal of roles, Proctor elected to live near Sundown in a teepee because that was the only way his model would agree to pose for him. The teepee served as Sundown's guesthouse, and the price was right, the location convenient, and the structure large enough for a full gaggle of Proctors. A magnificent mature buffalo bull would probably have been the last animal in a herd that Plains Indian hunters would have selected. They preferred cows or young bulls and heifers for their relatively tender meat.

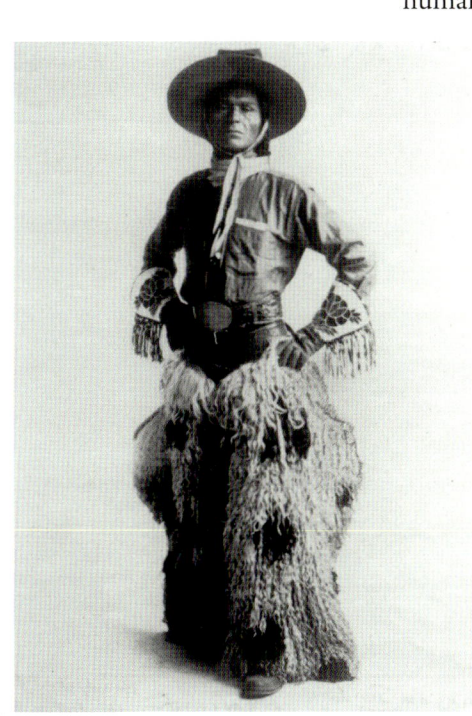

[PLATE 10.1]

ALEXANDER PHIMISTER PROCTOR

Jackson Sundown, ca. 1915

Photograph, b&w
Alexander Phimister Proctor Collection, MS 242, Harold McCracken Research Library, Buffalo Bill Center of the West, Cody, Wyoming. P.242.761

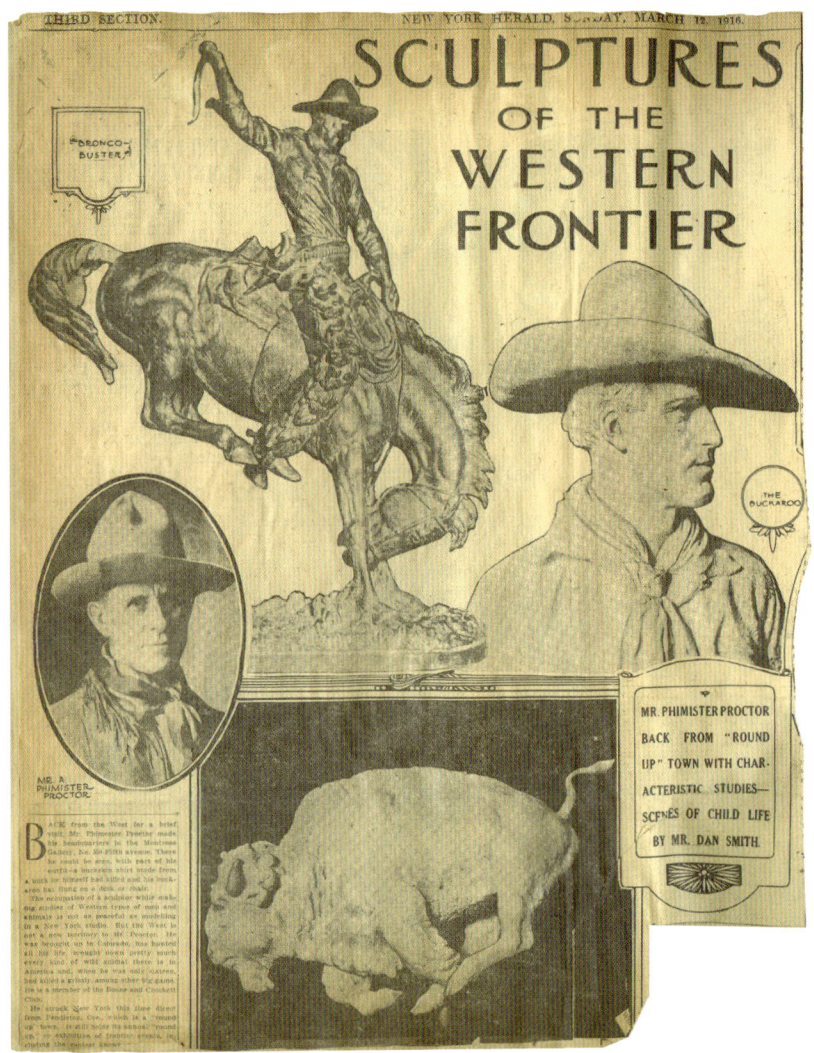

[PLATE 10.2]

ALEXANDER PHIMISTER
PROCTOR

Running Buffalo,
(study for Buffalo Hunt*)*, 1916

Plaster
Illustration in *New York Herald* (March
12, 1916, 3rd sec.)
Alexander Phimister Proctor Collection,
MS 242, Harold McCracken Research
Library, Buffalo Bill Center of the West,
Cody, Wyoming. MS242.OS10.01.16

[PLATE 10.3]

ALEXANDER PHIMISTER
PROCTOR

Buffalo Hunt, ca. 1916

Plaster, 7 ⅞ in. (height)
Buffalo Bill Center of the West, Cody,
Wyoming. Gift of A. Phimister Proctor
Museum with special thanks to Sandy
and Sally Church. 11.06.486

[PLATE 10.4]

ALEXANDER PHIMISTER
PROCTOR

Buffalo Hunt, 1917

Bronze, 18 ¼ in. (height)
Buffalo Bill Center of the West, Cody,
Wyoming. Gift of A. Phimister Proctor
Museum with special thanks to Sandy
and Sally Church. 4.08.3

Proctor began his buffalo hunt sculpture by portraying a running buffalo, which he completed by the spring of 1916 and illustrated in the *New York Herald*.[1] [PLATE 10.2] As a singular work of art, the plaster was superb. The beast's legs were tucked under him as he thundered across the presumed prairie floor.

It is thought that Proctor next conceptualized the full hunt scene as a plaster relief. [PLATE 10.3] It is a remarkably spirited work. When the buffalo was combined with the Indian rider in the three-dimensional sculpture, though, the scene was freighted with noticeable disparities. [PLATE 10.4]One critic pointed to the extraordinary "energy, activity and unusual alertness" of the Indian, while the buffalo was knotted up with "fear and anger." The "huge bulk of the bison" was also contrasted with the "slender grace of the horse."[2] There appeared to be a hierarchy

1 Dan Smith, "Sculptures of the Western Frontier," *New York Herald* (March 12, 1916). See also Ebner, *Sculptor in Buckskin*, 168.

2 Frank Owen Payne, "Two New Bronzes by A. Phimister Proctor," unidentified clipping, c. 1917, Proctor Archives.

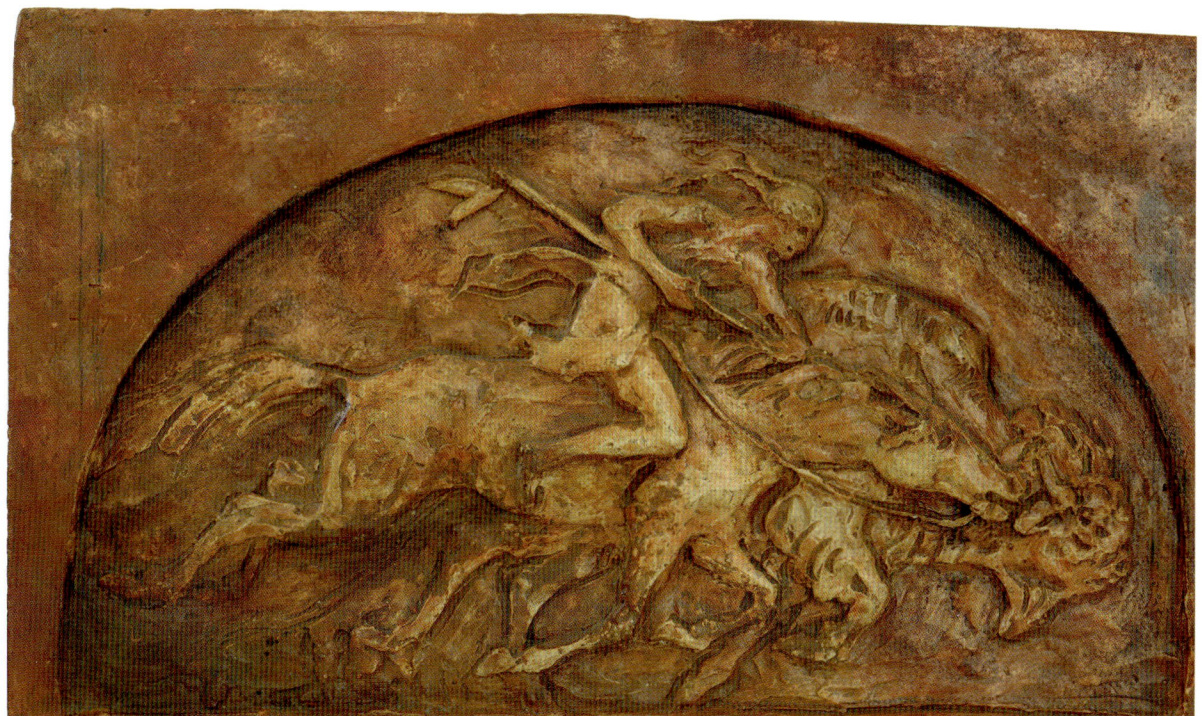

of players, the vigilant hunter subverting the lumbering prey. The work suggested to the same critic an opportunity not just for grading within the narrative structure of the piece but for an assessment of creative forces as well. Proctor was said in this work to have "a fine feeling for artistic values"—contrary, he extolled, to what he regarded as the "erratic" shortcomings of Frederic Remington's sculptural work.[3]

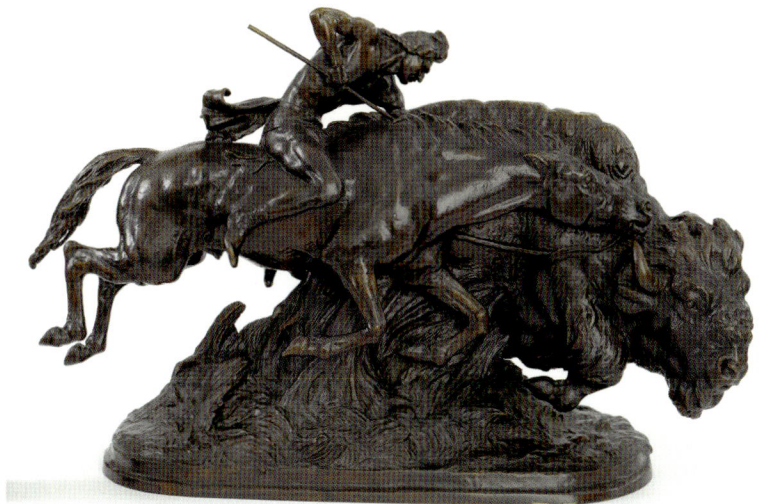

The dramatic ensemble, titled *The Buffalo Hunt*, was cast in 1917 and copyrighted the same year. Most viewers took it for what it was, a remembrance of times gone by, and regarded it as an example of the age-old myth of the vanishing Indian. As one reporter wrote in 1917, "Mr. Proctor has come to be recognized as indeed an historian, his sculptured works of fast disappearing western types being a link between what is soon to be the past, and the future."[4] Ironically, although the author suggested in the title of his article that Proctor was to make Sundown, the grand winner

3   Ibid.

4   "Proctor's Sculpture Will Make Immortal Winner at Round-Up," *Portland Oregon Journal* (February 11, 1917).

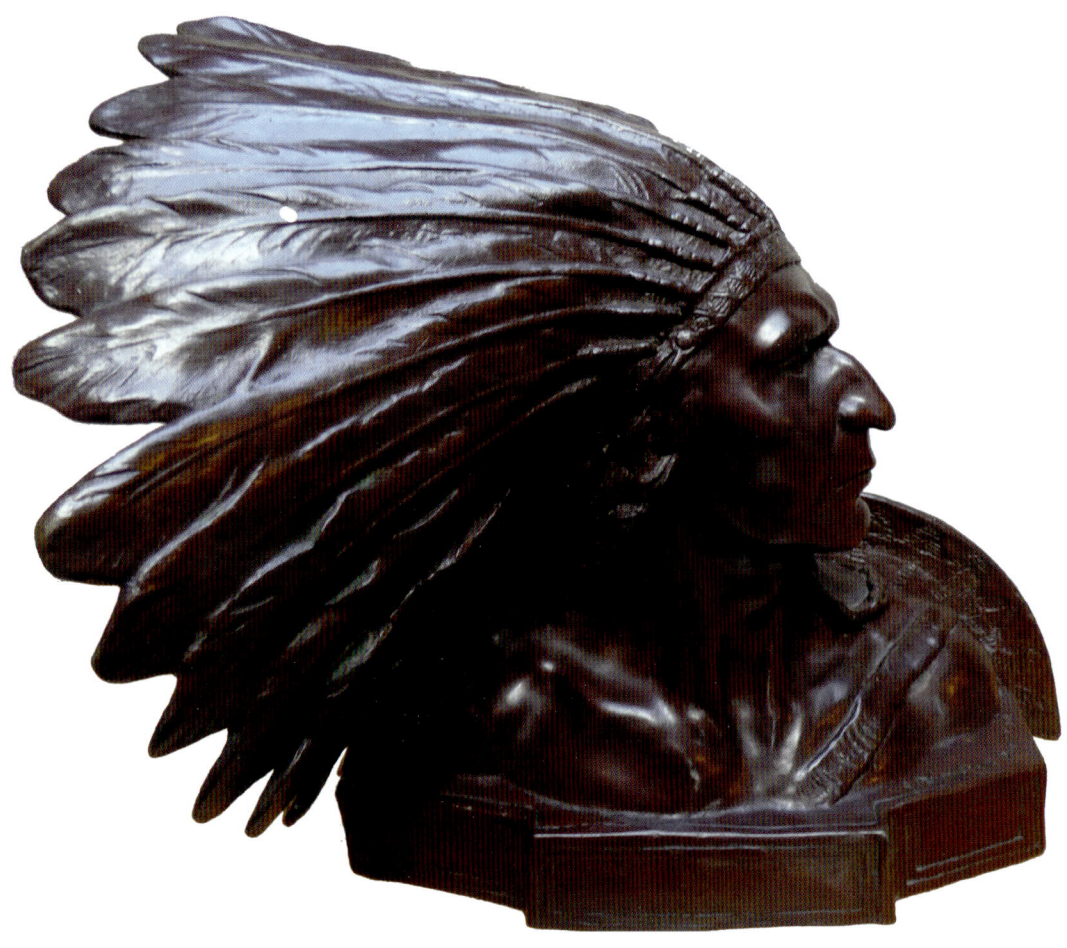

[PLATE 10.5]

ALEXANDER PHIMISTER PROCTOR

Sundown, Nez Perce Chief, 1917

Bronze, 11 ½ in. (height)
Buffalo Bill Center of the West, Cody, Wyoming. Gift of A. Phimister Proctor
Museum with special thanks to Sandy and Sally Church. 18.08.5

of that year's Pendleton Round-Up, "immortal," it was not as a bronc rider that the eternal recognition befell him, but as a staged "type" from a bygone era. Nonetheless, Sundown was proud to play the role and even posed in a feather bonnet for a companion bust portrait that Proctor titled *Sundown, Nez Perce Chief*. [PLATE 10.5]

A three-dimensional plaster of *The Buffalo Hunt* was exhibited in the spring of 1917 at the Art Institute of Chicago as *The Chase* and illustrated in the museum's *Bulletin*.[5] Most of the known subsequent bronze versions of *The Buffalo Hunt* were produced as sand casts by Gorham Co. Founders. One of the earliest such castings was acquired by the Corcoran Gallery of Art in 1918 and is now in the collections of the National Gallery of Art. It was purchased directly from an exhibition at the Corcoran, *Works in Sculpture by A. Phimister Proctor*, which ran through most of March of that year.[6] Considering that the United States was deeply immersed in World War I at the time, this was a fortunate and timely sale.

The Christian Science Monitor, which reviewed Proctor's Art Institute showing, claimed that he seemed to be "continually hampered because the medium of sculpture will not allow his animals to run in mid-air."[7] Yet not only the buffalo but also the horse and rider are suspended above the ground by the introduction of a large, sweeping bunch of sagebrush. Proctor had, indeed, achieved his goal of supplying verisimilitude in action.

---

5   *Small Bronzes by A. Phimister Proctor* (Chicago: Art Institute of Chicago, 1917), no. 33, and *Bulletin of the Art Institute of Chicago* 11 (April 1917), 308.

6   *Works in Sculpture by A. Phimister Proctor* (Washington, D.C.: Corcoran Gallery of Art, 1918), no. 13.

7   "Chicago Institute of Art Has Seven One-Man Shows," *Christian Science Monitor* (April 6, 1917).

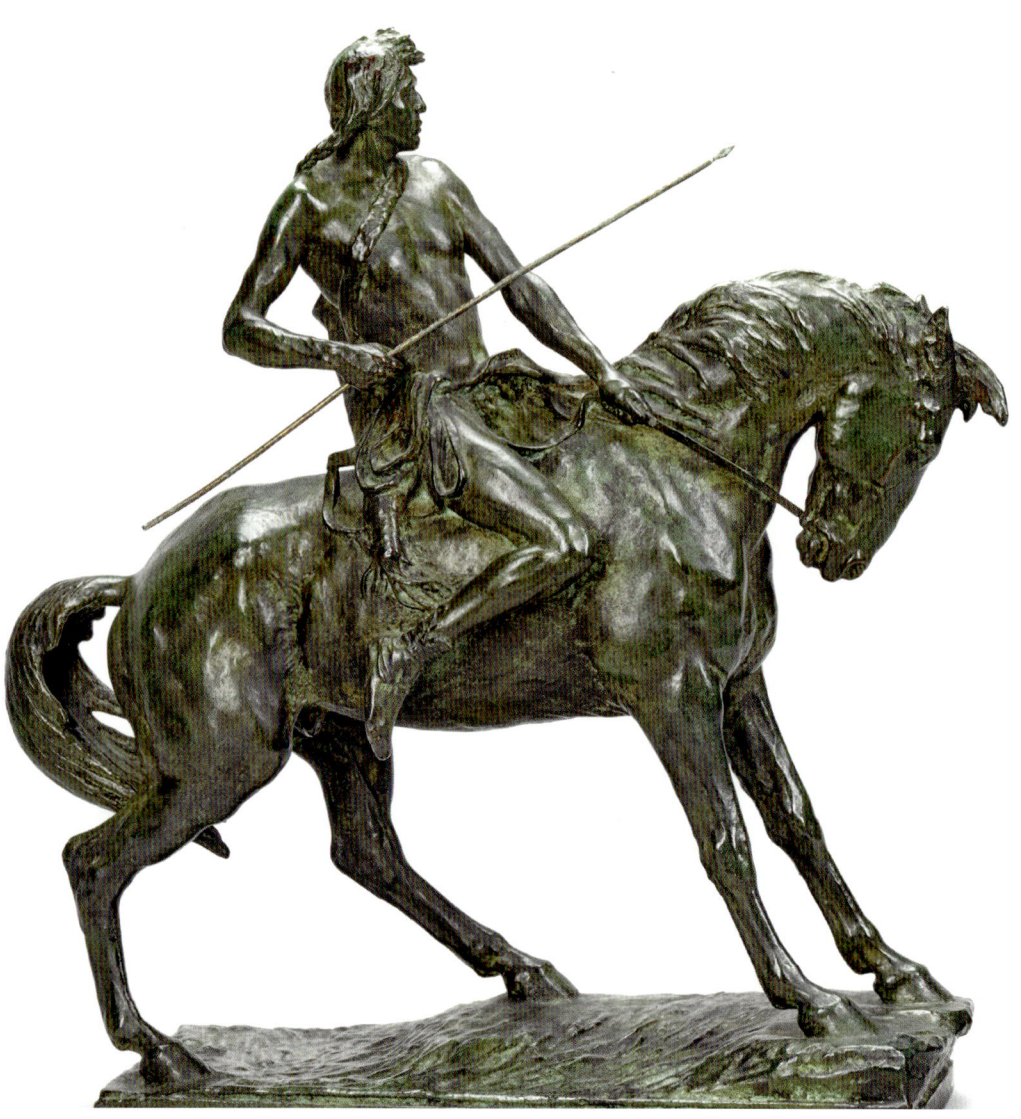

ALEXANDER PHIMISTER PROCTOR, *On the War Path*, 1928. Bronze, 20 ¾ in. (height). The Rees-Jones Collection, Dallas, Texas

ON THE WAR PATH

On the Warpath; On the War Trail; The Scout

On the first of May 1893, the gates of America's grandest nineteenth-century extravaganza, the World's Columbian Exposition, swung open to an eager public. As visitors—and there were millions of them that summer—wandered among the elaborate grounds and waterways and marveled at the exhibits and architectural wonders, they would have passed about a dozen monumental plaster sculptures of western wild animals, such as moose, elk, and mountain lions, that decorated the abutments of bridges provided to carry crowds over the fair's many lagoons. They would also have encountered two heroic-sized plasters of epic western equestrian figures, one called *Cowboy* and the other titled *Indian*. [PLATE 11.1] These monuments were all the work of a thirty-three-year-old New York sculptor named A. Phimister Proctor who had a reputation as a westerner, having been raised in Colorado, and as a fine artist, having studied at the National Academy of Design and the Art Students League.

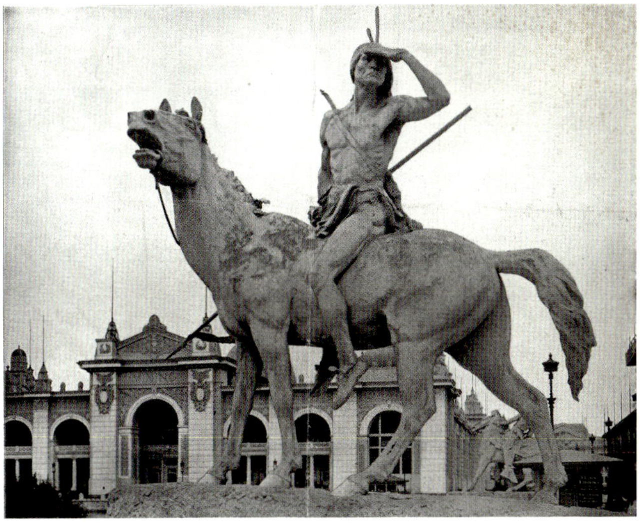

Proctor's *Indian* was deemed by the critics to be one of the more successful of his works at the fair, though they almost all garnered quite favorable mention.[1] He had used as a model none other than the son of the famous Sioux chief Red Cloud, Jack, who was part of Buffalo Bill's Wild West troupe, which performed in an arena adjacent to the world's fair grounds. He also adapted from one of Buffalo Bill's posters the pose of a mounted and fully armed Indian warrior scanning the horizon with one hand shading his eyes against the prairie sun. [PLATE 11.2] Proctor chose to portray the man and his horse in a dramatic fashion. The rider turns to the left in a gesture of immediate urgency, as if alerted to some danger in the distance. His horse, striding forward with a lifted, extended tail, is further animated as he twists his head and neck to the left acknowledging a similar threat.

[PLATE 11.1]

UNKNOWN PHOTOGRAPHER

Indian (monumental plaster by Alexander Phimister Proctor), 1893

Photograph, b&w
Alexander Phimister Proctor Collection, MS 242, Harold McCracken Research Library, Buffalo Bill Center of the West, Cody, Wyoming. MS242.OS3.2.3

---

1 Coffin, "The Columbian Exposition—I," 81.

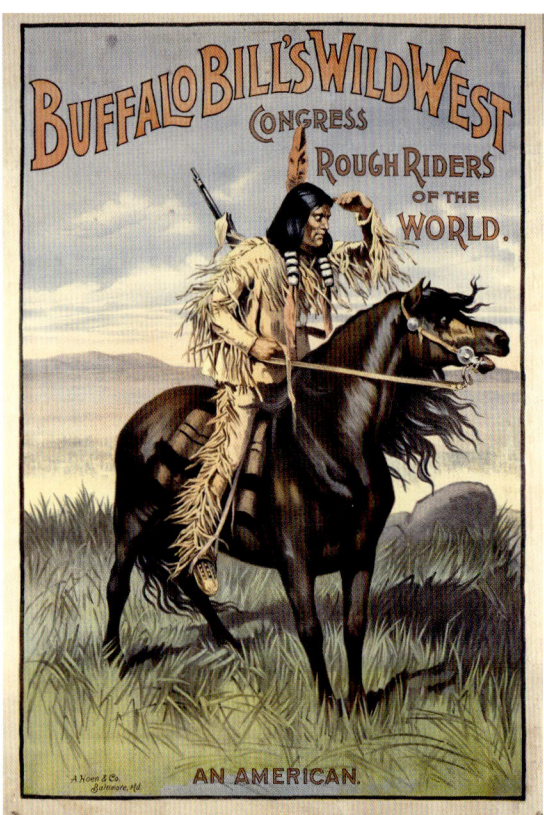

[PLATE 11.2]

A. HOEN & CO.,
LITHOGRAPHERS

Baltimore, Maryland

An American, 1893

Lithograph, four-color poster, 38 ½ x
27 ½ in.
Buffalo Bill Center of the West, Cody,
Wyoming. Gift of The Coe Foundation.
1.69.51

An inveterate hunter, Proctor had many close encounters with wild animals of the Rocky Mountains as a young man. He had also rubbed shoulders with many cowboys in his day, as well as Indians. When in his late teens, in September 1879, he was hunting near Grand Lake on Colorado's western slope, the Ute Wars broke out. Although not directly involved, Proctor was close to the action and later wrote a full, detailed chapter about the events in his autobiography.[2] Proctor's sentiments seemed to favor the intractable agent for the White River Utes, who was involved, Nathan C. Meeker, yet he also evidenced a certain compassion for the lead figure in the Ute insurrection, Chief Colorow. It was a portrait of Colorow that illustrated Proctor's chapter (6, "Colorado Indians"), not one of Meeker or those from the military who attempted to rescue him. Proctor was, in fact, so enamored of the Ute chief that, in the 1940s, he made a dry point etching of Colorow. [PLATE 11.3]

During the Ute Wars, Colorow's tribe was first bullied into abandoning its traditional hunting practices (continuing them would have competed with the likes of Proctor and his cronies), and then, after the tribe resisted, it was attacked twice by the formidable forces of the U.S. Cavalry. The attitude that Proctor selected for his monumental *Indian* at the World's Fair was one of militant opposition, pride, and vigilance, reminiscent of Colorow's actions. It was a stance that would inform Proctor's later work, including the spirit of *On the War Path*.

When the world's fair concluded in 1894, the city of Denver asked to have two of its hometown artist's works brought home to Colorado's capital. *Indian*, along with *Cowboy*, were placed in Denver's new City Park. There, despite their fragile medium, they remained into the mid-teens. They were still fresh in the public's mind when Proctor proposed a couple of monumental western bronzes for the city's emerging new Civic Center in 1917. Denver's visionary mayor Robert Walter Speer pressed to have the earlier works replaced with new ones using the same themes but cast in enduring bronze. By the following summer, Proctor had begun work on his second Indian monument, what would be titled on the plinth at the time of its dedication in 1923 as *On the War Trail*.

Proctor first completed the horse in March 1919 and then the full maquette by late that fall. Its evolution showed how much devotion Proctor felt for that first Indian sculpture he had produced back in 1893 for Chicago. In both of the two early sketches for the new piece, [PLATE 11.4] the warrior peers out while shading his eyes, as in his world's fair

2 See Ebner, *Sculptor in Buckskin*, 41–45.

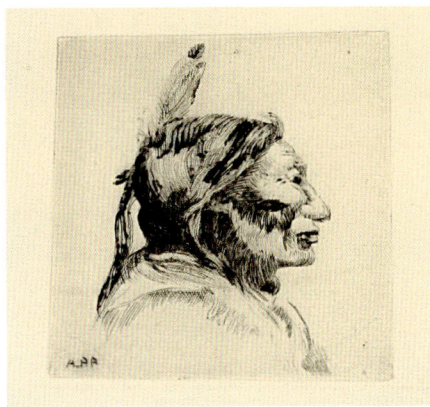

Indian plaster, in a posture of reconnaissance. But more than his initial work influenced this fresh interpretation. The Indian's horse has been pulled to an abrupt stop with its forelegs extended stiffly forward, and the warrior tucks his legs and feet back toward the horse's rump, all similar to the pose employed by Proctor's contemporary Cyrus Dallin in his 1904 bronze *Protest*.

[PLATE 11.5] Dallin's *Protest* had been displayed at the 1904 world's fair in St. Louis, the Louisiana Purchase Exposition, where it had won a gold medal. Proctor was no doubt quite familiar with it.

Proctor used three Indian models as he developed the Denver Civic Center monument and its various reductions. Jackson Sundown, the Nez Perce model for his *Buffalo Hunt*, began the process. However, Sundown grew homesick after a while and returned to Idaho before the final concept for the piece had matured.[3] Proctor then found a Blackfeet model named Spotted Eagle in Glacier Park, Montana.[4] But that association did not endure, and he had to look even farther afield. For the final iteration of the piece, he retained an accommodating, handsome, and good humored man from the Blackfeet Reservation. His name was variously noted as Big Beaver and Red Belt.[5]

The final prototype for Proctor's tribute to native resistance changed the Indian's gesture from one of hesitant scouting to one of full-scale belligerence. As with the story of Chief Colorow, the protagonist here is prepared to stand his ground and fight. Unlike Dallin's version, in which the chief raises his fist in futile desperation, Proctor's interpretation reflects Colorow's existential heroism when he defeated the first surge of U.S. military and stood resolutely, though ineffectually, against a much larger subsequent force sent to subdue him. Proctor met the old chief a few

[PLATE 11.3]

ALEXANDER PHIMISTER PROCTOR

Chief Colorow, ca. 1940

Etching on paper, 9 x 6 ½ in. Buffalo Bill Center of the West, Cody, Wyoming. Gift of A. Phimister Proctor Museum with special thanks to Sandy and Sally Church. 11.06.410

[PLATE 11.4]

ALEXANDER PHIMISTER PROCTOR

On the War Trail (early model), ca. 1919

Photograph, b&w
Alexander Phimister Proctor Collection, MS 242, Harold McCracken Research Library, Buffalo Bill Center of the West, Cody, Wyoming. P.242.838

---

3 "World Artist, Executing Indian Scout Statue, Busy in His Los Altos Studio," *San Jose Mercury Herald* (March 23, 1919).

4 See "Carries His Indian Model with Him," *The Spectator* (Portland, Ore.), December 1919.

5 "'Red Belt,' Indian Model of Sculptor Discovers Pacific," *Daily Palo Alto Times* (October 27, 1919).

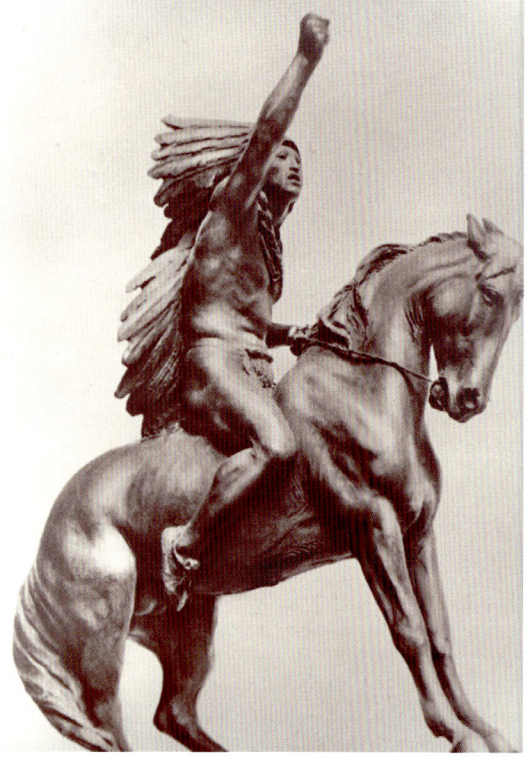

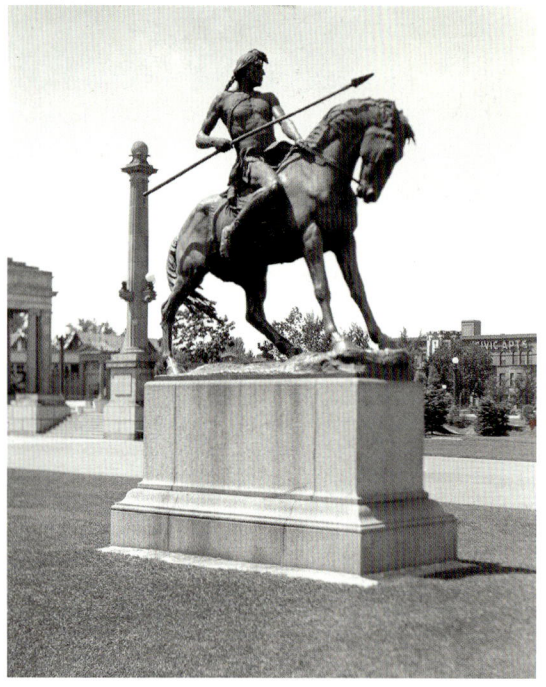

years later, and in the artist's autobiography, he wrote admiringly of Colorow's perspicacity and valor.[6] In the monumental version of the sculpture as situated in Denver, a belligerent warrior faces the city center. [PLATE 11.6] The city was filled with Anglos who had profited from the government's decision after the Ute Wars to remove the White River Utes to a remote corner of Utah. There the Indians would pose no threat. Their ancestral land could then serve as a rich resource for ranching and mining. The bronze warrior with his spear aspired to metaphorically pierce that bubble of greed and messianic Anglo assumptions about removal and acculturation.

Perhaps because of Proctor's not-so-subtle message with this bronze, small versions of the work were never big sellers. The piece was cast in two sizes, a 20-inch-high version and one that measured 48 inches, derived from a plaster that had served as the maquette for the monument. There are about four known copies of the smaller piece and just one of the larger.

On the War Path has had several titles over the years. Its first known mention as a tabletop-sized bronze appeared in the *San Francisco Chronicle* in November 1919 as the *Scout*.[7] A month later the *Denver Post* referred to it as *On the Warpath*.[8] By 1922, the same year the monument was dedicated in Denver as *On the War Trail*, Proctor began showing smaller, tabletop versions of the work from coast to coast. That year, the National Academy of Design in New York and the Bohemian Club in San Francisco both presented castings in their galleries, the former as *On the War Trail* and the latter as *On the War Path*.[9] Proctor finally copyrighted the piece in May 1923 as *On the War Path* (the title chosen here as the primary one).

Proctor cast examples of the 20-inch version of *On the War Path* with Roman Bronze Works, probably around 1928 (Rees-Jones Collection); Gorham Co. Founders in 1928; and in Brussels with Ancienne

6   Ebner, *Sculptor in Buckskin*, 45.

7   "Artist Takes Indian Model East with Him," *San Francisco Chronicle* (November 30, 1919).

8   Arthur Frenzel, "A. Phimister Proctor, One of the Early-Day Westerners, Will Put Up Monument Where Once He Played Ball," *Denver Post* (December 26, 1919).

9   See Peter Hastings Falk (ed.), *The Annual Exhibition Record of the National Academy of Design*, 1901–1950 (Madison, CT: Sound View Press, 1990), 426; and "Statues by Proctor Mark Club Exhibit," *San Francisco Chronicle* (January 25, 1922).

Foundeur National Bronzes, L. Petermann, also around 1928 (Gilcrease Museum). The Petermann cast produced in Brussels is thought to be the first in the series. It is marked with a signature and Dutch inscription "A P Proctor. Remodelert." [PLATE 11.7] It is thought that Proctor took the large plaster of the monument maquette to Rome and Brussels with him and did the reduction in the latter city. *Remodelert* is Dutch for "remodeler." There are no substantial differences between the three known small versions except for patinas and the fact that the Petermann example is sand cast and the other two lost wax. When he cast the one known example of the 48-inch version, he used Roman Bronze Works and the lost wax method. [PLATE 11.8]

[PLATE 11.5]

CYRUS EDWIN DALLIN
(1861 – 1944)

A Protest, 1904

Bronze
Illustration in *Arts & Decorations Magazine* (February 1914), 153
Buffalo Bill Center of the West, Cody, Wyoming

[PLATE 11.6]

UNKNOWN PHOTOGRAPHER

On the War Trail (monumental bronze by Alexander Phimister Proctor), ca. 1919

Photograph, b&w
Alexander Phimister Proctor Collection, MS 242, Harold McCracken Research Library, Buffalo Bill Center of the West. P.242.880

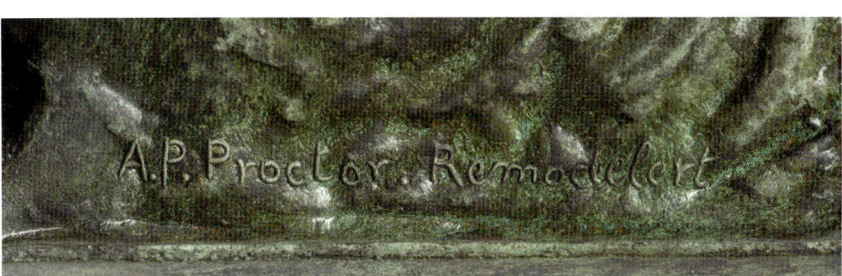

[PLATE 11.7]

ALEXANDER PHIMISTER PROCTOR

On the War Path (detail – foundry mark), ca. 1928

Bronze
Gilcrease Museum, Tulsa, Oklahoma. Philip Cole Collection. GM 0137.81

[PLATE 11.8]

ALEXANDER PHIMISTER PROCTOR

On the War Path, ca. 1921

Bronze, 48 in. (height)
Art Institute of Chicago, Chicago, Illinois. Bequest of Arthur Rubloff. 2004.1155

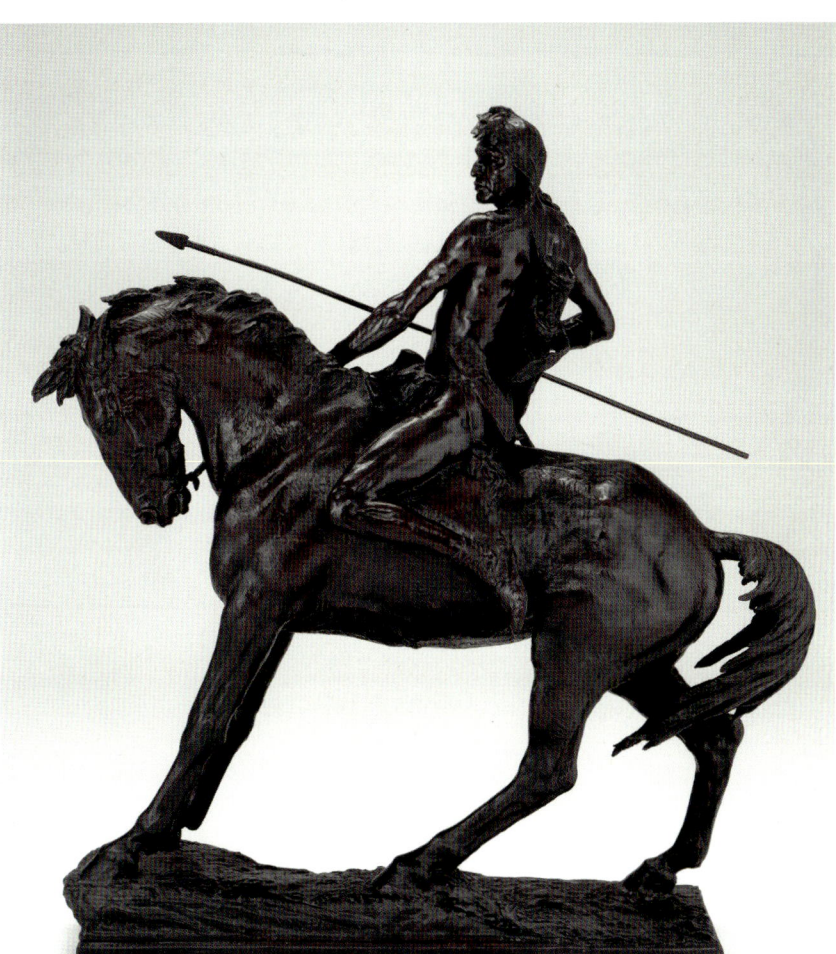

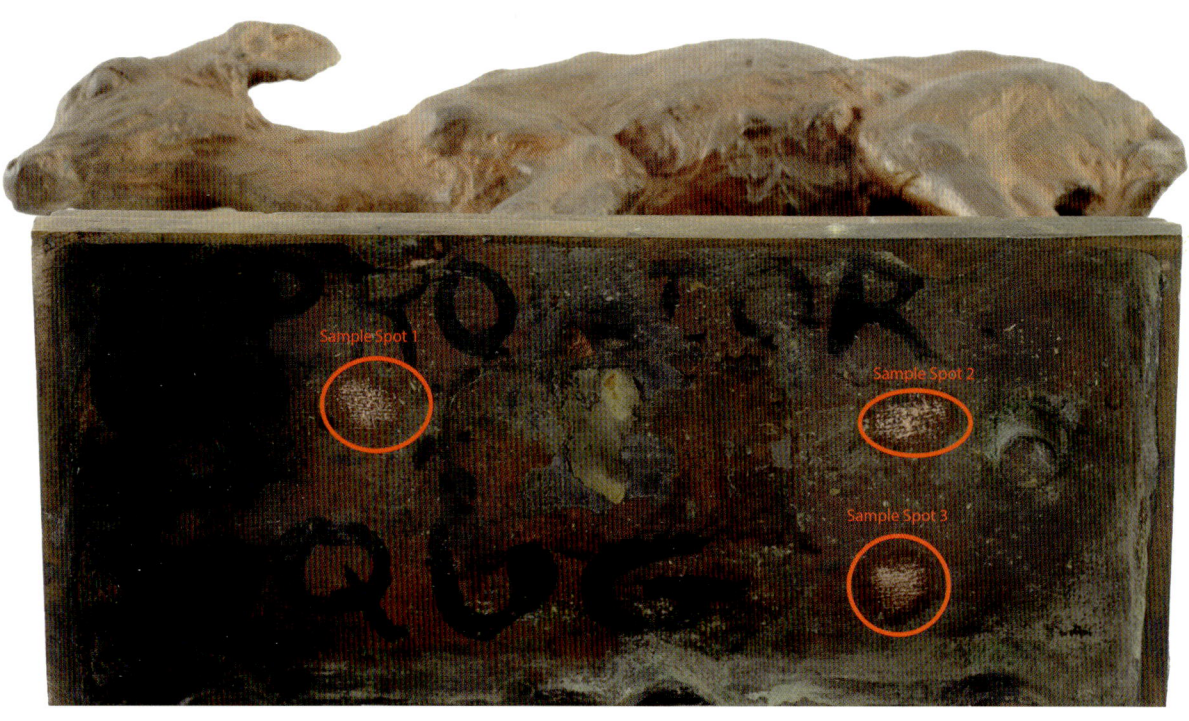

ALEXANDER PHIMISTER PROCTOR, *Fawn* (first model) (Gorham, detail – underside, XRF testing areas noted), ca. 1889. Bronze. Buffalo Bill Center of the West, Cody, Wyoming. Gift of A. Phimister Proctor Museum with special thanks to Sandy and Sally Church. 4.08.8

FINDING PROCTOR'S FOUNDRIES USING XRF ANALYSIS

By Allison Rosenthal, with Bruce Kaiser, and Beverly Perkins

As the previous essays amply demonstrate, Proctor's creation of bronze sculptures was not a solitary pursuit, but rather a collaboration with the foundries he employed. Castings of the same work can vary greatly in quality depending on the casting technique, degree of surface finishing, and patination.[1] These variations can be characteristic of certain foundries, but they also occur in bronzes known to be cast by the same foundries, which can give clues about when a sculpture was cast or about personnel changes within the foundry.[2]

The foundry that cast a bronze sculpture is therefore a key part of the artwork's provenance. Since January 2014, the Buffalo Bill Center of the West has been collaborating with Bruker Elemental and the Proctor Foundation on a project that aims to identify elemental patterns among the alloys, or compositions, of Proctor's bronze sculptures. Testing using X-ray fluorescence (XRF) spectroscopy[3] has been conducted on 122 of Proctor's lifetime castings throughout the United States and Canada.[4] This testing allows us to draw a connection between the alloy composition of a bronze and the foundry that cast it, and then use this information in conjunction with other analytical techniques—including

---

1 A bronze sculpture's patina is the layer on the outside of the sculpture that provides its color and finish. A patina is a chemical reaction that can happen naturally as the elements in a bronze alloy interact with their surroundings, and also intentionally as part of the casting process.

2 See Janis C. Conner, "Introduction to Cast Comparisons," in Captured Motion: The Sculpture of Harriet Whitney Frishmuth; A Catalogue of Works, by Harriet W. Frishmuth, Janis C. Conner, Leah R. Lehmbeck, Thayer Tolles, and Jerry L. Thompson (New York: Hohmann Holdings, 2006), 101–25.

3 XRF is a nondestructive analytical technique frequently used to determine the elemental composition of cultural heritage objects.

4 Of the 122 lifetime castings analyzed, 29 were tested at the Buffalo Bill Center of the West in July 2016 with the same instrument. The remainder of the sculptures were tested between January 2014 and August 2016 using approximately twenty-five different instruments. All of the instruments were Bruker Tracer III-SD XRF spectrometers with the same tubes and detectors, and all of the testing was done at 40 kV and 11.60 µA using the yellow filter.

visual inspection and archival research—to extrapolate previously unknown provenance information about many of Proctor's sculptures.

We have been using XRF spectroscopy to analyze Proctor's bronzes in a two-step process. By first exciting the photons of each element, a step we call detailed elemental presence analysis, we have identified the elements present in the alloy and patina of each tested bronze. We are then able to compare the relative amounts of copper, zinc, tin, lead, and iron in the second step, which we call relative elemental concentration studies.[5] This process is a pioneering approach in the field of XRF analysis, and in using these methods, we have been able to identify trends that are characteristic of certain foundries over time. Visual inspection has also allowed us to learn how a bronze was cast and then to confirm many of our hypotheses by finding casting records in foundry archives. We are using this information to deduce the foundry histories of some of Proctor's unidentified bronzes, and we have noticed especially distinct trends among the alloys of bronzes cast by four of the foundries Proctor worked with: Gorham Co. Founders, the Roman Bronze Works, Eugene Gargani & Sons, and Jno. Williams, Inc. Bronze Foundry.

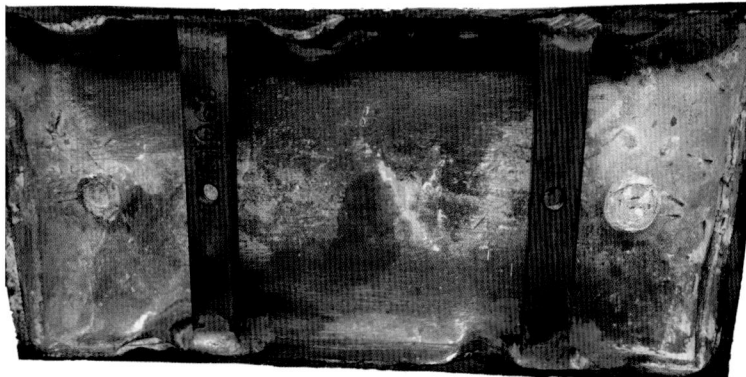

[PLATE 12.1]

ALEXANDER PHIMISTER PROCTOR

Fawn (first model) (Gorham, detail – underside), 1914

Bronze
R. W. Norton Art Gallery, Shreveport, Louisiana

The white residue indicates a plaster mold casting.

GORHAM CO. FOUNDERS

Gorham Co. Founders of Providence, Rhode Island, started off as a jewelry business in 1818 and evolved into a silver manufacturing company. By 1865 it had become the world's largest manufacturer of fine silver. In the 1880s, the company started casting ecclesiastical furnishings and other decorative works in bronze using sand casting, a method its workers were already employing to cast silver. Within the next decade they began casting bronze sculpture.[6]

5   We are expressing the data in unitless photon ratios. Absolute quantitative analysis is not possible or appropriate for patinated bronzes, because the alloy of a bronze sculpture is nonuniform in both depth and relative location in the bronze. Instead, XRF analysis relies on detailed analysis of a bronze sculpture's raw photon spectra using Bayesian deconvolution and subsequent elemental presence analysis and comparison of the ratio of photons gathered from the elements present. This ratio is directly proportional to the elemental concentrations. Thus, this study utilized the ratio of the net number of photons from each element, producing an accurate unitless quantity independent of everything but the absolute ratio of those two elements. Because of this accuracy we can directly relate that ratio from every bronze to every other bronze. This relationship allows us to identify particular characteristics and patterns accurately and observe elemental trends among foundries. For more information, see Lee Drake, "XRF User Guide," www.xrf.guru (accessed October 10, 2016).

6   For more information on the Gorham Co. Founders Bronze Division, see Janis Conner, "Harriet Whitney Frishmuth and Her Foundries," in *Captured Motion*, 52–99.

With the exception of a failed attempt to create a lost-wax casting facility in 1907, Gorham used two techniques to cast bronze sculpture: sand casting and its own technique, called the plaster mold process.[7]

Both processes would have begun in a similar fashion: the artist would make a model of his sculpture out of wax or clay and then have it cast as a plaster model. This plaster model would begin the sculptor's collaboration with the foundry. If the sculpture was to be sand-cast, the founder would build up a piece mold out of hard-packed sand; this negative mold could then be removed in pieces and assembled. The founder used the piece mold to make another copy of the model out of sand and shaved down this copy to create a casting core. Next, the founder baked the negative mold and core with pins inside to hold the core just the right distance away from the mold. Molten bronze was then poured into the space between the mold and core,

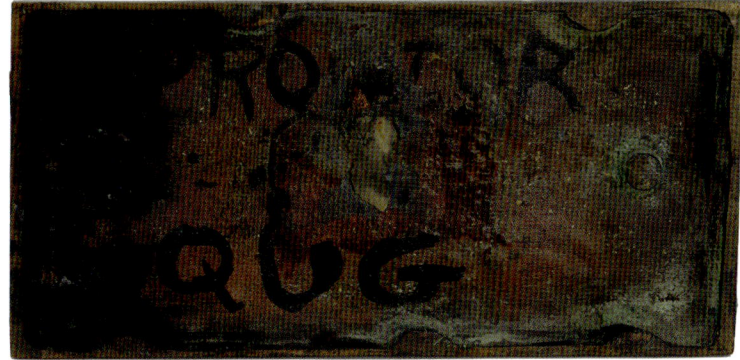

after which the mold and core were removed, and the bronze was chased and most likely patinated. Gorham's plaster mold process was similar to sand casting in many ways, except that the piece mold and core were created out of plaster mixed with asbestos rather than hard-packed sand.[8]

Gorham did not note which casting method was used in recording a job in its ledgers; indeed, the founders wrote surprisingly little on the specifics of their plaster mold process. However, we can differentiate between Gorham's two casting methods by visually inspecting the underside of a sculpture's base. [PLATE 12.1 and PLATE 12.2] If a bronze sculpture is known to have been cast by Gorham, it is possible to tell a sand from a plaster mold casting by the white residue left by the plaster core on the base's underside. We used XRF spectroscopy to test fifty-three known Gorham sculptures, a sample size larger than that of any other foundry included in the study. Sixteen of those sculptures are plaster mold castings, and thirty-seven are sand castings.

Gorham also frequently created bronze models for sculptures when

[PLATE 12.2]

ALEXANDER PHIMISTER PROCTOR

Fawn (first model) (Gorham, detail – underside), 1888

Bronze
Buffalo Bill Center of the West, Cody, Wyoming. Gift of A. Phimister Proctor Museum with special thanks to Sandy and Sally Church. 4.08.08

The residue of sand from the sand core, as well as a smoother overall surface, is characteristic of sand casting.

---

7 For excellent illustrated descriptions of both the lost-wax and sand-casting techniques, see Michael E. Shapiro, *Bronze Casting and American Sculpture, 1850–1900* (Newark: University of Delaware Press, 1985), and Malvina Hoffman, *Sculpture Inside and Out* (New York: W.W. Norton & Co., 1939). For a photographic walkthrough of the lost-wax casting process, see Harry Jackson, *Lost Wax Bronze Casting: A Photographic Essay on This Antique and Venerable Art* (Flagstaff, AZ: Northland Press, 1972). For an incredible visual of Proctor himself casting his monumental statue *The Rough Rider* using the lost-wax method, see The Metropolitan Museum of Art, *The Making of a Bronze Statue*, http://www.metmuseum.org/metmedia/video/collections/aw/making-of-a-bronze-statue, accessed December 5, 2016.

8 The authors thank Paul Cavanagh, owner of Paul King Foundry, Johnston, Rhode Island, for describing the differences between sand-casting and plaster mold casting, which he was able to observe as the son of one of Gorham's silver chasers employed in the 1920s. Author's conversation with Paul Cavanagh, August 25, 2016.

its founders were producing an edition.[9] They referred to those models as "metal patterns."[10] Ten of the fifty-three tested Gorham sculptures are metal patterns, and all of these are sand castings.

The conclusions we have drawn through analysis of the alloys of the tested sculptures are based on their ratios of copper photons to zinc photons and the ratios of copper photons to tin photons. Copper is the main element of a bronze alloy, and the remainder of the alloy is composed of varying proportions of tin, zinc, and lead, with traces of other metals. A bronze alloy is preferable to pure copper for casting because its melting point is much lower, it is less porous than pure copper, and it cools and contracts less rapidly. The addition of zinc, tin, and lead lowers an alloy's overall cost, lowers its melting point, and allows it to be cast with greater fluidity, which allows for crisper surface detail.[11]

Our analysis indicates that different foundries used different alloy formulations, and the degree of consistency with which they used them varied from foundry to foundry. While Proctor had his bronzes cast at Gorham from 1909 to 1930, the company appears to have used a few different alloy formulations. It used two alloy formulations exclusively for sand casting, one with comparatively more zinc and less tin, and the other with comparatively less zinc and more tin. The company also had a third alloy formulation, with little to no zinc, which it used for both sand and plaster mold casting.

These data suggest that Gorham's mysterious plaster mold casting process was much more precise than its sand-casting process. A 1952 Gorham publication titled "Statuary to Electronics via Plaster Molding" illuminates the need for a specific alloy formulation in the plaster mold casting process:

> The casting in plaster of solid solution alloys and others, for that matter, requires special attention to gating, feeding, etc., because the mold material is an excellent insulator, causing the casting to have a much slower rate of solidification than if cast in sand. The permeability of plaster is very low; therefore it is essential that all precautions possible be taken to provide adequate venting for the free passage of gases which may be in the metal or generated within the mold at pouring. . . . Metal pouring temperatures are very critical and require close control. The typical pouring range is between 1275 and 1375°F; however, each casting has its own best pouring temperature whether in sand or plaster, but pin

9   For more information about the role of models in the bronze casting process, see Ann Boulton, "The Making of Matisse's Bronzes," in *Matisse: Painter as Sculptor*, by Dorothy M. Kosinski, Jay M. K. Fisher, Steven A. Nash, and Henri Matisse (Baltimore: Baltimore Museum of Art, 2007), 73–97.

10   Gorham Manufacturing Company, Bronze Division, ledger, 3680, Amon Carter Museum of American Art (microfilmed by the Archives of American Art, Smithsonian Institution).

11   See Robert Tyler Davis, "Bronze," in *Master Bronzes, Selected from Museums and Collections in America* (Buffalo, NY: Buffalo Fine Arts Academy and Albright Art Gallery, 1937); reprinted, Long Island City, NY: General Bronze Corporation), 1.

pointing the proper pouring temperature is paramount when using the plaster process.[12]

Foundry workers likely added zinc in small amounts or omitted it entirely from the alloy for plaster mold casting in order to keep the pouring temperature within that specific range. This would not have been as much of a concern with sand casting, where we see a much greater proportion of zinc, allowing for a cheaper alloy. The lower proportion of zinc also offers an explanation for the three typical alloys we see in Proctor's Gorham castings: an alloy already melted down for plaster mold casting could be repurposed for sand casting to save time and money, but the reverse could not be done with an alloy already melted down for sand casting, because it would have contained too much zinc to achieve a proper pouring temperature for a plaster mold casting.

Another conclusion we can draw from analysis of these sculptures is that Gorham preferred one of its standard alloy formulations for its metal patterns. All of the metal patterns examined in this study were sand-cast, the majority with Gorham's standard sand-casting formulation of more zinc and less tin. The foundry preferred this alloy formulation probably because it was strong and comparatively cheap, using less expensive zinc to harden the copper alloy. Gorham's metal patterns were cast in parts and were not originally meant to be finished sculptures (though many were eventually assembled, patinated, and sold during times of financial stress). The founders' priorities while casting patterns would have been to obtain a detailed casting and to create a durable surface that would hold up to multiple reproductions.

ROMAN BRONZE WORKS

During the nineteenth century, the art of lost-wax casting was a mystery to American founders. The key innovation of this method is the flexible glue mold, as distinguished from sand casting's rigid sand mold. During lost-wax casting, the founder places the plaster model into a container and pours gelatin or glue into it, allowing the gelatin or glue to capture a negative impression of the model. The flexible mold can then be separated from the model. Next the founder applies a layer of melted wax to the interior of the glue mold and pours a core of investment material inside. Then he removes the glue mold and attaches wax runners and gates to the wax positive to allow the molten bronze to flow into the mold. He surrounds the wax positive with an outer mold made from investment material similar to the core. The mold is then fired, allowing the investment to harden and the wax to melt and run out the bottom, leaving a negative space for the molten bronze. The founder then pours molten bronze into the mold and lets it cool. Finally, the sculpture is chased and patinated.

---

12 Frank Pfister, "Statuary to Electronics via Plaster Molding," reprinted from *The Foundry*, Gorham Manufacturing Co. (Providence: A Penton Publication, September 1952), 144–45.

Lost-wax casting was a highly sought-after technology, as the liquid glue mold could easily capture surface detail that would take a lot of work using the sand-casting technique, and foundry workers could save a great deal of time by pouring an investment core rather than meticulously shaving away a sand core to achieve an exact duplicate of the original sculpture. By the turn of the twentieth century, lost-wax casting was an established method in Europe, but the few times it was successfully attempted in America, the founders used the "French method," which cobbled together both a glue mold and a shaved core, making the technique too laborious and time-consuming to implement on a large scale. All that changed when Ricardo Bertelli established the Roman Bronze Works in Brooklyn in 1899. Bertelli brought with him a staff of mostly Italian-trained foundry workers who were familiar with the "Italian method" of making cores.[13] Suddenly, American sculptors could have lost-wax castings made reliably and relatively quickly, and Roman Bronze Works began to attract a variety of prominent sculptors as clients.[14]

Proctor began using the Roman Bronze Works as early as 1904, and continued to use the foundry periodically throughout his career as late as 1935. Sixteen of the sculptures tested in this study are documented Roman Bronze Works castings (with a Roman Bronze Works foundry mark, an entry in Roman Bronze's casting ledger, or other documented provenance), and all were cast using the lost-wax method.

Roman Bronze Works appears to have had a standard alloy formulation, but approximately one-third of the sculptures tested are deviations from this formulation, with either more zinc, less zinc, or less tin than the standard. These exceptions could have been special formulations for the particular sculpture or variations in practice among foundry workers, and do not correspond to any chronological patterns. Nevertheless, the sculptures cast with Roman Bronze Works' standard alloy formulation are highly consistent.

EUGENE GARGANI & SONS

In 1927, a Roman Bronze Works foundry worker named Eugene Gargani left Bertelli's employ to start his own lost-wax bronze foundry in Brooklyn. Gorham, who did not have the facilities for lost-wax casting and felt the pressure of Roman Bronze Works' competition, appealed to the new

---

13   The authors thank Ann Boulton, Associate Conservator at the Gilcrease Museum, for a wonderful workshop on bronze casting history and bronze sculpture examination. Interested readers can watch her tour of "Frontier to Foundry: The Making of Small Bronze Sculpture in the Gilcrease Collection," an exhibit she curated at the Gilcrease Museum, on YouTube at https://www.youtube.com/watch?v=uuwIiVRRGQE (accessed October 15, 2016). Author's conversation with Ann Boulton, August 16, 2016.

14   For more information on Roman Bronze Works, see Janis Conner, "After the Model: Bessie Potter Vonnoh's Early Bronzes and Founders," in *Bessie Potter Vonnoh: Sculptor of Women*, by Julie Aronson, Bessie P. Vonnoh, and Janis C. Conner (Cincinnati: Cincinnati Art Museum, 2008): 225–47. For more information on the history of lost-wax casting in the United States, see Shapiro, *Bronze Casting and American Sculpture.*

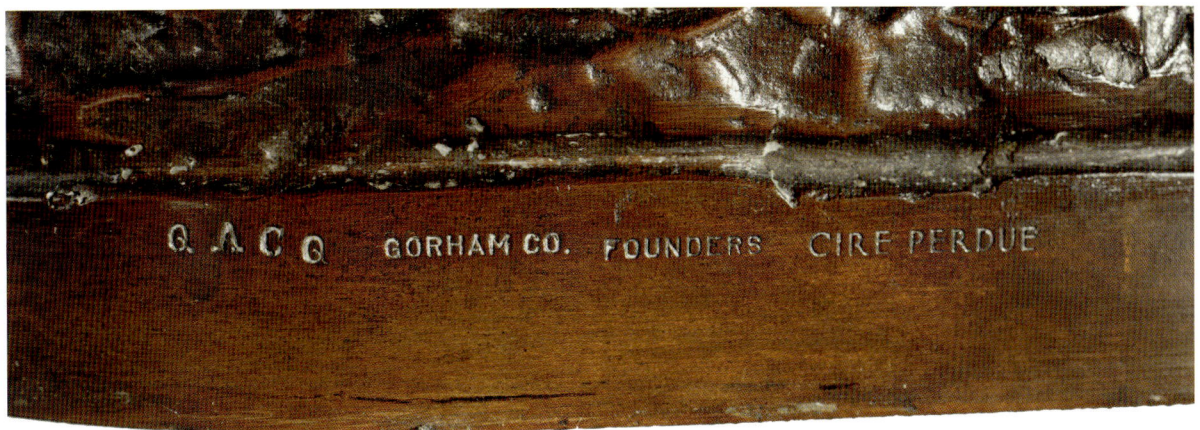

foundry to begin a mutually beneficial partnership. From June 1929 to May 1934, Gorham sublet some of its jobs to Gargani to be cast using the lost-wax method. Interestingly, these sculptures cast by Gargani still bear the Gorham foundry mark.[15] There are no obvious physical markers of a Gorham-sublet Gargani casting, but they can be identified by cross-referencing the records in the Gorham casting ledgers, by examining the bases of sculptures with Gorham foundry marks for indications that they are lost-wax castings,[16] or by using XRF analysis. Another telltale sign is that some of the Gorham-sublet Gargani casts have both the Gorham foundry mark and an inscription reading "CIRE PERDUE," which is French for "lost wax." [PLATE 12.3]

Five of the tested Proctor bronzes are Gorham-sublet Gargani casts. Their alloy formulations are fairly consistent and extremely similar to the Roman Bronze Works alloys—the result, most likely, of Gargani's former employment at Roman Bronze Works.

JNO. WILLIAMS, INC. BRONZE FOUNDRY

Jno. Williams Foundry was started in 1875 by John Williams, a former designer for Tiffany & Co. In 1905 he incorporated the foundry and changed the name from John Williams, New York, to Jno. Williams, Inc. Bronze Foundry. Proctor was collaborating with Jno. Williams before the company's incorporation in 1905. He would continue to work with it until 1911, at which time he became unsatisfied with the declining quality of its work and chose to take his business elsewhere. Ten of the sculptures tested in this study are documented Jno. Williams, Inc., castings. Jno. Williams, Inc., used the sand-cast method exclusively, and testing reveals that the company had a highly consistent alloy formulation, with more zinc and less tin than was standard for either Gorham or Roman Bronze Works.

[PLATE 12.3]

ALEXANDER PHIMISTER PROCTOR

Buckaroo, ca. 1915

Bronze
Denver Art Museum Collection: Funds from William Sr. and Dorothy Harmsen Collection by exchange, 2005.12.
Photography © Denver Art Museum

---

15   For more information on Gorham's partnership with Gargani, see Conner, "Harriet Whitney Frishmuth and Her Foundries," 73–76.

16   For more detail, see Conner, "Introduction to Cast Comparisons,"

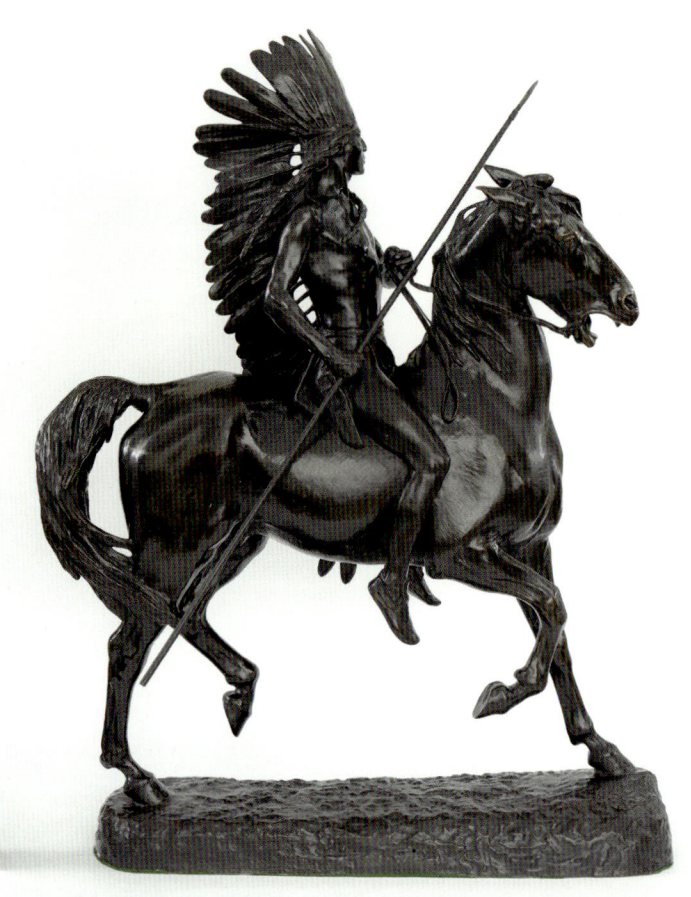

[PLATE 12.4]

ALEXANDER PHIMISTER
PROCTOR

Indian Warrior, 1900 – 1902

Bronze, 38 ⅝ (height)
Buffalo Bill Center of the West, Cody,
Wyoming. Gift of A. Phimister Proctor
Museum with special thanks to Sandy
and Sally Church. 4.08.2

OTHER FOUNDRIES

Proctor employed a variety of other foundries throughout his career. In this study, we've tested bronzes cast by A. Bruno in Rome, Italy; Batardy in Brussels, Belgium; the Henry-Bonnard Bronze Company in New York; Petermann in Brussels, Belgium; Pompeian Bronze Works in New York; Thiebault in Paris, France; Tiffany in Queens, New York; and Verbeyst in Brussels, Belgium. Because we have only tested one or two sculptures from each of these foundries, it is difficult to draw conclusions about the alloy formulations they used.

IDENTIFIED BRONZES

Using a combination of visual inspection of the undersides of bases, comparison of the elemental data, and archival research, we have identified the foundries of thirteen bronze sculptures whose casting history was heretofore unknown. We identified five as cast by Roman Bronze Works, two by Pompeian Bronze Works, and six by Jno. Williams, Inc., Foundry. The following is an example of the process we have used to identify previously unknown foundries.

We tested ten of Proctor's large *Indian Warrior* sculptures. [PLATE 12.4] Two of those (the castings belonging to the National Gallery of Canada and the R. W. Norton Art Gallery) have clear foundry marks indicating that they were cast by Jno. Williams, Inc., Foundry. As Peter Hassrick explains earlier in this book, Jno. Williams, Inc., Foundry used a characteristic style of underpinning that matches three other castings with no foundry mark, those belonging to the Amon Carter Museum [PLATE 12.5], the Portland Art Museum [PLATE 12.6], and the Seattle Art Museum.

As noted earlier, Jno. Williams, Inc., Foundry's alloy formulation was extremely consistent. According to our analysis, the copper-to-zinc photon ratios and the copper-to-tin photon ratios for the castings held by the Amon Carter Museum, Portland Art Museum, and Seattle Art Museum all fall within the observed range for Jno. Williams, Inc., Foundry. We therefore determined that these three unmarked castings were done by Jno. Williams, Inc., Foundry.

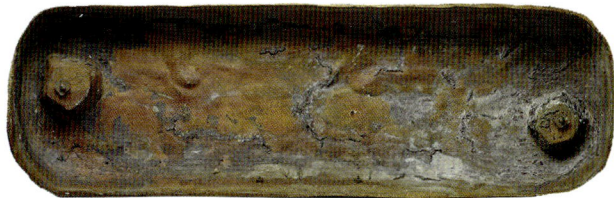

[PLATE 12.5]

ALEXANDER PHIMISTER
PROCTOR

Indian Warrior
(Jno. Williams, detail –
underside), ca. 1895

Bronze
Amon Carter Museum of American Art,
Fort Worth, Texas. 2002.5

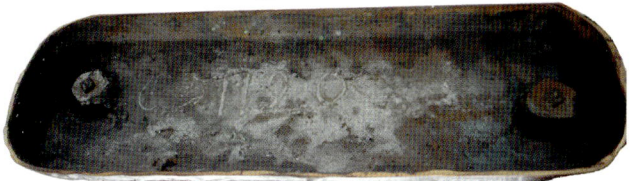

[PLATE 12.6]

ALEXANDER PHIMISTER
PROCTOR

*Indian on Horseback (Indian
Warrior)* (Jno. Williams, detail –
underside), 1898

Bronze
Portland Art Museum, Portland, Oregon.
Gift of Mrs. A.L. Mills, Mrs. T.H. Bartlett,
Henrietta E. Failing, Mary Forbush
Failing, Mrs. H.C. Cabell, Charles Francis
Adams, John C. Ainsworth, William D.
Cartwright, and T.B. Wilcox. 11.2

CONCLUSIONS

The method outlined here for identifying elemental presences,
utilizing the ratios of key elements, and comparing relative elemental
concentrations using XRF analysis has revealed key patterns among
Proctor's foundries. This information, coupled with visual analysis and
historical research, has helped us identify the foundries that cast some
of Proctor's bronzes with previously unknown provenance histories. As
our data pool continues to grow, we will be able to recognize additional
patterns that will lead to further discoveries about Proctor and his
relationship with his foundries.

We will continue our testing to gather more information on the
foundries underrepresented in this study and perhaps new ones for
which we do not have any data yet. We will also expand our data pool
to include bronzes cast by Proctor's contemporaries who were using the
same foundries, and will publish a comprehensive scientific review of
our findings.[17]

17   The authors wish to express their deepest gratitude to Phimister Proctor "Sandy"
Church for his support and knowledge throughout the research process, and to Perrine Le
Saux, Vanessa Ocaña-Mayor, Nicole Schmidt, and Michael Tusay for their help with the
testing and analysis. Many thanks are also owed to Ann Boulton, Kate Galatian, and Sarah
Gilcrease at the Gilcrease Museum; Jon Frembling, Rachel Panella, Sam Duncan, Jodie Utter,
Fernanda Valverde, and Stacey Kelly at the Amon Carter Museum; Arlen Heginbotham
at the J. Paul Getty Museum; Dr. Lisha Glinsman at the National Gallery of Art; Lee
Drake at Bruker Elemental; Paul Cavanagh at Paul King Foundry; and Mark Ostrander at
Conner-Rosencranz.

INDEX

Note: Page numbers in **bold** refer to illustrative matter.